THE PHYSICAL DEVELOPMENT NEEDS OF YOUNG CHILDREN

With growing concerns over declining levels of school readiness and physical activity, this book highlights the importance of quality early movement experiences and explores the connection between poor early physical development opportunities and later difficulties in the classroom.

The book outlines the physical development needs of babies, toddlers and young children up to the age of eight, and suggests practical ways in which these can be provided for. It explores key concepts and terms, such as physical literacy, fundamental movement skills, sport, physical activity and Physical Education (PE), in relation to young children's physical development needs and discusses age-appropriate provision. Advice is given to prevent movement difficulties from occurring, but it is acknowledged that not all children follow a typical physical development pathway, and, where this is the case, suggestions are provided to help put children "back on course."

The Physical Development Needs of Young Children is important reading for all who work with or care for young children, including Early Years practitioners, primary school teachers, students who are studying to join these professions and parents.

Rebecca Duncombe is a Neuro-developmental Therapist helping individuals and schools. Her recent research has focussed on Physical Development in the Early Years, and she jointly developed "Movement for Learning," a daily programme of developmental exercises aimed at children in reception and Year 1.

THE PHYSICAL DEVELOPMENT NEEDS OF YOUNG CHILDREN

Edited by Rebecca Duncombe

Routledge
Taylor & Francis Group

LONDON AND NEW YORK

First published 2019
by Routledge
2 Park Square, Milton Park, Abingdon, Oxon OX14 4RN

and by Routledge
52 Vanderbilt Avenue, New York, NY 10017

Routledge is an imprint of the Taylor & Francis Group, an informa business

British Library Cataloguing-in-Publication Data
A catalogue record for this book is available from the British Library

Library of Congress Cataloging-in-Publication Data
A catalog record has been requested for this book

ISBN: 978-1-138-60193-2 (hbk)
ISBN: 978-1-138-60194-9 (pbk)
ISBN: 978-0-429-46983-1 (ebk)

Typeset in Bembo
by codeMantra

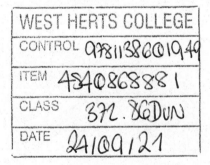

MIX
Paper from
responsible sources
FSC
www.fsc.org FSC™ C013985

Printed in the United Kingdom
by Henry Ling Limited

This book is dedicated to my father, Graham Wells. Thank you for giving me the confidence to take on a challenge and for always being there just in case it went wrong! We miss you.

CONTENTS

FIGURES

TABLES

CONTRIBUTORS

Sue Allingham is an experienced teacher and Local Authority Adviser. She is an independent consultant, author and trainer, and Consultant Editor of Early Years Educator publication EYE. Whilst working as a Local Authority Early Years Adviser, Sue wrote a "Healthy Settings" accreditation process for the area. She is also an active member of the International Physical Literacy Association.

Carol Archer is a Movement-Play Practitioner/Consultant in the United Kingdom and overseas. She has supported staff in Children's Centres and at voluntary and private nurseries in implementing movement-play in their settings and delivers central training and in-service training to staff working in early childhood education and care (ECEC) and early primary education.

Janine Coates is a Lecturer in qualitative research methods in the School of Sport, Exercise and Health Sciences at Loughborough University, United Kingdom. Her research focusses on children, specifically those with special educational needs and disabilities, and their experiences of physical activity and sport. Janine is also a member of the British Psychological Society.

Sue Gascoyne is a leading thinker and writer on sensorial engagement, therapeutic play and enabling materials and environments for children across the ages. She works within the United Kingdom and internationally. Sue is an active contributor to early childhood policy and a regular speaker at the European Early Childhood Education Research Association (ECEERA) and other national and international events. She is Founder and Creative Director of multi-award-winning sensory equipment company Play to Z Ltd. A qualified Creative Arts and Play Therapist working with children with emotional and behavioural issues, Sue specialises in messy play, sensory processing, autism and sensory attachment, and particularly favours the use of creative media to explore and express emotions, build resilience and change behaviour.

Sally Goddard Blythe is a member of the International Alliance for Childhood and the former "Open EYE" campaign, and Patron of Toddler Kindy GymbaROO. She has lectured on the role of infant reflexes in development and later learning problems to many different groups throughout Europe, including to a working party on child well-being at the European Parliament in Brussels and in different parts of the United States. She is also a member of the educational panel for Dyspraxia awareness.

Gerald Griggs is Head of Academics at the University Campus of Football Business (UCFB), Manchester, United Kingdom. His teaching and research interests are concerned with primary Physical Education and the Socio-cultural aspects of sport. Gerald is both a Fellow of the Royal Society for the Encouragement of Arts, Manufacturers and Commerce, and a Fellow of the Higher Education Academy.

Mike Jess is Senior Lecturer and Deputy Head of the Institute of Sport, Physical Education and Health Sciences at the University of Edinburgh, United Kingdom. He is Director of the Developmental Physical Education Group (DPEG). He is an honoured member of the Association for Physical Education and a member of the International Advisory Board for the World Bank-funded Renovation of General Education Project (RGEP) in Vietnam and is working on the UNESCO-funded Pre-Service Teacher Reform Project in Myanmar.

Lala Manners has enjoyed a long and varied career promoting the importance of Early Years movement development and physical activity as educator, teacher, consultant and presenter both in the United Kingdom and abroad. She has designed and delivered a range of accredited courses to Speech/Language therapists, EY students and practitioners, health professionals and sports and swimming coaches. She is a proactive member of the all-party parliamentary group (APPG) "Fit and Healthy Childhood" committee and a frequent contributor to early year's publications.

Dorothy Marlen is Course Leader of the Level 3 Holistic Baby and Child Care (EYE) Diploma. She originally trained as a Steiner Early Years teacher and a counsellor in Psychoanalytic Child observation, and more recently at the Pikler Institute in Budapest. She runs pioneering parent and baby support groups, and co-founded the Pikler UK Association, of which she is the chairperson. She offers freelance consultancy and workshops to mainstream and Steiner/Waldorf birth to three care settings, training courses and schools.

Carolynne Mason is Lecturer in Sport Management within the School of Sport, Exercise and Health Sciences at Loughborough University, United Kingdom.

Her research is concerned with better understanding the role of sport and physical activity in enhancing the lives of children and young people, and promoting social justice. Her research approach is participatory and child-centred, and draws on child-rights frameworks.

Patricia Maude is Emeritus Fellow at Homerton College in the University of Cambridge. She has enjoyed a long career promoting Early Years movement development and has worked as a Physical Education teacher, advisory teacher and teacher trainer; as a sports coach; and through research, publications and consultancy in the United Kingdom and abroad.

Cathy Parvin trained as a Registered General Nurse and an Orthopaedic Nurse, and completed the Further and Adult Teachers Certificate. She is Director of Dyspraxia Education and a visiting university Lecturer for SENDCo Award, P.E, PGCE, BA honours and Early Years courses, and has delivered conference seminars and keynote speeches both nationally and in Europe.

Kim Pott is Director and Founder of Kimble's Music and Movement. For the last 15 years she has worked with parents, teachers and children, facilitating classes in movement to music through sensory play. Having studied an MA at the Centre for research in Early Childhood, Kim linked theory with practice, and her training and music company Funky Feet Music was born.

Pat Preedy has been a global Chief Academic Officer for early childhood education, Executive Principal of a school catering for pupils from 3 months to 18 years with boarding, Head Teacher of one of the first Beacon Schools in the United Kingdom and a lead Inspector for ISI (Independent School Inspectorate). Pat has spearheaded a wide range of projects, including developing school leadership and the impact of Neuro-Developmental Delay on young children's learning. As Honorary Research Consultant for Tamba (Twins and Multiple Births Association), Pat has conducted extensive research into meeting the educational needs of multiple birth children, including the Movement for Multiples Project.

Vicky Randall is Senior Fellow for Knowledge Exchange at the University of Winchester, United Kingdom, and Subject Coordinator for Physical Education. As a former teacher, she has taught across primary and secondary age phases in Physical Education and continues to support teachers through professional development and consultancy. Her research interests are concerned with the development of teacher knowledge, curriculum development for teacher education and primary Physical Education policy. She has been a member of the Physical Education Expert Subject Advisory Group and the All Party Parliamentary Group for a Fit and Healthy Childhood, representing primary Physical Education initial teacher education at a national level.

Arja Sääkslahti is Senior Researcher in the University of Jyväskylä, Faculty of Sport and Health Sciences. Her main research interests focus on children's motor development, physical activity, well-being and health during early childhood. She has been involved in different intervention studies trying to create more child-centred pedagogy for early childhood. She also teaches in the University of Jyväskylä. She has been involved in creating the Finnish Physical Education curriculum and has a leading role in the Association Internationale des Ecoles Superieures d'Education Physique (AIESEP) special interest group for early education.

Rachel Sandford is Senior Lecturer in Young People and Sport in the School of Sport, Exercise and Health Sciences at Loughborough University, United Kingdom. Her research broadly covers issues related to young people's attitudes towards, experiences of and development in/through sport and physical activity.

Ruth Smith is an EYFS practitioner, Forest School leader, consultant and Assistant Head at Woodland Grange Primary School in Leicester, United Kingdom. She has 14 years teaching experience in the Early Years and has most recently set up a Pre-School within Woodland Grange. She is a Specialist Leader of Education advising on school improvement. She also delivers bespoke training for Early Years settings on a range of subjects, including Physical Development. She is a tutor on the Leicestershire School Centred Initial Teacher Training (SCITT) programme, mentoring students and teaching on best practise in Early Years.

Julie Stirrup is Lecturer in Physical Education and Sports Pedagogy at Loughborough University, England. As a former PE teacher, she teaches and writes on issues relating to equity and identity, embodiment and education within the Early Years and throughout the schooling process.

Margaret Whitehead is Visiting Professor at the University of Bedfordshire, United Kingdom, and Adjunct Professor at the University of Canberra, Australia. She retired from De Montfort University Bedford, United Kingdom, from the position of Associate Head of School of Physical Education, Sport and Leisure. She is currently President of the International Physical Literacy Association. She is a member of The Laban Guild, The Association for Physical Education, the British Philosophy of Sport Association and the International Physical Literacy Association.

ACKNOWLEDGEMENTS

To my children – Joshua, Jacob and Toby – without whom, I am certain, I would never have embarked upon this journey. Thank you for trusting Mummy enough to let her help you and for being very willing research subjects over the last few years. I love you all and am proud of the people you are becoming.

To Andy – my husband – who has just about tolerated this adventure, I hope you can now see exactly what I have been doing when you come home, and I appear to have done nothing all day! Apologies for the state of the house on these occasions.

To my mum, brother and sister – Christine, Dominic and Hannah – and to my best friend – Julie. We should never underestimate the value of supportive and fun family and friends. I have been very lucky.

And, finally, to everyone who has helped me to write this book: all of my co-authors who have met my numerous demands and deadlines; Toni O'Donovan for her feedback on Chapter 8; and Elaine Cowley for providing me with some valuable data and information for Chapter 8.

INTRODUCTION

Rebecca Duncombe

As somebody who has never really been all that "taken" with children, I was quite surprised when, at the age of 21, I made the surprising discovery that I wanted to work in some capacity with them. I had just finished my degree in psychology and sociology and had, without really thinking about it, selected a number of modules that related to education. Thus, having left university with absolutely no idea of what I wanted to do when I grew up, I started to look into careers that might involve working with children and, more specifically, careers that might draw on what I had already learnt in psychology and sociology. I formulated a plan. I would train to become an Educational Psychologist. At the time, this meant that I had to first train to become a teacher and then teach for a minimum of two years, at which point, I could apply to study to become an Educational Psychologist. So, I set off on this journey, completed my PGCE in primary education, taught as a supply teacher for a term and then secured my first proper teaching job as a year 4 teacher with responsibility for PE. I lasted for five terms (two terms in year 4 and a whole academic year in year 3)! It was not the teaching that I did not like – it wasn't even the children! In fact, the best bit about the job was helping them to learn and experience the joys associated with this, but I did not enjoy the constraints within which I was expected to work: filling in paperwork, dealing with parents, attending staff meetings (often discussing things for hours that had already been decided upon), listening to and sympathising with other members of staff who were all feeling the same way and watching children struggle day after day knowing that there was very little that I or "the system" could do to help them. In relation to this final point, two children spring to mind. Two children who I still, to this day, feel enormous guilt about because I was not able to help them. Knowing what I do now, I am certain that one was very dyslexic and one had severe symptoms associated with developmental coordination disorder (DCD)/dyspraxia. Both struggled academically in numerous ways and I was powerless to help (despite a degree in psychology and a desire to become an Educational Psychologist). I jumped through all of the hoops to get them assessed and some help put in place but, although an Educational Psychologist had visited and assessed them, absolutely nothing changed. It was at this point that I realised that educational psychology (in its format at the time and that remains today) was not the job for me. I wanted to help children, not merely assess and monitor them. And that realisation quickly ended two careers – that of teaching and that of educational psychology.

Yet, here I am today, approximately 18 years later, writing a book about the physical development needs of young children that has numerous links to education and learning difficulties. I like to think that what has happened in the meantime has been a "stepping stone" or "springboard" back to a career that I chose so many years ago and that I am now in a position where I can do more than assess and monitor – I can advise and implement changes that will actually make a difference. There are probably three key experiences or events that have helped me to return to this point: the research I conducted whilst working at Loughborough University; the difficulties that my own children faced in terms of their gross and fine motor skills (and the difficulties that this caused them at school); and a chance meeting with Pat Preedy approximately six years ago.

In relation to the first point or "stepping stone," I was in a fairly unique position at the University where I chose to conduct research rather than follow the more typical path of lecturing. I was employed as a research associate in The Institute of Youth Sport, where I worked on and led numerous research projects linked to PE, sport and physical activity. The majority of these either related to the ways in which sport and PE could be used to develop young people (in terms of their behaviour, social skills and academic outcomes) or ways in which physical activity could be provided for or promoted to young people. The teachers, parents and young people who participated in these research projects frequently told me how sport and PE had improved their lives but also how difficult it was to motivate oneself to engage in physical activity. Thus, on the one hand, I was being told that engaging in sport, PE and physical activity was beneficial, but, on the other hand, I was being told the numerous ways in which this was problematic. This gave me a background in PE, sport and physical activity in relation to young children but also extensive research experience that would prove very useful later in my career.

The second "stepping stone" was born in 2006, and his twin brothers were born in 2009. I will outline some of our experiences in a later chapter so won't repeat them in too much detail here. We are and always have been a very active family, and family members on both sides have enjoyed a fair amount of sporting success. I believed, when my children were little, that I was doing everything right (or as right as was possible) and that my children were progressing nicely along their physical development journey. They all pretty much met their physical development milestones at approximately the right time, nursery never alerted us to any concerns that they might have and I certainly had very few worries about any of them before they started school. However, between them they had difficulties with fine motor skills (reflected in their handwriting), balance, coordination and spatial awareness. Two of them had strongly retained primitive reflexes and one had traces. My eldest struggled at school right from the start. We were called in almost every day, and, on his first parents' evening, we were told that they weren't "quite sure what to do with him." This led me to start looking into what was going on – he had no difficulties in learning to read, his maths was above average for his age, but his behaviour and physical skills were well below what we expected. It was at about this time that I listened to Sally Goddard Blythe from the Institute for Neuro Physiological Psychology (INPP) presenting at a conference and realised that the symptoms she was describing very much fitted with what we were seeing at home and what teachers were reporting in school. Completely by chance a few months later, I was sat next to Dr Pat Preedy at a Twins and Multiple Births Association (TAMBA) meeting where we were both honorary consultants. Pat had trained with Sally at the INPP.

At this time, Pat was a complete stranger to us, yet she was the only person willing and able to help, thus, to describe her as the 'third stepping stone' is, perhaps, a little inappropriate and would underestimate both her kindness and the enormity of what she did for us. Needless to say though, I would not be here now if it was not for her, and Josh would not be engaging well in a range of sports and achieving way above expectations at his new secondary school. Pat, not only helped him, but she invited me to collaborate on the "Movement for Learning" research project, which we worked on together for approximately three years, assessing children's physical skills at the start and end of reception and investigating whether the Movement for Learning programme had an impact on the children involved. In 2016, Pat persuaded me to apply for the INPP course, which I completed in 2017, qualifying to treat children with retained reflexes and associated symptoms typically linked to dyslexia, DCD/dyspraxia, Attention Deficit Disorder, Asperger's and sensory processing disorder. Thus, my interest in the Early Years was sparked and my fascination with educational psychology renewed.

I was approached to write this book shortly following a press release from the Movement for Learning research that identified a worrying number of children now starting reception with low levels of physical development. Originally, I was asked to focus on Physical Education in the Early Years, but it quickly became apparent that this was not a suitable term, and, thus, the focus shifted to physical development and to a wider age range of children (0–8 years). Drawing on the experiences outlined earlier, I hope that this book will: (1) alert the reader to the importance of physical development in the Early Years, (2) highlight the link between poor physical development and learning/behavioural difficulties in the classroom, (3) outline a number of "barriers" to providing appropriate and adequate physical development opportunities for young children and (4) identify how parents and practitioners might overcome these barriers. An underlying message is that physical development isn't "fixed," and, whilst it is best to get things right from the start (as detailed in Chapter 6), later provision and interventions can be used to help put children back on track.

The book is structured into three sections: the first traces the origins and evolution of physical development as a term in early childhood, explores key concepts such as physical literacy, fundamental movement skills and physical activity, and outlines differences in provision in Finland (when compared to the United Kingdom); the second section highlights the physical development needs of and ways in which these can be provided for babies, toddlers, children in the EYFS, children in KS1 and children experiencing physical or learning difficulties once they start school; the final section looks at the ways in which sports, the physical environment and play (both indoors and outdoors) might be adapted or structured to provide appropriate physical development opportunities, and four different approaches/interventions are then presented alongside data to support their effectiveness. The focus of this book is on "The Physical Development Needs of Young Children," and I hope that, through reading it, all who have a role to play in bringing up children will be enabled and empowered to meet these needs.

1

THE ORIGINS AND EVOLUTION OF PHYSICAL EDUCATION AND PHYSICAL DEVELOPMENT IN EARLY CHILDHOOD 0–8 YEARS

Rebecca Duncombe and Lala Manners

Personal reflection

As I was writing this book, I was given two "historic" publications: *Moving and Growing: Physical Education in the Primary School, part 1*, and *Planning the Programme: Physical Education in the Primary School, part 2*, both published in 1952. I'd been aware of both of these because a chapter of my PhD (on Primary School teachers' continuing professional development in Physical Education [PE]) had included an overview, but I had never been lucky enough to access hard copies before this time.

Browsing through the two books, I was amazed at the content and particularly surprised by the photos. Perhaps most astonishing are the number of pictures of young children without their tops on and even some who are wearing no clothes at all, something that clearly would be hugely problematic today. Also, the majority of photos are of children being active outside (e.g. climbing rocks, jumping off tree stumps, clambering over crates, playing at the seaside, horse riding and hanging off monkey bars/tree branches).

Dance and gymnastics feature strongly, and, interestingly, the document recognises the importance of providing movement opportunities to support fluent handwriting. The following extract, in which good physical provision for young children in nurseries is described, portrays a situation that, in my experience, we do not see often enough in settings today:

> The day will not consist of periods in a classroom interspersed by a period or two in the playground; the children will be constantly in and out of doors, and there will be ample opportunity for all the natural (untaught) movements of running, climbing, swinging and throwing. It is most unlikely that the playground will be a bare yard; there will probably be a garden, a

sandpit, natural obstacles or apparatus on which to climb, crawl and swing and, perhaps a pool... Young children learn much seeing and hearing, but perhaps most of all by doing things. Shapes are not only seen but must also be handled, and attempts must be made to fit or build them together; colours must be used, tools tried out, materials smoothed, squeezed, patted or pressed... because the day is arranged with reference to the needs of the children for activity, fresh air, food, rest, and quiet, there is space and time for children to move freely at their own time and in their own way.

(Ministry of Education and the Central Office of Information, 1952, pp. 66–67)

If this was common knowledge in 1952, how has provision for children to move and learn changed so dramatically, and what may be needed to return to this life-enhancing approach?

Introduction

The aim of this chapter is to explore the origins and evolution of physical training (PT), PE and Physical Development (PD) as official terms in provision for young children's physical activity, health and well-being. Evolution implies change, progress and improvement. However, factual and anecdotal evidence concerning children's PD, health and well-being suggests that provision for movement, physical activity and active play is demonstrably less effective now than it was in 1952.

Changes in the education system from 1870 to the present day will be documented with specific reference to PT (a term used historically to describe early PE), PE for children in Year 1 onwards (ages 5+) and PD for nursery and Reception classes (ages 0–5).

The origins and evolution of PE in early childhood (0–8 years)

"Elementary" education was introduced following the Forster Act of 1870. Compulsory schooling was provided for children aged 5–12 (later extended to 14), but not until 1944 was the current Primary and Secondary schooling system created. Throughout this period, new approaches to learning created by pedagogical luminaries such as Freidrich Froebel and Maria Montessori were filtering into classrooms, but large class sizes often made it hard for teachers to implement these ideas, and teaching remained relatively didactic, with little room for discovery and investigation.

In 1931, two reports were produced by the Hadow Committee, led by Sir W. H. Hadow – the second of which focussed on the Primary School. These reports were influenced by the ideas of John Dewey and recommended that innovative teaching approaches be implemented:

Dewey's aim was to promote individuality, to base education on the concept of children as children, not as future adults, on the idea of growth in children as an end in itself, not as a preparation. The experience of the child must be real; learning, in the most famous of Deweyite slogans, must be by doing.

(Lawson & Silver, 1973, p. 398)

The Hadow Committee recommended that "the curriculum should be thought of in terms of activity and experience rather than of knowledge to be acquired and facts to be stored" (Lawson & Silver, 1973, p. 387).

Between 1870 and the end of the war in 1945, PE was also changing. Its origins may be traced back to 1876, following three recommendations from William Jolly (one of Her Majesty's Inspectors, HMI), who had identified the significant health benefits associated with structured PT. This was partly initiated by clear evidence of the poor physical state of young men signing up to fight in the Boer War.

Jolly's recommendations are as follows:

1. PT should be part of a payment by results scheme (teachers were paid according to the results they achieved). This change in policy meant that teachers would be paid for the results they achieved in PE.
2. Health should be studied by children as a subject at school.
3. PT should be a compulsory component of teacher training (Kirk, Penney, Burgess-Limerick, Gorely, & Maynard, 2002).

In addition, HMI started to inspect the "exercise grounds" that were available to children in schools, as they were termed at the time, though they later became playgrounds (as we generally refer to them today).

During this time, elite public schools were also developing their own system of PE that was based on sports such as cricket and rugby. The aims of PE in public and elementary schools thus differed:

> In the boys' public schools, organised games and athleticism developed into a cult of overriding importance in the education which was provided by those schools. In the elementary schools, drill and drill-like exercises were evolved to meet the exigencies of appalling facilities and huge classes of unruly children.
>
> *(McIntosh, 1952, p. 133)*

Although PT in the form of military drills was popular in the early part of the 20th century, many innovative ideas were filtering through from Europe concerning the efficacy of movement and gymnastics (with and without apparatus), and PE colleges were created to explore and disseminate new teaching approaches. There was also a growing belief in the wider benefits of PE to improve health, promote better morals, engender deeper empathy with others and support social skills (McIntosh, 1952). PE was arguably evolving to resemble a model we might recognise today due in part to the number of publications produced by the Board of Education. Specific syllabi were created in 1904, 1909, 1919 and 1933 to encourage provision of a greater range of activities in PE. McIntosh (1952) identifies 11 publications that helped to shape PE at this time and states that:

> Real progress too was made with the modification of exercises to suit younger children. Working to command and formal exercises gave place to activities and the use of apparatus, such as attractive coloured balls and bands. The climbing frame and the 'junglegym' made their appearance in playgrounds, while the work of Dalcroze and Ann Driver resulted in the extensive use of music and natural movement for young children.
>
> *(McIntosh, 1952, pp. 202–203)*

The Syllabus of 1933 represents a further shift away from the emphasis on military drill (PT) in previous decades:

> It contained fresh exercises and new teaching methods 'with a view to the special encouragement of good posture and flexibility of muscles and joints', but a large number of simple games were described and many free and vigorous 'activity' exercises were included. Its popularity as a handbook among teachers led to a great improvement in the physical education of children.
>
> *(McIntosh, Dixon, Munrow, & Willetts, 1981, p. 214)*

PE after the Second World War slowly evolved to include a wider range of activities. Whilst gymnastics and dance remained popular, increasing emphasis was placed on other activities as Primary school playgrounds started to include nets, walls and ropes. Apparatus for gymnastics including balls and hoops was increasingly utilised, and there was a conscious shift in the terminology used. Whereas "posture" had been a popular term in the previous period, it was now replaced by "movement": "The term movement, and phrases incorporating movement such as the art of movement, movement training, movement education came to be used more and more in place of dance" (McIntosh et al., 1981, p. 226). Swimming and games/sports were included in provision, and "movement" began to be viewed as primarily dance and gymnastics.

A new PE syllabus was introduced in 1952, and the two booklets cited previously were produced to accompany it: *Moving and Growing* and *Planning the Programme*. These further contributed to the growing recognition that a more child-centred approach to teaching, including PE, was required. This thinking culminated in the Plowden Report of 1967, which was heavily influenced by the ideas of Piaget and new research into child development. It extended the suggestions present in the 1952 PE syllabus and promoted the expressive opportunities offered by dance and "movement." Plowden also recommended that competitive games (sports) should only be introduced at the end of Primary School and suggested there were important differences between girls and boys, whose needs could be met through teaching them different games.

During the 1960s and 1970s, an increased focus on fitness and the health benefits of physical activity became a significant part of the zeitgeist. These ideas found their way into PE provision, as reflected in the following quote from the Sports Council in Britain:

> Parents and schools have an important role to play in fostering positive attitudes to exercise in all young people and not merely in the sporting elite, in the hope that active lifestyles which are established early, will last into maturity and old age.
>
> *(Sports Council in Britain, cited in McIntosh et al., 1981, p. 231)*

The Education Reform Act was passed in 1988 and established a framework for the National Curriculum, which, despite a number of revisions, has remained largely the same to this day. It was structured round the "key stages," as they are now known, and included the *core* subjects of English, Mathematics and Science, and the *foundation* subjects of art, geography, history, music, PE and technology (and foreign languages from age 11). PE had, therefore, secured a place in the National Curriculum and was now a compulsory component for all 5–16-year-olds. The National Curriculum for PE was, however, not implemented until 1991. It was then revised in 1995, 1999 and 2014. The specific content of these curricula is documented in Griggs (2015) and so will not be repeated here in full. A brief summary of each and an identification of the main changes will, however, be provided.

The Education Reform Act in 1988 marked the start of Key Stage 1 (KS1) (ages 5–7) and Key Stage 2 (ages 7–11) within Primary school provision in the United Kingdom. The 1991 curriculum states that pupils should experience six activity areas: athletic activities, dance, games, gymnastic activities, outdoor and adventurous activities, and swimming. Within athletics, for example, KS1 pupils should "Experience and be encouraged to take part in running, jumping and throwing activities, concentrating on accuracy, speed, height, length and distance" (DES, 1991). However, in the school context, it soon became apparent that the breadth of knowledge demanded by each of the nine curriculum subjects made their delivery unmanageable, and, following the Dearing Review, the curriculum for each subject was reviewed and revised in 1995 (Griggs, 2015).

The general requirements for the KS1 PE curriculum of 1995 were:

1. To promote physical activity and healthy lifestyles;
2. To develop positive attitudes;
3. To ensure safe practice.

These were to be delivered through three areas of activity: games, gymnastics and dance. A number of developments at this time led to the 1995 revision focussing almost entirely on games/sport (Penney & Evans, 1999). In response, the

National Curriculum was further revised in 1999, and more of a balance between the activity areas was restored. Whilst the activity areas remained the same as in the 1999 version (with the addition of swimming), specific guidance was included that related to what should be covered within these activities.

Teachers were expected to teach the following through the identified activity areas:

- Acquiring and developing skills;
- Selecting and applying skills;
- Tactics and compositional ideas;
- Evaluating and improving performance.

The Physical Education, School Sport and Club Links (PESSCL) strategy was launched in 2002, with an overall objective of increasing the take up for sporting opportunities by 6–16-year-olds and an aim of engaging children in at least two hours of "high quality" PE and sport each week (DfES/DCMS, 2003). The strategy consisted of eight strands to help fulfil its objective: Specialist Sports Colleges, Sport Co-ordinators, Gifted and Talented, Investigating PE and School Sport, Step into Sport, Professional Development, School/Club Links and Swimming. Following this, the Physical Education and Sport Strategy for Young People (PESSYP) was introduced, creating the idea of a five hour offer of PE and sport for young people (to be delivered through PE and school clubs).

The National Curriculum for PE, whilst contested, remained in its 1995 format until a review in 2011, and the current version was implemented in 2014. The purpose of PE provision was now identified as:

> A high-quality physical education curriculum inspires all pupils to succeed and excel in competitive sport and other physically demanding activities. It should provide opportunities for pupils to become physically confident in a way which supports their health and fitness. Opportunities to compete in sport and other activities build character and help to embed values such as fairness and respect.
>
> *(DfE, 2013)*

The subject content for KS1 was described as follows:

> Pupils should develop fundamental movement skills, become increasingly competent and confident and access a broad range of opportunities to extend their agility, balance and coordination, individually and with others. They should be able to engage in competitive (both against self and against others) and co-operative physical activities, in a range of increasingly challenging situations.

Pupils should be taught to:

- Master basic movements including running, jumping, throwing and catching, as well as developing balance, agility and co-ordination, and begin to apply these in a range of activities;
- Participate in team games, developing simple tactics for attacking and defending;
- Perform dances using simple movement patterns

(DfE, 2013)

From this, we can see that sport and health discourses have permeated their way into the current PE curriculum, ideas that have, arguably, evolved from the changing purpose of PE since 1870.

The origins and evolution of PD in the Early Years

The previous section traced the broad developments in PE since the Forster Education Act of 1870. Early acknowledgement of the PD needs of nursery-aged children may be noted in the two documents published in 1952. The approach at this time focussed on providing a range of fairly unstructured, plentiful and challenging outdoor opportunities for active play that promoted a "movement-rich" environment. This section will now track the evolution of provision for PD in the Early Years through to its presence as a "prime area" of learning in the current Early Years Foundation Stage (EYFS) framework.

Although private nurseries had been in existence since the late 1800s, and various educational thinkers, such as the McMillan sisters, had developed new child-centred pedagogies, no state funding had ever been allocated for educating this age group. In 1972, the white paper "A Framework for Expansion" (DES, 1972) proposed that nursery education should be available for all children and that by 1980, 50 per cent of three-year-olds and 90 per cent of four-year-olds should be awarded nursery places. During this time, Maria Montessori's beliefs about the importance of learning through play were becoming increasingly influential, and Lev Vygotsky's concept of the Zone of Proximal Development had alerted nursery educators to the innate potential of adults to guide children towards their own discoveries and understandings. However, the economic downturn that followed between 1973 and 1975, and again in the early 1980s meant that, despite nursery provision being firmly on the agenda, the figures proposed in this white paper were never achieved.

The Education Reform Act of 1988 introduced a formal curriculum for schools to implement. Although it applied to children from five years upwards, there was an implicit acknowledgement that children starting school should be ready to do so, and attention should be given to the possible role of nurseries in supporting future academic achievement. In 1990, the Rumbold Report

"Starting with Quality" (1990) was published and stated that nursery education needed to be increased and improved; the report also identified eight areas of learning:

- Aesthetic
- Human and social
- Language and literacy
- Mathematics
- Physical
- Science
- Spiritual and moral
- Technology

"Physical" in this context meant PD and concerned "developing manipulative and motor skills, physical control, coordination and mobility. It involves knowledge of how the body works and establishes positive attitudes towards a healthy and active way of life" (Rumbold Report, 1990, p. 42). A successful programme of physical provision for under-fives was further described as:

- Increasing fine control through the use of large and small equipment; learning to use paint brushes, pens, pencils and other tools safely and with increasing precision, and modelling and construction materials with increasing dexterity and skill;
- Control, coordination and mobility through opportunities to climb, run, jump, hop, skip, swing and balance; to manipulate large toys, building blocks, planks, steps, plastic crates and the like; and to respond physically to stimuli such as sounds, songs, music and stories;
- An understanding of how to keep healthy through, for example, eating sensibly, caring for teeth and hair and engaging in physical activity.

(Rumbold Report, 1990, p. 42)

This report also includes an example of how this may be provided:

In addition to the fixed climbing equipment, a wide variety of materials and equipment was provided in the outdoor play area. These included planks, steps, boxes, plastic crates, waste materials and dressing up clothes. The children decided to make a boat using the scramble net as rigging. They worked co-operatively deciding how to organise areas of the boat for sleeping, eating and working. They lifted wooden blocks and planks setting them out to form a space for each activity. Using waste materials, they made telescopes and flags. Equipment was carried from the domestic play area to furnish the eating and sleeping areas. The children took turns to carry out various tasks, cooking the meals, discussing what they would need to eat to be strong climbing the rigging to be the lookout and raising and lowering the flag. Subsequently they were taken to see some boats in the local harbour and recorded what they had seen using a variety of drawing, painting and modelling materials. They listened and responded in movement and dance to sea songs and music.

(Rumbold Report, 1990, p. 43)

The "Start Right Report" was produced in 1994 – a few years after the Rumbold report of 1990. This report stressed the critical importance and value of early learning. Drawing on extensive available research, it criticised previous provision and recommended that more and better-quality nursery provision be provided, acknowledging that "Poor pre-school education is almost as little use to children as none at all" (Ball, 1994, p. 6).

Thus, the way was paved for a comprehensive investigation into what actually constitutes effective nursery provision, and the "Effective Provision of Pre-school Education" (EPPE) project, led by Professor Kathy Sylva, began in 1997. This longitudinal study followed the experiences and outcomes of 2,800 children who had attended pre-schools and 200 children who were raised solely at home.

The initial findings were published in 2004, and the cohort were then followed through to their GCSEs as part of the "Effective Pre-School, Primary & Secondary Education" (EPPSE) Project. The focus of the EPPE study was not on PD, and it is hard to find any mention of this area in the reports. However, they illustrate the potential positive impact that good pre-schools and nurseries may have on a child's overall development (especially their language development) as they enter school and that good quality pre-school provision is particularly beneficial for disadvantaged children (Sammons et al., 2004).

Key findings from the longer-term EPPSE study suggest that:

- Having attended any pre-school was a positive predictor of total GCSE scores at age 16, more full GCSE entries, better grades in English & maths and a higher probability of achieving 5 A*-C GCSEs including English & maths. The impact is higher the longer children had spent in pre-school (in months) and if the pre-school was of high quality. But even lower quality pre-schools had a weak positive effect.
- The effect of attending any pre-school compared to none is equivalent to achieving an additional 7 grades at GCSE (i.e. the difference between getting 7 GCSE at 'B' grades versus 7 GCSE at 'C' grades, or 7 'C' grades versus 7 'D' grades etc). Attending pre-school for 2 years or more, or attending high quality pre-school, compared to none, is equivalent to an additional 8 grades.
- Pre-school can help to combat the effects of disadvantage. It has a particular impact for students of low qualified parents. For this group, if they had experienced a high-quality pre-school they had better grades in GCSE English (just under half a grade) and maths (a third of a grade) compared to similar

students who had not attended any pre-school. There was also some indication that effects of high quality were more notable for boys.

(Sammons et al., 2014, pp. 11–14)

Both the EPPE and EPPSE projects demonstrate that attendance at a good quality pre-school setting has a positive impact on overall development as children start school and on later GCSE results. The EPPE research in particular informed and underpinned the EY policy initiatives that followed.

Prior to the publication of the EPPE findings, "Birth to Three Matters: A Review of the Literature" was compiled and informed what would later become the EYFS framework for practice. Chapter 6 of this publication focussed on "a healthy child" and included underpinning knowledge and advice on PD. Within the summary section of this chapter, it is suggested that practitioners should:

- Understand children's dietary and physical needs;
- Provide opportunities to explore and play in a safe and secure environment (children's mobility and movement are important for their development);
- Know about brain development and the importance of 'nourishment' (a good diet – in both the form of food and of physical and psychological stimulation).

(David, Goouch, Powell, & Abbott, 2003, p. 146)

This focus on overall health and well-being, including "the physical," was later incorporated into the EYFS framework when it was first introduced in 2008. Within this, six areas of learning were identified and accompanied by specific Early Learning Goals (ELGs) that formed the assessment criteria:

- Personal, Social and Emotional Development;
- Communication, Language and Literacy;
- Problem Solving, Reasoning and Numeracy;
- Knowledge and Understanding of the World;
- Physical Development;
- Creative Development.

In relation to PD, children were expected to have met the following goals by the end of the EYFS in their Reception year:

- Move with confidence, imagination and in safety;
- Move with control and coordination;
- Travel around, under, over and through balancing and climbing equipment;
- Show awareness of space, of themselves and of others;
- Recognise the importance of keeping healthy, and those things which contribute to this;
- Recognise the changes that happen to their bodies when they are active;

- Use a range of small and large equipment;
- Handle tools, objects, construction and malleable materials safely, and with increasing control.

Although some attempt was made to include the different components of this area of development, there was little awareness of exactly how the goals could produce relevant or meaningful data: what does "move with confidence" or "show awareness of" actually look like or mean? Moreover, how many practitioners provide opportunities for children to actually develop these skills?

In 2012 the EYFS was reviewed and revised, and a companion document, "Development Matters," was produced. A table was provided for practitioners to refer to that detailed what babies and children may be expected to achieve at each age and stage, and ways in which adults could create the environment and resources to encourage this ("what adults could do" and "what adults could provide"). The 2012 version of the EYFS identified three prime areas (reduced from the six areas of the 2008 version), and PD was included, alongside "communication and language" and "personal, social and emotional development."

PD was described as follows:

> Physical development involves providing opportunities for young children to be active and interactive; and to develop their co-ordination, control, and movement. Children must also be helped to understand the importance of physical activity, and to make healthy choices in relation to food.
>
> *(DfE, 2008, p. 5)*

This overall premise was broken down into two separate yet symbiotic areas: "moving and handling" and "health and self-care."

Moving and handling

"Children show good control and co-ordination in large and small movements. They move confidently in a range of ways, safely negotiating space. They handle equipment and tools effectively, including pencils for writing" (DfE, 2012, p. 8).

Health and self-care

"Children know the importance for good health of physical exercise, and a healthy diet, and talk about ways to keep healthy and safe. They manage their own basic hygiene and personal needs successfully, including dressing and going to the toilet independently" (DfE, 2012, p. 8).

Further revisions were made in 2014 and 2017, but no changes were made to the prime areas or accompanying goals. In 2018, the ELGs were reviewed, and pilot projects have been implemented to determine how the proposed changes will impact on practice. Moving forward, the proposal is to reduce "Physical Development" to "Gross motor and Fine motor skills" and place "Health and self-care" under "Self-management." This puts the status of PD as a "prime area" in jeopardy, completely ignores the fundamental link between the two components, makes the implementation of any physical activity/movement guidelines extremely difficult and questions what sort of training model would be relevant if this area of learning is only about skill acquisition.

Conclusion

The purpose of this chapter is to outline the origins and evolution of the terms PE and PD, and how they are manifested in schools and Early Years settings. Although largely descriptive in nature, it is hoped that an awareness of the past may help generate an understanding of the present as well as provide lessons for the future.

The health and well-being agenda is now accepted as being of critical importance to children's overall learning experience. Yet we often see emphasis being placed on and funds being allocated to competitive sport and games initiatives. The title of this book is "The PD needs of young children" but we need to question whether we (parents, practitioners, policy makers and academics) can accurately identify what these needs are and whether/how past and current policies prevent or support good practice in relation to this.

Summary of key points

- PE in the Primary School has evolved since 1870 from the provision of military drill style exercises to a focus on posture, gymnastics, movement and sports – through to the current broad curriculum and wide range of activities experienced by young children.
- PD in an EY context has deep pedagogical roots, but there are significant issues around assessment and determining best practice in this field.
- The content of practice is often affected by political developments and current societal trends. The focus should be on the PD needs of young children and not accommodating wider agendas.

Suggested further reading

Ball, C. (1994). *Start right: The importance of early learning.* London: RSA.
Sammons, P., Elliot, K., Sylva, K., Melhuish, E., Siraj-Blatchford, I., & Taggart, B. (2004). The impact of pre-school on young children's cognitive attainments at entry to reception. *British Educational Research Journal, 30*(5), 691–712.

References

Ball, C. (1994). *Start Right: The importance of early learning*. London: RSA.

David, T., Goouch, K., Powell, S., & Abbott, L. (2003). *Birth to three Matters: A review of the literature*. London: DfES.

Department for Education (DfE). (2013). *The National Curriculum in England: Key stages 1 and 2 framework document*. London: Crown Copyright.

DfE (2008). Statutory Framework for the Early Years Foundation Stage. Setting the standards for learning, development and care for children from birth to five. London, DfE.

DfE (2012). Statutory Framework for the Early Years Foundation Stage. Setting the standards for learning, development and care for children from birth to five. London, DfE.

Department for Education and Skills/Department for Culture, Media and Sport (DfES/DCMS). (2003). *Learning through physical education and sport: A guide to the physical education, school sport and club links strategy*. London: DfES/DCMS.

Departments of Education and Science (DES) (1972). *White Paper: Education: A framework for expansion*. London: HMSO.

Department of Education and Science (DES). (1991). *Physical education for age 5–16*. London: DES.

Griggs, G. (2015). *Understanding primary physical education*. London: Routledge.

Kirk, D., Penney, D., Burgess-Limerick, R., Gorely, P., & Maynard, C. A. (2002). *A level physical education: The reflective performer*. Leeds: Human Kinetics.

Lawson, J., & Silver, H. (1973). *A social history of education in England*. London: Methuen.

McIntosh, P. C. (1952). *Physical education in England since 1800*. London: G. Bell.

McIntosh, P. C., Dixon, J. G., Munrow, A. D., & Willetts, R. F. (1981). *Landmarks in the history of physical education* (3rd ed.). London: Routledge & Kegan Paul.

Ministry of Education and the Central Office of Information. (1952). *Moving and growing: Physical education in the primary school, Part 1*. London: Her Majesty's Stationery Office.

Penney, D., & Evans, J. (1999). *Politics, policy and practice in physical education*. London: Taylor and Francis.

Rumbold Report. (1990). Retrieved from http://www.educationengland.org.uk/documents/rumbold/rumbold1990.html#15

Sammons, P., Elliot, K., Sylva, K., Melhuish, E., Siraj-Blatchford, I., & Taggart, B. (2004). The impact of pre-school on young children's cognitive attainments at entry to reception. *British Educational Research Journal*, *30*(5), 691–712.

Sammons, P., Sylva, K., Melhuish, E., Siraj, I., Taggart, B., Toth, K., & Smee, R. (2014). *Influences on students' GCSE attainment and progress at age 16: Effective pre-school, primary & secondary education project (EPPSE)*. London: DfE.

2

PHYSICAL LITERACY IN EARLY CHILDHOOD

Sue Allingham, Patricia Maude and Margaret Whitehead

Personal reflection

Musings on ways in which children learn and become physically competent have occupied scores of my waking hours. What are the triggers to success and how can we ensure that infants and young children achieve their full potential in physical competence and go on to establish active lifestyles that subsequently lead to lifelong engagement in physical activity? The following two reflections provide some answers. The first relates to flying a kite: kite flying was one of my keen aspirations as a child. The physical challenges demanded greater strength than I had at the outset, but that did not curtail my confidence or my eagerness. Persistence and determination were also essential ingredients to eventual success. The second reflection follows my observation of a child sitting with his mother, trying to tie his shoelaces. She patiently showed and helped him with each part of the process over and over again and he patiently tried, over and over again. She gave him ample time to work at it alone, only helping when he asked for another demonstration. After about 20 minutes he had succeeded several times and the two celebrated with a high five each time he was successful.

Significant physical development and physical competence are fundamental both to kite flying (which requires whole body strength and co-ordination) and to effective manipulation of shoelaces (which calls for fine motor control and manual dexterity). But these are just parts of the story of success. Other key factors include having: the motivation to want to get involved; the determination to persist and hopefully succeed; the confidence in one's own ability to achieve the task; and adequate levels of cognitive development to both gain knowledge about the task and understand how progress could be made.

In summary, physical competence and the ability to establish active lifestyles that lead to lifelong engagement in physical activity are significantly determined by motivation, confidence, knowledge and understanding. All of these factors have led me to a whole-hearted commitment to the importance of establishing and embedding physical literacy (a concept that embraces these factors) from birth and throughout early childhood.

Introduction

Physical literacy is defined by the International Physical Literacy Association (IPLA) as a personal disposition whereby an individual has the "motivation, confidence, physical competence, knowledge and understanding to value and take responsibility for engagement in physical activities for life" (IPLA, 2017). In unpicking the concept further, Pickard and Maude (2014, p. 22) identify that "Physical literacy should not be viewed as an end product to be aspired to, but rather a state in which we live throughout our lives." Physical competence and physical literacy are distinct but are closely related in that physical competence is just one constituent of physical literacy. It is a necessary but not sufficient constituent. Physical literacy depends also on evidence of affective and cognitive characteristics and, as such, motivation, confidence, knowledge and understanding must also be nurtured. In this sense, physical literacy is, therefore, more than just physical development and physical competence.

This chapter outlines the ways in which physical literacy can be nurtured from birth and throughout early childhood as infants set out and make progress along their lifelong physical literacy journey. First, a brief summary of the background to the development of the concept will be provided along with the definition, domains and attributes of physical literacy. An example of a child who is making good progress along her physical literacy journey is then provided and this is followed by identifying some of the ways in which physical literacy may be nurtured and, finally, potential barriers are explored.

Development of the concept of physical literacy: "why physical literacy?"

Since the turn of the century, concerns have been expressed over a lack of physical activity in children and adults and the detrimental effects that this might have on physical and mental health, leading to diminished quality of life. At the same time, questions were being asked about the aspirations of teachers of physical education (PE) and indeed the purpose of PE. These concerns and questions resulted in a proposal that one aspiration for involvement in physical activity should be a commitment to physical activity for life. Alongside this aspiration is the need to take account not only of developing physical competence in the Early Years but also of developing the confidence, motivation, knowledge and understanding that will enable this to happen. Physical literacy, therefore, is a "disposition," based on sound philosophical study, that should be maintained throughout the life course (Whitehead, 2010). Thus, it is important that efforts are made to nurture physical literacy from an early age.

What is physical literacy?

The definition set out earlier encompasses the aspiration of promoting physical literacy through participation in physical activity and suggests means by which this aspiration might best be achieved (i.e. through developing motivation, confidence, physical competence and knowledge and understanding). These means can be grouped into three domains (see Figure 2.1), namely the affective domain (motivation and confidence), the cognitive domain (knowledge and understanding) and the physical domain (acquisition of physical competence) (Whitehead, 2019).

To help clarify the nature of the three domains, some descriptors are suggested later to indicate "behaviours" that children in their Early Years and in Primary school might work towards or demonstrate, in making progress on their physical literacy journey. The following characteristics are closely aligned to the IPLA Physical Literacy Attributes (Whitehead, 2019).

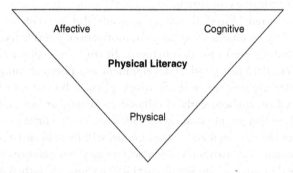

FIGURE 2.1 The three domains of physical literacy.

1. Characteristics related to The Affective Domain refer to behaviours that indicate that the individual is:
   • Motivated to be physically active;
   • Confident to choose and explore unfamiliar physical activities;
   • Confident when continuing to engage and learn in physical activities.
2. Characteristics related to The Cognitive Domain refer to behaviours that indicate that the individual:
   • Knows what leads to success in learning physical activities;
   • Understands how to improve performance in physical activities;
   • Knows how physical activity and an active lifestyle can enhance well-being.
3. Characteristics related to The Physical Domain refer to behaviours that indicate that the individual is:
   • Moving efficiently and effectively in an increasingly wide range of physical activities;
   • Developing an awareness of movement needs and possibilities in an increasingly wide range of physical activities;
   • Participating readily, both independently and with others, in physical activities.

Nurturing physical literacy in young children

The characteristics outlined earlier and in Figure 2.1 are general examples of ways in which children can be guided along their physical literacy journey but we should be mindful that this list is not exhaustive. Table 2.1 exemplifies further ways in which some characteristics of the affective, physical and cognitive domains can contribute to progress in physical literacy, throughout early childhood.

TABLE 2.1 Nurturing physical literacy with children aged 0–4 years and 4–8 years

Some characteristics of physical literacy	Children aged 0–4 years, through active play and physical activities	Children aged 4–8 years, through physical education
Being motivated to be physically active	Nurture eagerness to move; provide for frequent and varied active play; minimise sedentary time; play with child	Engage and sustain the interest, willing and active participation of learners, including frequent opportunities for at least moderate physical activity
Having confidence to choose and explore new physical activities	Encourage self-confidence, exploration and inquisitive discovery of ways of moving, balancing and manipulation	Build on existing confidence; encourage choice of new physical activities; assess moment of readiness to tackle increasingly challenging situations
Showing confidence when continuing to engage and learn in physical activities	Build on children's confidence in their current ability as they build new learning	Sustain learners in developing persistence, determination, resilience and self-regulation
Moving efficiently and effectively in an increasingly wide range of physical activities	Ensure exposure to a wide range of locomotion, stability and object control activities	Extend movement vocabulary, movement memory and movement quality; give developmental feedback on performance
Developing an awareness of movement needs and possibilities in an increasingly wide range of physical activities	Offer a range of resources, outdoor and indoor environments and activity types Promote diversity of activities	Provide a PE curriculum that builds towards athletics, dance, games, gymnastics, swimming, adventure activities and active recreation
Participate readily, both independently and with others, in physical activities	Support active play, alone, alongside and with others	Promote and develop solo, cooperative and competitive physical activities and appreciation of winning and losing

(Continued)

Some characteristics of physical literacy	Children aged 0–4 years, through active play and physical activities	Children aged 4–8 years, through physical education
Knowing what leads to success in learning physical activities	Encourage choice of challenging yet attainable activities; introduce repetition and practice in adding to success in learning	Help the learner to gain knowledge of, assess and select attainable progressions in learning physical activities; encourage personal evaluation and discussion of performance
Understanding how to improve performance in physical activities	Support learning through trial and error, repetition and practice	Promote questioning, give verbal feedback Facilitate personal analysis of performance Build the learner's observation skills
Knowing how physical activity and an active lifestyle can enhance well-being	Establish a healthy lifestyle of physical activity, rest, sleep and diet	Help learners to understand the values of active lifestyles. Promote health and well-being

Demonstrating progress along the physical literacy journey

Successfully flying a kite and doing up shoelaces were identified in the personal reflection at the start of this chapter as two ways in which physical literacy might be demonstrated by a young child. A further example is provided by Alma as she succeeds in her attempts to master a balance bike (bicycle with no pedals). At the age of two, Alma was physically competent in terms of postural control, locomotion in walking and running, and she was strong in both lower and upper limbs. She was a confident mover and well-motivated to be active and to play outdoors whenever possible. She was offered a balance bike, which she curiously explored, although tentatively to start with. To begin with, she walked beside the bike and eventually had the confidence to walk astride it. As she gained experience and understood more about how to balance and control the bike, walking became striding (see Figure 2.2) and, with increasing confidence, striding became speedier until she needed some parental guidance to ensure safe practice! She soon began to take her feet off the ground momentarily, whilst keeping her balance and then tried gliding with her feet off the ground for short and gradually longer distances (see Figure 2.3).

FIGURE 2.2 Alma striding on her balance bike.

FIGURE 2.3 Alma gliding on her balance bike.

Alma's achievements stemmed from her self-motivation, curiosity and positive "can-do" approach to independent learning, her eagerness to succeed and her willingness to keep trying. She could draw from her tacit knowledge from past experiences, in order to tackle the new demands of this activity and she had boundless energy to devote to the task in hand. In terms of her lifelong physical literacy journey, Alma was then almost all set for a lifetime of active travel. She was soon ready to transfer to a pedal bike, to venture further afield, biking with her family. The next steps in this journey might be to use cycling as a form of active travel, a recreational activity, a competitive sport, an extreme sport or for exploring the world. Thus, we can see how early steps and progressions lay the foundations for future activities.

Physical literacy from birth: brilliant beginnings

The physical literacy journey for most children has a brilliant beginning! As Hoeger and Hoeger (1993, p. 148) state, "movement and physical activity are basic functions for which the human organism was created." Just watching a baby repeatedly striving to achieve a new movement provides evidence of the intrinsic motivation to "have a go," the confidence to engage in experimentation, persistence through trial and error and then either to succeed or happily abandon that activity. At the same time, physical competence is progressing at an amazing rate, from being a relatively minimal mover at birth to becoming an independent and physically active explorer of the world around in just a few months! Noam (see Figure 2.4) was a very active child from birth, eager to be on the move and, on

FIGURE 2.4 Noam demonstrating enthusiasm for his new-found skill of walking.

his first birthday, when this photograph was taken, he was happily heading out across the garden, with upright posture, a sturdy gait and effective balance.

Physical development is evidenced by the growth in shape and size of the skeleto-muscular system and commensurate maturing of the internal body systems along with rapid development of the brain and neuro-muscular system throughout the early months and years. In infancy, learning is dependent on the early developing sensori-motor area of the brain and is achieved through moving, accompanied by the five senses of feeling, hearing, seeing, tasting and smelling. From birth, the brain continues to grow at an accelerated pace as the billions of brain cells (neurons) present at birth link up creating connections (synapses). Movement is the key to synaptic development. Ratey and Hagerman (2008, pp. 4 and 245) state that not only is exercise "the single most powerful tool to optimize brain function," but also "for brain function to be at peak performance, our bodies need to work hard!" Wolpert (2012) supports this when he suggests that the main reason that we have a brain is to produce adaptable and complex movements. This exemplifies how, for example, the randomly arm-waving, leg-kicking recumbent infant progresses from lying to sitting, to standing, to walking and then to running, whilst also discovering the use of the arms in powerful activities such as pushing up from a prone position (on the tummy), pulling up to standing and climbing onto furniture. Once a new movement is mastered and practised, it can be stored in the memory for future use, thus building up a vast bank of movement knowledge on which to draw and apply. By their first birthday, most children have achieved significant levels of co-ordination and have laid the foundations for the development of postural control and movement mastery. Much of this early development is physical in nature and represents the start of a child's physical literacy journey.

Physical literacy: from brilliant beginnings towards school readiness

Some children are lucky enough to have had a "brilliant beginning" to their physical literacy journey, although the way in which this may have been provided will have varied dependent on the setting in which the child experienced their first few years (be it at home, with a child-minder or in a nursery). Following their first three years of life, children who attend a setting away from the home will experience different approaches to their development as they enter the Early Years Foundation Stage (DfE, 2017). Wherever children are raised, be it solely in the home, at a nursery or preschool full time or experiencing a combination of these, it is beneficial to consider the following three points in order to optimise children's physical literacy:

1. An enabling environment;
2. Motivation;
3. Physical competence.

An enabling environment

To have an "enabling environment" is one of the four statutory themes of the Early Years Foundation Stage in England (DfE, 2017). This means that the provision of the environment must nurture physical, affective and cognitive development. As soon as infants are born, they start to explore and investigate the world around them both physically and affectively, and an "enabling" environment is crucial in supporting their early learning and development:

> ...movement is an integral part of life from the moment of conception until death, and a child's experience of movement will play a pivotal part in shaping his personality, his feelings, and his achievements. Learning is not just about reading, writing, and maths. These are higher abilities that are built upon the integrity of the relationship between brain and body.
>
> *(Goddard-Blythe, 2005, p. 5)*

Motivation

Successful learning depends largely on being motivated. Providing an "enabling environment" is the first step towards promoting motivation. The EYFS (DfE, 2017) identifies the following three characteristics of effective teaching and learning that may help foster an environment in which children are motivated to learn. First, children should be encouraged to play, explore, investigate, experience and "have a go"; second, learning should be active; third, children should be given opportunities to think critically and creatively, and to develop their own ideas as well as to make links between them.

Physical competence

Formal settings can build children's physical competence through providing frequent opportunities for active play and physical activity of at least moderate intensity throughout the day as well as at breaktimes and in PE sessions, whilst also minimizing sedentary time in the classroom. Table 2.1 provides some ways in which physical competence may be improved, for example, children should be enabled to:

- Move efficiently and effectively in an increasingly wide range of physical activities;
- Develop an awareness of movement needs and possibilities in an increasingly wide range of physical activities;
- Participate readily, both independently and with others, in physical activities.

It is argued in Chapter 8 that many children are starting school with lower than desirable levels of physical development and that they are not physically ready to start school. This suggests that some children's physical literacy journeys may have been "disrupted." The following two case studies are provided as examples of children who may need further support.

Case study 1: Matthew

In his Early Years, Matthew had a good vocabulary and was very eloquent. As an infant, he got around with a commando crawl and could go up and downstairs with ease. He was taught how to do this safely and rarely needed a stairgate. Health visitors started to question why he was late to walk (17 months), but his parents had not been concerned because, at the same time, Matthew was building complicated models with batteries and motors that were marketed for much older children. His fine motor control and ability to build very detailed technical models were completely missed and not appreciated at school. He did not find writing easy, and it was assumed that his fine motor skills were under-developed. The challenge for him, however, was that he did not like writing, was not motivated to write and was not inspired to try.

Case study 2: Joseph

When Joseph started in his Reception class, he immediately stood out because he was taller than the other children. He arrived at school without records from a previous setting, so it was assumed that he had not received any preschool provision. This was not the case. As time went on, his teachers became increasingly concerned about Joseph. Their observations showed that he did not seem to be in control of his limbs and found it difficult to negotiate the environment without bumping into furniture and children. Of course, the other children perceived this as deliberately hitting or kicking them, and they did not like it. He was unable to sit still on the carpet and could not understand how to "line up" because, in his mind, he was "in the line." This resulted in reprimands from other adults, especially those who did not know him.

After six weeks, there was a Parents' Evening. The staff needed to speak to Joseph's parents about their concerns. His parents had always known that there was something different about him, but had felt that no one was listening to them. He had been to preschool; in fact, he had been to more than one, but he had been asked to leave them all as he was perceived to be "naughty," and the settings were not prepared to support him (this was

(Continued)

why, on transition, he had no previous preschool notes). After the Parents' Evening discussion, actions were put in place, and it was not long before a diagnosis of dyspraxia was made, and strategies were given to support him. For example, along with all the children in his class, Joseph started on a programme of physical activities.

Thinking about the children in these two case studies, to what extent were they provided with an enabling environment, how much were they motivated to learn and develop their physical skills and would we describe them as physically competent? At an early age, Matthew was labelled by health visitors as having a movement delay because he started to walk later than many children. However, he had well developed manual dexterity, where his interest lay in activities such as constructing complex models. Joseph, on the other hand, experienced movement difficulties and was branded as being naughty, whereas his movement challenges were due to dyspraxia (see Chapter 10 for more details on dyspraxia/ Developmental Co-ordination Disorder).

These case studies aptly illustrate the crucial importance of acknowledging the uniqueness of each child, noting their abilities and achievements, their strengths and areas for development in relation to physical development and physical literacy via the physical, affective and cognitive domains.

Barriers to physical literacy

In order to successfully nurture physical literacy in young children, such as in the examples provided earlier in the chapter (kite flying, tying shoelaces and riding a balance bike), it is helpful to explore some of the barriers to this. Not surprisingly, there is an overlap here between barriers to physical development and barriers to physical literacy. Perhaps, the key difference is in the domains that physical literacy covers and the ways in which they interrelate. There seem to be at least five key barriers to developing physical literacy. The first of these can occur when practitioners focus solely on the physical domain, whilst neglecting the affective and cognitive domains. For example, a young child who presents as inactive may have become inactive due to a lack of confidence, self-motivation, resilience and/or well-being. As another example, young children who are physically well developed and have experienced frequent success in physical activities such as balance, locomotion and object control are likely to be confident in the movement capabilities of their body. This does not, however, mean that they will necessarily succeed within the cognitive domain (for example, they may not understand how to improve their performance). Thus, to facilitate physical literacy, all three domains need to be considered and promoted.

A second barrier arises when a child is deprived of adequate movement opportunities. Within the physical domain, young children should engage frequently throughout the day in physical activity and keep sedentary time to a minimum. Added benefit is gained from exposure to a wide variety of environments (indoors, outdoor, in water) as well as through opportunities to play with many and varied resources and toys, with which to gain manipulative experience and object control. The greater the movement experience, the greater is the possibility of enhancing the affective and cognitive domains.

A third barrier is created when insufficient attention is given to developing the specific essentials of the child's balance, stability and postural control. At this early age, mastering balance and developing good posture are central to physical success. Goddard-Blythe (2005, p. 12) states that "balance is the primary sense with the task of enabling the body to function within the force of gravity." Secure balance is essential for postural control and postural control is essential for efficient functioning throughout life. Upright posture, whether sitting or standing, involves the ability to align the segments of the body in a vertical stack, like a plumb line, as seen in Figure 2.5. As far back as the Physical Education Syllabus of 1933, "posture" was a core requirement and was allocated frequent practice with the aim of developing "lightness and spring," "body flexibility" and "securing of good health" (Maude, 2001, p. 94). Although "wobbleyness" seems to be the order of the day for most young children, through active play and frequent practice, the strength and co-ordination needed to hold static positions gradually develop, resulting in the ability to be steady, centred, poised and rooted. Good upright posture often correlates with self-confidence, self-esteem and a sense of well-being (Figure 2.5).

A fourth barrier to developing physical literacy can be created when young children lack the involvement of significant others both as playmates and as interested and supportive participants. Whilst self-directed, spontaneous, free play is a very significant medium of learning in the Early Years, peer and adult interventions can add richness to active, creative play and enhance motivation. The provision of appropriate guidance and encouragement can scaffold the building of new experiences, provide positive feedback, aid learning and support the building of confidence. Peer and adult involvement can also help to develop the cognitive domain of knowledge and understanding, and also strengthen the affective domain of well-being.

The final barrier relates to a general lack of knowledge and understanding amongst practitioners (Conkbayir, 2017, p. 17). This may, in part, be due to a lack of knowledge and understanding of progression in child development within official guidance. Presently, what we expect of children is not clearly defined and is inconsistent from one source to another. Adults working with children in early childhood need to understand how to develop children's balance, locomotion, whole-body control and co-ordination through frequent physically active play. All "on entry" and "baseline" assessments used when a young child enters a new setting must be heavily weighted towards these and to what needs to be done to support and develop them. Tick lists of whether a child can throw, catch or kick

FIGURE 2.5 Standing posture (adapted from The Physical Education Syllabus, His Majesty's Stationery Office, 1933).

are spurious in assessing physical competence unless the fundamentals of balance, stability, control and co-ordination are sufficiently mature and that account is also taken of the affective and cognitive domains of physical literacy.

Conclusion

In conclusion, Ratey and Hagerman (2008, p. 3) assert that "we are born movers" and suggest that "we are at risk of dulling the brains of the next generation" if we fail to ensure that every young child engages frequently in energetic physical activity. Physical activity is the key factor in both the development of the brain and the achievement of physical competence.

Fostering physical literacy depends on capitalising on the three domains of affective, cognitive and physical. Nurturing the affective domain helps to ensure well-being, self-esteem, resilience and a "can do" attitude in physical activity. Stimulating the cognitive domain helps to increase tacit knowledge (Gill, 2000) and promote inquisitiveness and curiosity as a mover. Providing frequent opportunities for moderate to vigorous physical activity, with interventions suited to maximising individual physical development and physical competence, paves the way for young children to achieve their fullest potential in the physical domain.

Purposeful fostering of the brilliant beginnings and exciting potential seen in infancy can ensure that children are successfully launched on their physical literacy journey. With on-going encouragement as they transition from one phase of childhood to the next, they are well-placed to make continuous progress on their physical literacy journey and maintain a physically active lifestyle.

Summary of key points

1. Make provision for optimum physical development and physical competence throughout early childhood, by providing for the unique needs of each individual.
2. Develop the affective and cognitive domains alongside the physical domain to promote physical literacy.
3. Provide enabling environments.
4. Enable significant others to embrace the three domains of physical literacy in their work with children throughout early childhood.

Suggested further reading

Brodie, K. (2018). *The holistic care and development of children from birth to three.* Abingdon: Routledge.

Conkbayir, M. (2017). *Early childhood and neuroscience. Theory, research and implications for practice.* London: Bloomsbury Academic.

Maude, P. (2001). *Physical children, active teaching.* Buckingham: Open University Press.

Whitebread, D., & Coltman, P. (2015). *Teaching and learning in the early years* (4th ed.). London: Routledge.

Whitehead, M. E. (2010). *Physical literacy: Throughout the lifecourse.* London: Routledge.

References

Board of Education. (1933). *Syllabus of physical training for schools.* London: HMSO.

Department of Education (DfE). (2017). *Statutory framework for the early years foundation stage. Setting the standards for learning, development and care for children from birth to five.* London: HMSO.

Gill, J. G. (2000). *The tacit mode.* Albany: State University of New York Press.

Goddard-Blythe, S. (2005). *The well balanced child*. Stroud: Hawthorn Press.

Hoeger, M., & Hoeger, S. (1993). *Fitness and wellness*. Belmont, VA: Wadsworth.

International Physical Literacy Association (IPLA). (2017). Retrieved from www.physical-literacy.org.uk

Pickard, A., & Maude, P. (2014). *Teaching physical education creatively*. London: Routledge.

Ratey, J., & Hagerman, E. (2008). *SPARK: The revolutionary new science of exercise and the brain*. New York, NY: Little Brown and Company.

Whitehead, M. E. (Ed.). (2019, in press). *Physical literacy across the world*. London: Routledge.

Wolpert, D. (2012). A moving story. *Cambridge Alumni Magazine*, Issue 66, Easter.

3

THE COMPLEX NATURE OF EARLY CHILDHOOD MOVEMENT SKILLS DEVELOPMENT

Mike Jess

Personal reflection

Thirty years ago, after teaching in high schools for almost a decade, I became a Primary School Physical Education (PE) specialist. The experience was new to me and I struggled. My multi-activity sport background made me feel like a square peg in a round hole, particularly when working with the younger children. The first year in this new role was difficult and it was not until I began to read the literature on children's motor development and developmentally appropriate practice that I started to make some sense of my predicament. Gradually, I began to understand and acknowledge the importance of children's fundamental or basic movement foundation. Because PE was a marginal subject in the eight Primary Schools in which I worked each month, my classes soon became my personal "laboratory." I set out to explore children's movement learning, particularly in the younger children, and spent the next few years concentrating on the travelling, object control and balance-related movements of almost one thousand children. It was a revelation. I learnt that children's movement learning was much more complex than I had imagined. Over time, the physical, cognitive, social and emotional responses of the children were so different. Some loved the movement tasks I offered, took part enthusiastically and practised movements between my visits. Others were withdrawn, bored or even frightened and did not really engage. I was amazed at how well some of the young children worked in groups, while others argued, fell out or were just locked in their own world. From a movement perspective, some children demonstrated a high degree of flow, rhythm and timing, while others were stilted, uncoordinated and timid. When offered the opportunity to explore, some were creative, while others played it safe or reluctantly tried out different ways of moving. While some children could demonstrate the "mature" movement criteria I had read in the text books, I noted how there were few examples of children presenting this in "real life" movement scenarios. In fact, these "mature" movements were more the exception than the rule. During this period of my career, while I was immersed in young children's movement learning I couldn't quite get my head around it all. It was all very complex. Thirty years on, as I now reflect on these experiences through a complexity lens, I think I have a much better understanding of the movement foundation that these young children were grappling to develop on a daily basis.

Putting Early Years movement in context

During their Early Years of schooling (ages 4–7), children's movement development and learning begin to focus on the fundamental movement skills (FMS) that act as the foundation for an active life. Movement learning, however, has often been on the margins of preschool and Primary Education and this is unlikely to change until a number of long-held misconceptions and barriers are addressed. For more than a hundred years, thinking that splits the mind and body into separate entities has dominated views of education and schooling in the West. Literacy and numeracy have remained the focus of most school systems around the world with the result that movement development and learning are not considered to be of any significant educational value. This marginal status has not been helped by some key developments across the movement and PE worlds. In the 1920s and 1930s, motor development researchers presented a maturational view that suggested children's movement development "just happens" (e.g. Gesell & Thompson, 1938). While FMS may indeed emerge "naturally" during the Early Years of life, most children need regular opportunities and appropriate teaching to develop a movement foundation that is efficient (Gallahue, Ozmun, & Goodway, 2012). Unfortunately, the "just happens" viewpoint has tended to dominate in education circles and has sustained the low status of PE in these Early Years. Later, as PE and sport programmes evolved during the second half of the 20th century, these developments tended to exacerbate this marginalisation issue by "compartmentalising" PE on the more specific and complex movement skills needed in various physical activities, particularly team games (O'Connor, Alfrey, & Payne, 2012). For many young children, these specific movements are developmentally outside of their reach.

More recently, however, holistic views that acknowledge the complexity of children's movement development are being introduced. Frameworks focussed on children's FMS are becoming increasingly popular in many parts of the world (e.g. Donnelly, Mueller, & Gallahue, 2017). These frameworks generally focus on three categories of FMS that are believed to act as the foundation for the more complex physical activities children take part in as they grow older e.g. games, sports and dance. These movement categories are defined by Logan, Ross, Chee, Stodden, and Robinson (2018) as:

- Locomotor/travelling (e.g. walking, running, jumping, galloping, sliding, skipping);
- Balance/stability (more static skills like bending, dodging, stretching, swinging, turning and twisting);
- Object control/manipulative (e.g. throwing, catching, dribbling, kicking, striking).

Significantly, most of these FMS approaches present a more integrated and educational framework focussing on the connections between the fundamental movements and children's cognitive, social and emotional learning. Valuable development work is being carried out in the motor development, motor control and PE communities but progress has generally been slow because of the deep-rooted misconceptions discussed earlier. This chapter presents a complexity-informed framework to support practitioners' understanding of young children's movement. It will first introduce background about complexity thinking before discussing how key ideas from complexity can help frame our understanding of children's movement development. The chapter will conclude by briefly presenting key ideas for practitioners as they seek to support young children's movement development.

What is complexity?

While most people readily acknowledge the complexity within our world, there is some confusion about the meaning of the term. This confusion stems from the belief that complexity is primarily viewed as something that is difficult. As a concept, however, complexity is much more than something that is difficult. Across the academic, professional and policy worlds, many are beginning to argue that complexity represents a way to view how the world works, particularly the social world. Almost 20 years ago, the world-renowned scientist Stephen Hawking was reported to say that "I think the next (21st) century will be the century of complexity."

Systems thinking is a good starting point to understand complexity. Systems are collections of different parts that interact to achieve something. These include large systems like countries, forests, the earth and even the universe and smaller systems like cars, televisions and watches. Human beings can be viewed as systems because our physical, cognitive, social and emotional parts come together (or integrate) to support our development and learning over time. Central to the idea of complexity is the difference between two types of systems that are often confused as being the same thing: complicated systems and complex systems (Ovens, Hopper, & Butler, 2013). Traffic lights, fridges and televisions are good examples of complicated systems. In a complicated system, the interaction between the different parts of the system is pre-programmed, and there is little or no relationship with the environment in which the system is functioning. Watching traffic lights continue to pass through their timed sequence, even when an accident has stopped all the traffic, is a good example of the pre-programmed and closed nature of a complicated system. Complicated systems do not change over time because they function in a linear way that produces outcomes with a high degree of predictability, even certainty. Anyone who works regularly with young children is unlikely to describe them as pre-programmed, predictable and never changing systems!

While complex systems may appear to have some similarities with complicated systems, they have one key difference. Within a complex system, some of the parts are able to organise themselves in different ways. This ability to self-organise is the big difference between the complicated system and the complex system and is witnessed in many human behaviours, including movement behaviours (Chow, Davids, Button, & Renshaw, 2015). For example, self-organising behaviours in humans range from short term decisions, like how to move their body when walking on a wet pavement, through to long term life changing decisions focussed on the types of physical activity we choose to take part in at different times of our lives. Critically, it is this ability to self-organise that means humans can be predictable at times and unpredictable at other times in their behaviours. It is this capacity to be unpredictable and do the unexpected that separates humans as complex systems from pre-programmed complicated systems. As such, this chapter takes the view that young children's movement development is a complex process (Savelsbergh, Davids, van der Kamp, & Bennett, 2003): a process that evolves in an emergent, non-linear and often "messy" trajectory.

Complexity and young children's movement

Building on this short introduction to complexity, the main section of the chapter considers how four concepts relating to complexity can help practitioners develop an understanding of young children's movement development. These four concepts are: the self-organising nature of young children's learning; the negotiation of boundaries; connections; and the long term and "messy" process that ultimately leads to movement development.[1] First, examples highlighting how young children continually self-organise as they seek to work out their movement potential will be presented. However, it is critical to recognise that self-organisation is not an "anything goes" process for the child. Children are not in a position to do whatever they want to because this self-organising process always takes place within boundaries. As such, the second complexity concept, self-organising within boundaries, focusses on what is meant by boundaries and considers the implications of young children continuously negotiating boundaries as they attempt to move. Linked to the notion of self-organisation within boundaries, the third concept considers how children's interactions with the different boundaries result in a range of multiple connections that, over time, have a significant impact on the nature of children's movement development. Finally, by integrating these three complexity concepts, the fourth concept highlights how children's movement development cannot be viewed as a simple, linear and short term process but one that is a long term, non-linear and differentiated phenomenon. The chapter concludes by briefly considering how practitioners can start to use complexity ideas to inform their teaching of young children's movement skills.

A self-organising process

If you watch young children move, you will observe them "self-organising-in-action" as they attempt to connect and coordinate different parts of their body into movements. While they may occasionally decide to move for the pure enjoyment of moving, their movement efforts are usually for a specific reason. The baby reaching for the toy, the toddler trying to take their first steps, the three-year-old attempting to hit a moving balloon or the six-year-old skipping or galloping to keep in time with the music are all examples of children's self-organising efforts as they try to move for a reason. Some of these efforts will be successful and others less so and, if the children revisit these movements sometime in the future, the outcome of their efforts may be quite different. Movements are not simply repeated in exactly the same way, time after time, in the linear, closed-loop manner of the complicated system: they tend to develop in ways that are messy and non-linear through a mix of successes, surprises, repetitions, mistakes and possibly the occasional disaster.

However, it is not only the physical parts of the child that self-organise as they learn to move. If a group of children go outdoors and a variety of small and large equipment is placed on the ground, the self-organising process is immediately more than physical. Cognitively, the children self-organise by deciding who they want to play with, what equipment they want to play with and what they do with the equipment. Some may decide to keep repeating the same action, others may try a range of different movements while some may try something original and be creative. Socially, some may play alone, others may stick with their friend, while others may change partners often or play in a larger group. Emotionally, some may get excited, others may be withdrawn and some may just be bored and disinterested. As the children take part in their movement experiences, their self-organising becomes a more holistic experience also involving cognitive, social and emotional behaviours. But, as we now discuss, this complex self-organisation process does not happen in an isolated "bubble" from the rest of the world; there are many boundaries that need to be negotiated!

Negotiating boundaries

Boundaries are a significant part of children's movement development. As children make their way through each day they are constantly negotiating different boundaries (sometimes called barriers or constraints) i.e. they self-organise within boundaries. Critically, boundaries either act to help or hinder children's movement efforts and come in three main forms: personal boundaries, boundaries in the immediate environment and boundaries that are part of the tasks the children are attempting. Examples of children negotiating boundaries are limitless, but in the following scenario, "Tig" is used as an example to describe how these three types of boundaries can help or hinder young children in their efforts to move.

Playing the game of 'tig'

Most adults know the game of 'tig' or similar. It is a relatively simple chasing game that can be played in many different ways with children in the early years of schooling. Within a group of children, one child is designated 'it'. The task for 'it' is to let the other children run away, chase them and 'tig' one of the children by touching them above the waist and below the head. This child then becomes 'it' and takes over the role of the chaser. The child who was previously 'it' is now free and can be chased. The game continues in this manner until someone decides it is time to stop. While 'tig' may appear to be a simple game to an adult, it involves young children in a complex self-organising process as they interact with, and negotiate, the many boundaries they meet. Examples from each of the 3 categories of boundary help us understand the complex nature of the game for young children.

Personal boundaries: From a physical perspective this game involves locomotor and balance movements. These include running, dodging, weaving and even stopping. Alongside these FMS, children also need to: understand and remember the rules of the game (cognitive); play within a large group of children (social); and hopefully enjoy the experience of chasing or being chased (emotional).

Environmental boundaries: These include the size and limits of the space in which the game is being played and the different obstacles within this space. These obstacles can include equipment placed around the hall and the other children who are moving within the space. These all act as environmental boundaries to be negotiated as the game progresses.

Task boundaries: During the game, the task boundaries change as the child takes on different roles. One minute they may be a chaser whose task is to run towards the other children, while a minute later their task is to flee from the chaser. The boundaries of these tasks quickly change and need to be negotiated by the child.

Children negotiate boundaries in their own way. The same boundary may act to hinder one child's movement behaviour while it might help another child. Thus, boundaries are described as *ambiguous*. For example, in the game of tig, running, dodging and weaving are key task boundaries influencing children's participation in the game. Children whose running action is immature may find it difficult to change speed or dodge and weave when they are running. For them, these movement boundaries are barriers to their participation. However, for children who can change speed and dodge quite easily, these movement boundaries help them access the game. Movements, however, are not the only boundaries affecting children's participation in tig. The rules of the tig and the "rough and tumble" nature of the game are examples of cognitive and emotional boundaries that will affect children in different ways. The key is that boundaries are a constant feature of children's movement experience that sometimes act to hinder their development and, at other times, are helpful in the development process. The positive and negative influence of boundaries on children's movement development can be explained by considering where the children's self-organising efforts take place in relation to the boundaries: inside, around and outside the boundaries (see Table 3.1).

TABLE 3.1 Children's self-organising efforts in relation to boundaries

	Supporting development	Hindering development
"Playing safe" **inside** the boundaries	Consolidates	Bores
"Pushing" **around** the boundaries	Challenges	Stresses
"Exploring" **beyond** the boundaries	Creative	Breaks down: chaos!!

"Moving along a bench" is one example that helps explain how young children's movement development involves a complex mix of their self-organising efforts inside, around and outside different boundaries. This example will now be used to illustrate the three possible options mentioned earlier.

"Playing safe" inside the boundaries

"Playing safe" inside the boundaries is an important part of children's movement development because it helps children to consolidate movement behaviours. The children are not taking risks and are not being particularly challenged. For some children, sliding or crawling along the bench on their fronts or walking along the bench represents "playing safe" inside the boundaries. Walking along the bench may be something they have not done very often and it may take time for them to become more confident in this movement situation before they are ready to challenge themselves. "Playing safe" helps them consolidate this movement behaviour. However, if children "play safe" in the same predictable way for too long, there is a good chance they will become bored with the activity. For practitioners, recognising those children who are "playing safe" to consolidate behaviours and those who are becoming bored because the task is now easy is an important part of the support and teaching process.

"Pushing" around the boundaries

Self-organising *around* boundaries is also an important part of a child's movement development process because it challenges their current behaviours and helps move the development process forward. For example, a child may "push their boundaries" by walking halfway along the bench, turning around 180 degrees and then walking backwards to the end of the bench. For many young children, changing the locomotor movement or adding the turning action halfway along the bench makes the movement task more challenging, is likely to extend their movement capacity but may also lead to a few mistakes as they push too far. In addition, if children are consistently "pushing the boundaries" too far and too often, their movement behaviours will likely begin to break down. For practitioners, deciding when and how to challenge each child by "pushing their boundaries" is a key feature of their support repertoire.

"Exploring" beyond the boundaries

Self-organising **outside** boundaries is also an important part of the movement development process because it offers children the opportunity to be creative in their movement behaviours. Children explore movement possibilities by intentionally trying movements that are different. Their movement behaviours become less predictable and less certain. For example, children may include different locomotor styles and balances as they roll or jump along the bench and add different shapes or spinning movements as they move. They may even try this with a partner. However, while exploring beyond the boundaries can be a very positive and creative feature of the development process it can also be quite chaotic and even dangerous. For practitioners, offering children the opportunity to explore movement possibilities "beyond their boundaries" is an important part of the teaching process but one that needs to be carefully monitored for safety reasons.

As is now discussed, supporting children's movement development over time is a complex process for practitioners. Striking a balance of "playing safe" to consolidate behaviours, "pushing the boundaries" to challenge behaviours and offering opportunities to explore movement possibilities are key factors in supporting children's movement development.

Connections

From a movement perspective, practitioners have always been aware of the importance that the different connections between children's body parts make to their movement development. However, traditional PE and sports programmes have unfortunately been designed as if children are complicated systems whose body parts are pre-programmed to connect in an order that leads to predictable movement outcomes. Before each lesson, the teacher decides the desired movement outcome and transmits specific "gold standard" information on how the body parts connect to achieve this outcome. Children's movement development is, therefore, viewed as a "one-size-fits-all" phenomenon: a view that ignores two key points. First, it ignores the individual differences between each child: their previous experiences and their current physical, cognitive, social and emotional development. Second, and just as important, it ignores the fact that, while children, young people and adults need to develop some degree of movement efficiency, they also need to be adaptable and creative in their movement behaviours to take part in most physical activity contexts (Jess, Keay, & Carse, 2016; Sandford, Duncombe, Mason, & Butler, 2015).

The FMS of over arm throwing can be used to highlight the importance of efficiency, adaptability and creativity in children's movement development. From the perspective of movement efficiency, a number of key movement features help young children throw efficiently e.g. stepping forward with the opposite foot from the throwing arm (see Donnelly et al., 2017 for more information). However, in most physical activity situations, children will need to throw objects of different sizes in different directions, at different heights and at different speeds. They rarely, if ever, need to connect the different parts of their body in exactly the same way time after time. They need to be adaptable in their throwing action. In addition, and particularly when playing games, throwing the ball in ways that are unpredictable can be used to confuse or surprise opponents e.g. pretending to throw a ball one way but actually sending it in another direction. Throwing, therefore, is not about meeting a rigid "gold standard" but developing a flexible repertoire of body part connections to be efficient, adaptable and creative in different contexts.

The complexity concepts presented earlier are helpful here. By opening and closing boundaries, practitioners can help children develop efficiency, adaptability and creativity in their movement behaviours. As discussed earlier, closing boundaries to focus on key movement features or movement concepts (e.g. directions, levels and speeds) will help children consolidate their movement efficiency and adaptability in different contexts. However, by opening the boundaries and introducing new movement features, new movement concepts or designing new movement tasks, practitioners can challenge the children by "pushing around their boundaries." These challenges are designed to extend the children's movement repertoire and add to their ability to be adaptable in their movement behaviour. Finally, by encouraging children to move beyond or outside the boundaries, children have the opportunity to explore different movement possibilities and be creative. By opening and closing the boundaries at appropriate times, practitioners can offer an appropriate mix of experiences that help children develop the connections between their physical body parts to be efficient, adaptable and creative as their movement behaviours develop. Unlike the predictable and limited connections of the complicated system approach, this complexity-informed example highlights how young children's movement development involves a much wider range of connections between different body parts.

Long term and messy

Movement development is not a "quick fix" that "just happens" but a long process that evolves over time in ways that are sometimes quite stable and, as we have discussed throughout this chapter, at other times messy and unpredictable. As babies pass through infancy into early childhood, the increasing size of their bodies helps them move. Likewise, with the right opportunities (many of which are discussed in this book), babies and toddlers should achieve levels of physical development that will act as the foundations upon which future, more complicated movements, such as the FMS identified in this chapter, can build. If these physical development foundations are in place, young children should gradually begin to demonstrate better balance, travel through space in a range of different ways and manipulate objects with different parts of their bodies, particularly their hands and feet. However, while this increased size, shape and strength act as a platform to support the emergence of most movements, the FMS efficiency, adaptability and creativity that are so important for current and future participation do not "just happen"; it needs opportunity and appropriate teaching. Time, opportunity and appropriate teaching are therefore key features of children's movement development because they help children revisit movement experiences and gradually build a movement repertoire that acts as the foundation for their current and future engagement in physical activity throughout life. This revisiting process is called *recursive elaboration* (Davis, Sumara, & Luce-Kapler, 2008) and has a significant impact on children's movement efficiency, adaptability and creativity. As we have discussed, complexity concepts offer an opportunity to move beyond the short term "one-size-fits-all" approach of traditional movement-related programmes and move towards a more recursive approach that supports children's movement development as both long term, non-linear and emergent.

Conclusion

This chapter has identified the complex nature of young children's mastery of FMS (e.g. running, throwing, catching, jumping). The development of these more advanced skills assumes that children's physical development needs were adequately met when they were babies and toddlers; the ways in which these needs can be met are identified throughout this book. Fundamental movement skills require a solid foundation upon which to develop and this chapter assumes that these are in place before more complex skills are taught. This chapter presents a view that young children are complex, self-organising systems who are consistently negotiating a range of ever-changing personal, environmental and task-related boundaries and offers examples that demonstrate how young children's movement development evolves in a non-linear and messy manner over a long period of time. At the heart of this complex learning process is the children's developing capacity to self-organise inside, around and outside the different boundaries they meet in order to build a movement foundation that incorporates an evolving mix of efficient, adaptable and creative movements.

Summary of key points

This chapter makes the case that children's movement development is a complex, long-term and emergent process. Practitioners may wish to consider the following points:

- Carrying out an initial or baseline assessment to establish children's previous movement experiences and their current level of development (physically, cognitively, socially and emotionally) can assist in planning "next steps."
- Children's movement development is unpredictable so learning intentions may need to be amended accordingly.
- Opening and closing "boundaries" may help children consolidate, be challenged and be creative in their movements.
- Revisiting movements can help build efficiency, adaptability and creativity across a range of physical activity contexts.

Suggested further reading

Donnelly, F. C., Mueller, S., & Gallahue, D. (2017). *Developmental physical education for all children* (5th ed.). Champaign, IL: Human Kinetics.

Jess, M. (2017). Start young: The possibilities of primary physical education. In M. Thorburn (Ed.), *Transformational learning in physical education* (pp. 77–92). London: Routledge.

Ovens, A., Hopper, T., & Butler, J. (2012). *Complexity thinking in physical education: Reframing curriculum, pedagogy and research.* London: Routledge.

Note

1 More background on these concepts can be found in Davis et al. (2008) and Ovens et al. (2013).

References

Chow, J., Davids, K., Button, C., & Renshaw, I. (2015). *Nonlinear pedagogy in skill acquisition: An introduction.* London: Routledge.

Davis, B., Sumara, D., & Luce-Kapler, R. (2008). *Engaging minds: Changing teaching in complex times* (2nd ed.). New York, NY: Routledge.

Gallahue, D. L., Ozmun, J. C., & Goodway, J. (2012). *Understanding motor development infants, children, adolescents, adults.* New York, NY: McGraw-Hill.

Gesell, A., & Thompson, H. (1938). *The psychology of early growth including norms of behavior and a method of genetic analysis.* New York, NY: Macmillan.

Jess, M., Keay, J., & Carse, N. (2016). Primary physical education: A complex learning journey for children and teachers. *Sport, Education and Society, 21*(7), 1018–1035. doi: 10.1080/13573322.2014.979142

Logan, S., Ross, S., Chee, K., Stodden, D., & Robinson, L. (2018). Fundamental motor skills: A systematic review of terminology. *Journal of Sports Sciences, 36*(7), 781–796. doi: 10.1080/02640414.2017.1340660

O'Connor, J., Alfrey, L., & Payne, P. (2012). Beyond games and sports: A socio-ecological approach to Physical Education. *Sport, Education and Society, 17*(3), 365–380.

Ovens, A., Hopper, T., & Butler, J. (Eds). (2013*). Complexity thinking in physical education: reframing curriculum, pedagogy and research.* London: Routledge.

Sandford, R., Duncombe, R., Mason, C., & Butler, C. (2015). Ability to be active: Exploring children's active play in primary schools. *International Journal of Play, 4*(2), 149–162. doi:10.1080/21594937.2015.1060569

Savelsbergh, G. J. P., Davids, K., van der Kamp, J., & Bennett, S. (Eds.) (2003). *The development of movement coordination in children. Application in the field of sport, ergonomics and health sciences.* London: Taylor & Francis Group.

4

PHYSICAL ACTIVITY IN THE EARLY YEARS

Julie Stirrup and Rachel Sandford

Personal reflection

We have written this chapter as academic researchers with both professional and personal interests in how we can critically reflect on practice to ensure learners get meaningful, equitable experiences. Reflecting on our personal experiences (teaching, family, research) we acknowledge that not all children arrive to their Early Years (EY) setting, school or higher education institution, with the same experiences and knowledge but how do we accommodate for this in our practice? If we take the example of numeracy or literacy from the EY right up to the end of secondary education, we as practitioners acknowledge that some children are "better" at these areas of education. We equally, as a society, recognise that numeracy and literacy are "important" and therefore scaffold our practice to meet the needs of our learners and ensure they develop appropriately based on what they arrive to our context with. However, do we do the same for Physical Development (PD)? If not, why not? As active performers in football and netball, we have both recently witnessed young children (3/4 years old) playing with a ball but never being shown or told how to kick or catch properly. Would this be the same if we witnessed a child wrongly counting animals on the farm? While there is much support (in academic, political and public debate) for increased physical activity (PA) time for young children – and the benefits that can accrue with regard to aiding health and well-being (and helping to address issues of childhood obesity) – there is perhaps less consideration given to the contribution such activities can play in supporting children's overall development (and the potential impact this may have on academic outcomes).

Our reflection here is not to argue that practitioners at all levels of education fail to differentiate, but rather that, in relation to PD and Physical Education (PE), we perhaps are less critical of our practice and in our acknowledgement that even from a young age, children "bring all aspects of themselves into the gym" (or educational context) (Hellison, 2010). With this in mind, our chapter looks to explore how research, policy and practice relating to PA in the EY are aligned and consider the value to practitioners of utilising a critical lens.

Introduction

Within the United Kingdom, as elsewhere, there is a recognition among policy-makers that PA has multiple benefits for society and, more so, that there is a specific need to nurture PD within the first five years of life. Furthermore, there is a significant amount of evidence to suggest that enrolling under fives in enrichment activities is now perceived to be a central aspect of "good" parenting among certain social groups (Evans and Davies, 2010; Lareau, 2003; Stirrup, Duncombe, & Sandford, 2015; Vincent & Ball, 2006, 2007). This chapter aims to identify what PA should and does "look like" in early childhood and draws predominantly on a small research project that the authors were involved in to map the PA landscape for young children. In doing so, a number of issues (or barriers) are exposed and discussed and possible ways that practitioners and parents may provide opportunities for children to be active are explored.

At this point, it is perhaps worth clarifying our use of terminology. While we recognise that there is some disparity between the use of terms, within this chapter we use the term PA to refer to child- or adult-initiated physical play or organised activities that involve gross and fine motor movements. This is different to PD but clearly connected. As endorsed within recent policy documents, PA is seen to be important for health and general well-being (DoH, 2018) but we acknowledge that not all PA may lead to PD, especially when PA opportunities are not age/developmental stage-appropriate or structured to meet the needs of the child. An example of this might be when a child is expected to play sport (they are being physically active) but they have not developed the eye tracking or fine motor skills required to catch a ball (their PD needs are not being met). Likewise, engaging children in activities like the daily mile (https://thedailymile.co.uk) may help contribute to their recommended daily minutes of PA but is unlikely to address underlying motor coordination issues. However, providing opportunities for babies to engage in floor-based play, or for slightly older children to climb trees and crawl through tunnels, should enable children to be physically active whilst also contributing to their overall PD.

What <u>should</u> physical activity "look like" in early childhood?

When considering the answer to this question, two key documents are relevant within the UK context. The first is the Early Years Foundation Stage (EYFS) framework and the second is the UK Physical Activity Guidelines (CMO, 2011).

The EYFS framework will be outlined in Chapter 8, so will only be covered briefly here. The framework itself focusses on three key areas of learning and development:

- Personal, social and emotional development;
- Communication and language;
- Physical development.

(DfE, 2017, p. 7)

Within the area of PD, two areas are focussed on:

1. Moving and Handling: referring to children's ability to show good control and coordination in small and large movement, moving confidently in a range of ways;
2. Health and Self-Care: whereby children know the importance of good health, of physical exercise and a healthy diet, and talk about ways to keep healthy and safe (DfE, 2017, p. 11).

The guidance document "Development Matters" was produced in support of this (although it is described as non-statutory guidance) and provides some examples of what the aforementioned areas might mean – and look like – in practice (see: https://foundationyears.org.uk/files/2012/03/Development-Matters-FINAL-PRINT-AMENDED.pdf for further details).

The second document, The UK Physical Activity Guidelines, was produced on behalf of the Chief Medical Officer in 2011. For the purposes of this book, three sections of the guidelines are of particular relevance: the guidelines for Early Years (under 5s) infants who are not yet walking; the guidelines for Early Years (under 5s) children who are capable of walking; and the guidelines for children and young people (aged 5–18 years). The recommendations relating to each of these three sections will now be outlined:

1. Infants who are not yet walking

i   PA should be encouraged from birth, particularly through floor-based play and water-based activities in safe environments.

ii All under fives should minimise the amount of time spent being sedentary (being restrained or sitting) for extended periods (except time spent sleeping).

For infants who are not yet walking, PA refers to movement of any intensity and may include:

- "Tummy time" – this includes any time spent on the stomach including rolling and playing on the floor;

- Reaching for and grasping objects, pulling, pushing and playing with other people e.g. "Parent and baby" swim sessions;
- Floor-based and water-based play encourages infants to use their muscles and develop motor skills. It also provides valuable opportunities to build social and emotional bonds.

2. Under fives capable of walking

i   Children of preschool age who are capable of walking unaided should be physically active daily for at least 180 minutes (3 hours), spread throughout the day.

ii All under fives should minimise the amount of time spent being sedentary (being restrained or sitting) for extended periods (except time spent sleeping).

At this stage, PA is likely to occur mainly through unstructured active play but may also include more structured activities. Activities can be of any intensity (light or more energetic) and may include, for example:

- Activities which involve movements of all the major muscle groups, i.e. the legs, buttocks, shoulders and arms, and movement of the trunk from one place to another;
- Energetic play, e.g. climbing frame or riding a bike;
- More energetic bouts of activity, e.g. running and chasing games;
- Walking/skipping to shops, a friend's home, a park or to and from school.

3. Children and young people (aged 5–18 years)

i   All children and young people should engage in moderate to vigorous intensity PA for at least 60 minutes and up to several hours every day.
ii   Vigorous intensity activities, including those that strengthen muscle and bone, should be incorporated at least three days a week.
iii All children and young people should minimise the amount of time spent being sedentary (sitting) for extended periods.

Moderate intensity PAs will cause children to get warmer and breathe harder and their hearts to beat faster, but they should still be able to carry on a conversation. Examples include bike riding and playground activities. *Vigorous intensity PAs*, on the other hand, will cause children to get warmer, breathe much harder and have their hearts beat rapidly, making it more difficult to carry on a conversation. Examples include fast running and sports such as swimming or football. Finally, *PAs that strengthen muscle and bone* involve using body weight or working against a resistance. Examples include swinging on playground equipment, hopping and skipping or sports such as gymnastics or tennis.

While this section has identified relevant UK documents/policies, it should also be noted that international comparisons can be drawn to similar guidelines from other countries. For example, in Canada, 24-Hour Movement Guidelines for the Early Years (0–4 years) have been produced (CSEP, 2017). Within Canada's guidelines, guidance is given to parents and care givers on children's recommended levels of movement, sleep and sitting. Whilst such guidelines can be useful and are, certainly within the United Kingdom, seen as a way of addressing sedentary issues within society, it should be noted that they are not without critique and concerns have been raised about, for example, the realistic nature of targets (bearing in mind diverse populations), the capacity for guidelines/campaigns to effect significant behavioural change and the challenge of monitoring trends over time when guidelines shift and change (e.g. Cavill and Bauman, 2004; Milton and Bauman, 2015). This, again, perhaps points to the need for practitioners to consider guidelines and policies through a critical lens, and consider their application in real-world contexts.

What does physical activity "look like" in early childhood?

Despite UK Government white papers (DoH, 2018; DfE, 2012) recognising the benefits of PA and acknowledging the need to nurture it within the first five years of life (Hall et al., 2009; Kato, 2006), there remains a lack of focus on such activities within the EYFS. In contrast, internationally there has been specific research into the opportunities children have to enjoy PA within various day care settings (e.g. child minders, public and private EY providers). In Australia, for example, Cashmore and Jones (2008) found similarities in the potential barriers pre-school children face to PA in both "family" day care settings (child minders) and "long day" childcare settings (private provision). Both studies found that practitioners see more developmental value in non-organised, child-initiated PA and highlighted several practitioner-perceived barriers to PA – including resources, training, health and safety and weather. Similar findings were highlighted by van Zandvoort, Tucker, Irwin, and Burke (2010) in their Canadian study on the barriers to PA in day care. Furthermore, these authors also noted that child-initiated "play" is not necessarily always physically active; for example, some children may choose to play on a computer whilst others may appear to be engaged in active play but are in fact standing still whilst doing so.

Certainly, our research and experiences to date suggest that policy rhetoric does not always translate into practice. For example, data generated during one nursery-based research project (which we discuss in more detail later in the chapter) suggest that EY practitioners and stakeholders certainly recognised the importance of daily access to or opportunities for PA for young children. Specifically, they raised the importance of providing a wide range of activities, including those both done indoors and outdoors, targeting gross and fine motor skills, and engaged with alone, under the supervision of adults (parents, family, EY practitioners) and/or with peers. Furthermore, they recognised the need for a reduction in "screen time" for young children in order to prevent more sedentary behaviour. However, our data also illustrated that despite appreciating the *importance of* PD and PA, practitioners also felt inadequately trained to facilitate this aspect of a child's development i.e. they did not always know *how* to create appropriate activities that would afford developmental opportunities. For example, we frequently observed practitioners putting on "sing and dance along" videos during rainy days instead of going outside as a way of addressing children's PD needs. Practitioners openly recognised that this was not how they addressed developmental needs with regard to numeracy and literacy (relating, perhaps, to the point made within the initial reflection at the start of this chapter) but argued that they felt better trained to support children in these areas when compared to their training in PD.

Stakeholder views on PA provision: the empirical data

Bearing in mind the previous points, the discussion will now move on to examine more closely some of the findings that emerged from this commissioned research project, which sought to examine the provision of PD and PA opportunities for children from birth to five years within the East Midlands of England (2015). The study involved two data collection methods; a short, online survey and telephone/face-to-face interviews with individuals identified as being involved in the management, design or delivery of PA provision for children from birth to five, within the identified geographical area. Twenty-eight participants completed the online survey and ten participants were interviewed. Participants' job roles varied but included: nursery nurses, a health visitor, school nurses, a GP, an occupational therapist, a foundation stage teacher, a play therapist, a developmental movement practitioner, a lecturer, a researcher, nursery staff and local authority staff (e.g. public health manager and healthy child programme manager).

Data from our survey and interviews illustrate that, across all stakeholders, PA was a high priority. However, the focus on PD provision for children from birth to five was relatively recent. Several interviewees, for example, suggested that it is only within the last four years that EY had become a priority work strand for many of them. This is perhaps not surprising when we consider the initial inclusion of PD as a prime area in the 2012 EYFS framework. All participants acknowledged the importance of daily access to or opportunities for PA, as demonstrated in some of the following illustrative comments:

> It is advised that young children need 1000 hours of floor time a year. This is seen as safe play with the encouragement to use all gross and fine skills.
>
> *(Lecturer)*

> They need to access daily activities – be it walking, playing or engaging in physical activities outside as well as at home.
>
> *(Nursery nurse)*

An opportunity to be outdoors to explore, run and climb. To be more active indoors − games etc. to aid movement rather than sedentary games...

(Member of health visiting team)

In unpacking this further, the importance of a wide range of activities was highlighted and this included those that were both indoors and outdoors, that targeted gross and fine motor skills, and that were engaged with alone and/or with others. Table 4.1 illustrates the comprehensive list of activities that participants suggested should be part of a child's physical activity offer. These are presented in order of the most frequently cited:

TABLE 4.1 Activities suggested as being an important part of young children's physical activity opportunities

Activity	Number of responses
Outdoor play/time outside (woodland, garden, park, playground)	14
Running	10
Climbing	8
Active play	7
Tummy time/floor play	6
Balancing activities	6
Walking	5
Swimming/active in water	4
Crawling	3
Indoor play	3
Sports (tennis, football, hockey, handball)	3
Bike rides/cycling	3
Jumping	3
Catching	3
Playing in mud/puddles	2
Hopping	2
Throwing	2
Kicking	2
Games (e.g. Duck, Duck, Goose; hide and seek; circle games)	2
Activities to develop co-ordination, speed, strength, agility	2
Bats and balls	1
Activities using left and right together (e.g. pom poms)	1
Dancing	1
Cheerleading	1
Skipping	1
Messy play	1
Swinging/hanging	1
Activities to develop core stability	1
Rhythmic movement	1
Apparatus	1

Outdoor play in natural environments (in all weathers) seemed a popular response from participants, as was an adequate amount of floor or tummy time for babies. Not surprisingly, therefore, a call for a reduction in "screen time" for young children and "unrestricted movement" (e.g. time spent in C-curve in baby bouncers and car seats) for babies was also made. Whilst practitioners recognised issues such as poor training for EY practitioners and parents being too busy to engage in these activities outside of the EY setting, they also felt that PA should be seen as "part of the norm," with "parents being shown the benefits of outdoor spaces" (nursery practitioner). As one nursery practitioner noted, "modern life has built up pressures and a culture of fear about the outdoors," and this was perceived to limit the PD opportunities presented to many young children. The lack of opportunities for PA was felt to be particularly problematic when coupled with the perception of young children's increased use of technology, as one local EY manager suggested:

> A pair of children's walking boots can cost much less than a kindle or smart phone!!

Thus, participants were able, between them, to identify a broad range of activities that they felt young children *should* engage in and which would offer opportunities for PD. During interviews, it also became apparent that many of these activities could be grouped into broader categories: PA/PD programmes; enrichment activities; PE (for children aged 5–7); and "other opportunities to be active." The sections that follow outline these in more detail and consider them in relation to broader literature.

Physical activity programmes

Concerns around the lack of appropriate movement opportunities for young children (Goddard-Blythe, 2005) and the impact of poor EY learning experiences on future education (Sammons et al., 2004), combined with increasing health concerns focussed on obesity and sedentary lifestyles (Marsden & Weston, 2007), have contributed to a growing awareness of the importance of PA/PD in the EY and a number of programmes (e.g. BUPA "Start to Move" (now TOPS) and BHF "Early Movers") have previously been implemented in an attempt to combat this. These programmes are designed to equip teachers/practitioners with the skills needed to teach high quality physical literacy/activity and development in the early and primary years. Looking specifically at "Start to Move," data from Morley's (2016) review suggest that such programmes can: improve children's fundamental movement skills (FMS) particularly where children have a low starting level; have a significant impact on schools within socially deprived areas; and increase both children's PA and teachers' confidence and competence in delivering EY and KS1 PE.

Enrichment activities

Enrichment activities such as music, sport and art activities/clubs have been described as a "booming" area, with provision and consumption increasing significantly over the last three decades (Vincent & Ball, 2006). The marketplace is saturated with franchises offering provision for preschool children, from the well-established "Tumble Tots" (a gymnastics-based physical play programme that has been running since 1979) to more recent activities, including "Water Babies," "Shakers Music" and "Jo Jingles." Certainly, the benefits of such activities are something our interviewees praised, with many suggesting that there was a need for more facilities (e.g. soft-play venues, swimming pools, community leisure centres) within the local area. It was suggested that some venues held "come and try" sessions, where young children and their parents could try new activities (e.g. climbing, canoeing, orienteering, cheerleading, swimming, horse riding, trampolining, cycling, gymnastics, ball games, yoga, etc.). The importance of these sessions being led by people trained in EY PA/PD was also stressed by participants.

It is worth noting, however, that whilst such sessions and enrichment activities are positive for both PD and PA, they come at a cost which not all can afford. In the United Kingdom, Vincent and Ball (2007) have highlighted that class divisions are clearly visible within the realm of child rearing, and they have illustrated how, with the aim of equipping their children with the necessary skills and resources to "succeed," middle class parents often enrol their children into such enrichment activities (outside of EY nursery settings) to develop their physical talents and abilities. In an increasingly privatised education system, which offers critical resources for sections of the population (i.e. middle class parents) to maintain their position in the "privatised" education market and in wider social and cultural hierarchies, questions need to be asked regarding what happens to those children whose parents are unable to buy into these resources. Where do these children get their PD or PA opportunities from? The following section goes someway towards exploring this question, looking at the influence of PE and beyond "formal" opportunities as well as the potential barriers faced by children and practitioners.

Physical education

Within the National Curriculum in England for primary education, PE is one of the foundation subjects and, as such, all children aged 4–7 have access to PE within KS1. It is up to schools to determine how much time is devoted to PE in the curriculum, but Government guidance recommends that schools should provide pupils with a minimum of two hours curricular PE per week. In addition to this, many schools offer after-school and lunchtime activities. In 2012, the UK Government announced the launch of "Primary PE and Sport Premium" (PPESP) funding (amounting to £450 million) for English schools, initially for three years (although later extended). This equated to an approximate payment of £9250 per school. The funding, it was claimed, would support the improvement of the quality of PE and sport (DfE, 2015). In its first two years, the funding reportedly enabled schools to:

- Upskill and train existing staff;
- Buy new equipment;
- Provide more extra-curricular activities;
- Employ new sports coaches;
- Introduce new sports in both curricular PE and extra-curricular sport;
- Increase participation in inter- and intra-school competitions.

(DfE, research report, 2015, p. 14)

This illustrates once again that while Government policy (within the UK, at least) is trying to promote PE, PA and PD, access to and engagement with relevant activities is still somewhat problematic (see Chapter 9).

"Other opportunities" to be active

Within the research study, several participants highlighted the significance for young children of having other "opportunities to be active" beyond those more formal encounters noted earlier. These included things such as physically active play (e.g. playing chasing games in the playground), active travel (e.g. walking/scooting to school or riding their bike to the shops) and opportunities to simply play outside in a garden or at a local park (with either specific play equipment or just making use of natural resources). As we see elsewhere within this book (Chapters 13 and 14), such activities can also be seen to hold developmental benefits for children and young people and should be recognised as a valuable part of their overall PA "offer."

Barriers to physical activity

There is a persistent argument, with a strong evidence base, that suggests a prescribed, outcomes-driven curriculum, focussed on formal skills in preparation for the next stage of education, is misinformed, developmentally inappropriate and potentially damaging (e.g. Anning, Cullen, & Fleer, 2004; Gulberg, 2009; House, 2011; Miller & Hevey, 2012; Moyles, 2012; Moyles, Payler, & Georgeson, 2014). In accordance with Moss (2007, 2013), Whitebread and Bingham (2014, p. 187) argue that "if we wish to improve the quality of early education for all children, particularly those who are disadvantaged in some way we need to locate the problem, not in the children, but in inappropriate provision." This issue of inappropriate provision was also raised by our participants, with a suggestion that better training for EY practitioners and additional education for parents were needed in relation to both PD and PE.

Making practitioners aware of the role that physical activity can play in child development was identified as a priority. Likewise, better and safer facilities (e.g. parks or soft-play centres) and activity groups were also seen to be important, especially if provided at reduced cost or for free.

> In my experience, many practitioners who have no background in sports, movement or dance, lack confidence in providing playful physical activities that are creative and child-led. Training and resources would need to be offered to support a new pathway.
>
> *(Play therapist)*

> Parents need to be shown the benefits of our parks and open spaces. I believe that modern life has built up pressures of time and a culture of fear about the outdoors.
>
> *(Nursery teacher)*

The concept of play, along with residual principles of child-centredness, is embedded in EY policy. Furthermore, the EYFS framework outlines the "competencies" within each "prime area" that children are expected to develop and ultimately display through play. As stated in the Statutory Framework:

> Each area of learning and development must be implemented through planned, purposeful play and through a mix of adult-led and child-initiated activity. Play is essential for children's development, building their confidence as they learn to explore, to think about problems, and relate to others. Children learn by leading their own play, and by taking part in play which is guided by adults. There is an on-going judgement to be made by practitioners about the balance between activities led by children, and activities led or guided by adults. Practitioners must respond to each child's emerging needs and interests, guiding their development through warm, positive interaction.
>
> *(DfE, 2012, p. 6)*

Esland (1971) argued that teaching involves directing children's consciousness towards the acceptance of the realities marked out in the curricula. Considering this, we can perhaps appreciate that children are presented with "bodies of knowledge" through the EYFS curriculum, with the practitioner making critical choices about how children should acquire this knowledge (different forms of play). Furthermore Esland, (ibid.) like Becker (1952) and many other researchers since, suggests that processes of teaching and learning are influenced by practitioner/child interactions, and the degree to which practitioners perceive children to be the "ideal" child in relation to "official" knowledge constructions. In the case of EY, the "competencies" outlined in the EYFS are "ideally" realised through a curriculum enacted within each setting as play. But which forms of "play" are valued and encouraged within settings is impacted by practitioners and how they recontextualise policy. Our observations and discussions with practitioners are suggestive of "academic" forms of play being valued over "physical" forms of play. The former referring to reading, counting and storytime and the latter referring to outdoor play. Such focus on "academic" play is perhaps a reflection on EY being seen as a place to ensure children are "school ready," but this also, in itself, becomes a barrier to children having access to high quality "physical" play, PD and PA. Furthermore, it is important to note here that current critical debates within the literature suggest that EY practitioners' pedagogy is increasingly framed by an intensification upon the "raising standards" policy context (e.g. Whitebread & Bingham, 2011; Roberts-Holmes, 2015). This, in turn, is undermining the unique, child-centred, play-based approach of the EY and providing additional barriers for some with regard to engagement in PA (Bradbury, 2012; Moss, 2013). The idea of settings focussing on "school readiness" as a barrier to PD is perhaps of particular interest if we consider children's PD and the potential implications if a play-based approach to learning is substituted for a more formal "scholification" of the EY. If our EY settings are increasingly driven by Government policy focussed on performative pedagogies and notions of school readiness, with an albeit narrow focus on numeracy and literacy, then we might ask to where do our children turn for PD?

Overall, the most significant finding from this scoping project was the lack of consensus about what constitutes good practice in delivering PD and PA for children from birth to five, and this is problematic for those charged with making effective decisions about prioritising efforts, given finite resources. In addition to uncertainties among participants about what constituted good practice, it was also apparent that there was a lack of agreement about the overarching aims of PA/PD "work". This was illustrated succinctly by one particular interviewee who felt that the "big story" was somewhat missing in the EY strand of her work. Moreover, she suggested that establishing a "shared vision" for PD within the EY was important to ensure that the needs of more children could be met.

Overall, our data suggest that the following were seen by stakeholders as key barriers to providing PA/PD opportunities:

- Practitioner knowledge and confidence;
- Practitioner experience and training in PD;
- Focus on school readiness and literacy/numeracy over PD;
- Social class issues linked to opportunity and access.

Conclusion

This chapter has outlined what young children *should* be doing in terms of PA and, drawing on data from a recent research project, has provided an overview of a number of different ways in which young children could be and are active within and beyond EY settings. It then identified a number of barriers as identified in the literature and from the participants in the research. Our data illustrated that there are many challenges impacting on physical provision for 0–5s in the geographical area under study and, drawing on broader literature, we can also see that this issue is faced by EY practitioners, settings and stakeholders more widely within England. These barriers included: a lack of coherent provision; limited training for practitioners in PD and PA; and some children's limited opportunities outside EY settings to be physically active. Whilst there is agreement that this area of work is extremely important, it is also apparent that there are very limited resources with which to address it, despite the apparent status of PD within the current EYFS framework. Current policy pushes practitioners to focus on getting children "school ready," which, in turn, impacts on the time available for meaningful PA that can enable children to develop appropriately. Whilst our participants acknowledged the role parents and enrichment activities can play in children's PD, we need to recognise that not all children have access to such resources outside of their EY setting. Therefore, to provide more equitable experiences, it would be wise to be critically reflective on our own practice to ensure children in the EY are being provided with positive and developmentally appropriate opportunities to be physically active.

Summary of key points

This chapter has set out to explore how PA is currently experienced in various EY settings, drawing on data collected from stakeholders. The chapter has explored how PA is taken up in both policy and practice, including some of the potential barriers to developing children's PD and meaningful PA in EY settings. The following suggestions offer some practical advice for both practitioners and parents:

- There is a need to recognise the variety of ways in which young children can be physically active and engage in developmental activities.
- Parents and practitioners also need to recognise their own role in supporting children's access to PA/PD.
- Practitioners should be encouraged to engage in relevant continuing professional development and ongoing training relating to PA/PD.
- There is a need for a review of current provision relating to EY PA/PD and for parents, practitioners and policy makers to consider where additional changes can be made.

Suggested further reading

Bradbury, A. (2012). Education policy and the 'ideal learner': Producing recognisable learner-subjects through early years assessment. *British Journal of Sociology of Education*, *34*(1), 1–19.

Goddard-Blythe, S. (2005). *The well balanced child: Movement and early learning.* Gloucester: Hawthorn Press.
Stirrup, J., Duncombe, R., & Sandford, R. (2015). Intensive mothering in the early years: The cultivation and consolidation of (physical) capital. *Sport, Education and Society, 20*(1), 89–106.

References

Anning, A., Cullen, J., & Fleer, M. (2004). *Early childhood education: Society and culture.* London: Sage.
Ball, S., & Vincent, C. (2007). Education, class fractions and the local rules of spatial relations. *Urban Studies, 44*(7), 1175–1189.
Ball, S., Vincent, C., Kemp, S., & Pietikainen, S. (2004). Middle class fractions, childcare and the 'relational' and 'normative' aspects of class practices. *The Sociological Review, 52*(4), 478–502.
Becker, H. (1952). Social-class variations in the teacher–pupil relationship. *Journal of Educational Sociology, 25*(8), 451–465.
Bradbury, A. (2012). Education policy and the 'ideal learner': Producing recognisable learner-subjects through early years assessment. *British Journal of Sociology of Education, 34*(1), 1–19.
Canadian Society for Exercise Physiology (CSEP). (2017). Retrieved from https://csepguidelines.ca/
Cashmore, A., & Jones, S. (2008). Growing up active: A study into physical activity in long day care centres. *Journal of Research in Childhood Education, 23*(2), 179–191.
Cavill, N., & Bauman, A. (2004). Changing the way people think about health-enhancing physical activity: Do mass media campaigns have a role? *Journal of Sports Science, 22*(8), 771–790.
CMO. (2011). UK Physical Activity Guidelines. Retrieved from https://www.gov.uk/government/publications/uk-physical-activity-guidelines
DfE. (2012). Statutory Framework for the Early Years Foundation Stage.
DfE. (2015). *The PE and sport premium: An investigation in primary schools research report.* Retrieved from https://www.gov.uk/government/publications/pe-and-sport-premium-an-investigation-in-primary-schools
DfE. (2017). *Early years foundation stage statutory framework (EYFS).* Retrieved from https://www.gov.uk/government/publications/early-years-foundation-stage-framework--2
DoH. (2018). Retrieved from https://www.gov.uk/government/publications/physical-activity-applying-all-our-health/physical-activity-applying-all-our-health
Esland, G. (1971). Teaching and learning as the organisation of knowledge. In M. Francis & D. Young (Eds.), *Knowledge and control: New directions on the sociology of education.* London: Collier-Macmillan.
Evans, J., & Davies, B. (2010). Family, class and embodiment: Why school physical education makes so little difference to post school participation patterns in physical activity. *International Journal of Qualitative Studies in Education, 23*(7), 765–785.
Goddard-Blythe, S. (2005). *The well balanced child: Movement and early learning.* Gloucester: Hawthorn Press.
Gulberg, H. (2009). *Reclaiming childhood: Freedom and play in an age of fear.* Abingdon: Routledge.

Hall, J., Sylva, K., Melhuish, E., Sammons, P., Siraj-Blatchford, I., & Taggart, B. (2009). The role of pre-school quality in promoting resilience in the cognitive development of young children. *Oxford Review of Education, 35*, 331.

Hellison, D. (2010). *Teaching personal and social responsibility through physical activity* (3rd ed.). Champaign, IL: Human Kinetics.

House, R. (2011). *Too much too soon. Early learning and the erosion of childhood.* Stroud: Hawthorne Press.

Kato, H. (2006). Our children deserve the best. *Childhood Education, 82*(3), 186.

Lareau, A. (2003). *Unequal childhoods: Class, race and family life.* Berkeley: University of California Press.

Marsden, E., & Weston, C. (2007). Locating quality physical education in early years pedagogy. *Sport, Education and Society, 12*, 383–398.

Miller, L., & Hevey, D. (2012). *Policy issues in the early years.* London: Sage.

Milton, K., & Bauman, A. (2015). A critical analysis of the cycles of physical activity policy in England. *International Journal of Behavioral Nutrition and Physical Activity, 12*(1), 8.

Morley, D. (2016). *Bupa start to move, executive summary.* Retrieved from https://www.youthsporttrust.org/TOPStart

Moss, P. (2007). Bringing politics into the nursery: Early childhood education as a democratic practice. *European Early Childhood Education Research Journal, 15*(1), 5–20.

Moss, P. (2013). The relationship between early childhood and compulsory education. A properly political question. In P. Moss (Ed.), *Early childhood and compulsory education: Reconceptualising the relationship* (pp. 2–49). London: Routledge.

Moyles, J. (2012). *Unhurried pathways. Early childhood action.* Winchester. Retrieved from http://www.earlychildhoodaction.com/docs/ECA%20EYF%20Unhurried%20Pathways.pdf

Moyles, J., Payler, J., & Georgeson, J. (2014). *Early years foundations: Critical issues* (2nd ed). Berkshire: Open University Press.

Roberts-Holmes, G. (2015). The 'datafication' of early years pedagogy: 'If the teaching is good, the data should be good and if there's bad teaching, there is bad data'. *Journal of Education Policy, 30*(3), 302–315.

Sammons, P., Sylva, K., Melishuh, E. C., Siraj-Blatchford, I., & Taggart, B. (2004). *Measuring the impact of preschool on children's social/behavioural progress over the preschool period.* London: DfE/Institute of Education, University of London.

Stirrup, J., Duncombe, R., & Sandford, R., (2015). Intensive mothering in the early years: The cultivation and consolidation of (physical) capital. *Sport, Education and Society, 20*(1), 89–106.

van Zandvoort, M., Tucker, P., Irwin, J., & Burke, S. (2010). Physical activity at daycare: Issues, challenges and perspectives. *Early Years: An International Research Journal, 30*(2), 175–188.

Vincent, C., & Ball, S. (2006). *Childcare, choice and class practices.* London: Routledge.

Vincent, C., & Ball, S., (2007). 'Making up' the middle-class child: Families, activities and class dispositions. *Sociology, 41*(6), 1061–1077.

Whitebread, D., & Bingham, S. (2011). School readiness: A critical review of perspectives and evidence. *TACTYC Occasional Paper No. 2*, TACTYC.

Whitebread, D., & Bingham, S. (2014). School readiness: Starting age, cohorts and transitions in the early years. In J. Moyles, J. Georgeson, & J. Payler (Eds.), *Early years foundations: Critical issues* (2nd ed., pp. 179–191). Berkshire: Open University Press.

5

FINLAND

An international approach to physical development

Arja Sääkslahti and Rebecca Duncombe

Personal reflection (Arja Sääkslahti)

As a Physical Education (PE) teacher, I have researched the area of early childhood physical development for 30 years. During this time, I have been fortunate to visit many different countries and cultures to explore the different ways in which education and PE is delivered. Through these international visits, it has been possible to see my own culture and the PE practices within it in a different light. The old expression "From the distance, it is possible to see more clearly" is relevant here, and my visits have helped me to clarify many things and to reflect on why and how we provide physical activity and physical development opportunities in Finland in the way that we do. I was asked to write this chapter to provide an international perspective, and I hope that the practical examples provided will be helpful to those attempting to meet the physical development needs of young children in different countries and different contexts. We are lucky in Finland as we have a culture that is based outdoors; it is normal to be outdoors and we are generally not put off by the weather! Being outside and enabling children to be outside are part of the ethos of the country, and this has not always proved to be the case in other countries that I have visited.

My informal observations of children playing, both indoors and outdoors, have helped me to reflect on the practices that do and don't encourage physical activity. Many Finnish Early Years settings have a large outdoor space as well as access to forests and woodlands. On average, our young children spend four hours a day outside engaged in active play. It would be hard for them not to be active with opportunities such as this provided for them! I have seen fidgety children play for hours, being constantly on the move until they have refined their gross and fine motor control over many months to a point where they can finally sit and stand still (a skill that is unbelievably hard until the body becomes physically developed enough to cope with it). There are many differences between our system and those of other countries including the United Kingdom; it is not my place to say which is the best approach but Finnish children are renowned for their educational success and I hope by sharing what I have learnt, others may be able to change some or all of their practice to better suit the children in their care.

Introduction

In 2013, the United Kingdom was ranked 24th (out of 29 "rich" countries) for its education and 16th for overall child well-being (UNICEF, 2013). This was in comparison to Finland (the focus of this chapter) which ranked 4th for both education and overall child well-being. The Programme for International Students Assessment (PISA) sheds further light on academic achievement in the two countries. PISA is a worldwide research programme focussing on the learning outcomes of 15-year-old students in 73 countries (www.oecd.org/pisa). The latest PISA results ranked Finland 5th and the United Kingdom 14th (PISA, 2015, Results in Focus, OECD 2018). The education ranking from both studies is of particular interest when you consider that Finnish children don't start (formal) school until they are 7, they typically have a shorter day with longer breaks and homework is minimal. In the years prior to formal schooling starting, approximately 70 per cent of young children (aged 0–6) in Finland attend preschool. Clearly there are some stark differences between the Finnish and the UK system with the Finnish approach appearing to take the lead in both education and overall child well-being. So, what is it that contributes to Finland's success? How can Finnish children do so well when they are at school for less time?

This chapter will attempt to highlight differences between the two educational systems by outlining the situation in Finland and then examining why this approach may be a more suitable one for young children's education, physical development and general well-being. The following are put forward:

- Education, teachers, PE and physical activity are valued;
- Education is continuous and progressive from ages 0 to 8;
- Appropriate pedagogies are employed;
- Facilities provide opportunities for physical activity and development;
- Clothing is appropriate for the outdoors;
- Physical activity and physical development are a requirement.

Education, teachers, PE and physical activity are valued

In Finland, teaching is a very attractive profession, with just 10 per cent of applicants admitted to be trained as teachers (Finnish National Agency for Education, 2017). Teachers for Early Childhood Education and Care (ECEC) study for three years at university gaining a Bachelor's degree and it is not uncommon for teachers to also hold a Master's degree (i.e. five years of study at university). The latest educational strategy in Finland has increased the number of teacher training places in early education and set a target of having half of the staff members in childcare centres with a university education. Teaching is valued as one of the top four professions in Finland (Suomen Kuvalehti, 2018), and PE teachers belong to this highly valued group requiring a five-year Master's degree. It is also a highly competitive profession with just 5 per cent of applicants being accepted to study PE in 2018. PE is considered one of the five main areas of the curriculum in Primary and Secondary Schools and accounts for a third of the total amount of lessons (after Finnish/literature and mathematics). Whilst a teacher training course at university level lasting 3+ years is commonplace in the United Kingdom for Primary School teachers, practitioners in nurseries typically do less than this. Likewise, much has been written about the low status of PE in English schools and especially in the primary setting (Duncombe, Cale & Harris, 2016; Griggs, 2007) – see also Chapter 9.

Another factor illustrating the value that is placed on teachers in Finland is the freedom they are given to teach in a way that they see fit. As such, there is no national inspection system, and teachers have autonomy to choose how they will fulfil the National Curriculum for the ECEC. In Finland, the quality of the education system and ensuring the curriculum is fulfilled are measured by a survey conducted in randomly chosen childcare centres and schools. The focus of this survey varies from year to year, for example, in 2017, the survey aimed to find out how communities implemented the new curriculum that was launched in 2016. In contrast, a very rigid inspection system is in place in the United Kingdom (Office for Standards in Education – OFSTED) with schools being inspected approximately every three years. Following the inspection, schools are given a qualitative judgement and reports about the inspection are published publicly on the inspection website for others to read.

Physical activity has always been valued in Finland but this has increased further in recent years. This has partially been fuelled by growing research evidence highlighting the link between physical activity and overall learning prerequisites (Donnelly et al., 2016) as well as learning outcomes in academic subjects (Haapala et al., 2018; Hillman, Kalaja, & Liukkonen, 2015). In support of this growing understanding of the link between physical activity and academic outcomes, the Finnish government launched "Joy in Motion" as part of their strategy in 2017. The purpose of this programme is to encourage all day care centres to take care of children's physical activity, and all childcare centres are supposed to follow this program by 2022.

The UK physical activity guidelines are outlined in greater detail in Chapter 4; these recommend that children capable of walking and aged 0–5 should engage in at least 180 minutes a day of physical activity and that children aged 5–18 should engage in 60 minutes each day. The Finnish physical activity guidelines follow the same recommendations (in terms of minutes of physical activity), but how do the two countries compare in relation to the percentage of children achieving these recommended amounts? Finland's Report Card on Physical Activity for Children and Youth (2018) identifies that approximately 40 per cent of Finnish children (aged 7–15 years) do achieve the 60-minute recommendations and that

54–59 per cent of younger children (<6 years) achieve the 180-minute guideline. In the United Kingdom, these figures are concerning: in 2012, just 21 per cent of boys and 16 per cent of girls, aged 5–15, met the 60-minute recommendation, whilst in the younger 2–4 age bracket, 9 per cent of boys and 10 per cent of girls met the 180-minute recommendation (Townsend, Wickramasinghe, Williams, Bhatnagar, & Rayner, 2015).

Education is continuous and progressive from 0–8

In Finland, early education covers the 0–8 age range and is designed to provide continuous and progressive education and care from the Early Years, to preschool (6 years) and through to the early part of Primary School (7–12 years). Early education is seen to be part of an important continuum of education that starts from the very beginning of life. The system in the United Kingdom is less progressive with numerous changes in the way in which education is provided for the 0–8 age range. For example, very young children and babies may be cared for in nurseries until they reach the age of three when they enter the Early Years Foundation Stage (EYFS) and their first experience of more formal schooling begins. Young children start school in the academic year that they turn four and continue with the EYFS but in a new setting. Just one year later, they enter Key Stage 1 (years 1 and 2, ages 5–7) and just two years after this, they enter Key stage 2 (Years 3–6, ages 7–11) and this is sometimes accompanied with another change of setting (some Primary Schools in the United Kingdom are split into Infant and Junior schools; each responsible for a different key stage).

Appropriate pedagogies are employed

The aim of ECEC in Finland is to promote the holistic growth, health and well-being of each child as determined by his or her age and development. This is delivered through pedagogical activities based on play, physical activity, the arts and cultural heritage. ECEC staff, in their training, are encouraged to provide developmentally appropriate activities that promote learning in a healthy and safe environment. Physical activity, physical development and movement are a core part of early childhood provision in Finland.

The aims of the EYFS in the United Kingdom are to provide:

- Quality and consistency in all Early Years settings so that every child makes good progress, and no child gets left behind;
- A secure foundation through learning and development opportunities which are planned around the needs and interests of each individual child and are assessed and reviewed regularly;
- Partnership working between practitioners and with parents and/or carers;
- Equality of opportunity and anti-discriminatory practice, ensuring that every child is included and supported.

(DfE, 2017)

Whilst there is an acknowledgement that provision should be based on the needs of individual children, the focus does not seem to be on the more holistic outcomes identified in the Finnish system. The aims of both "curricular" have been identified, but further differences will become evident in the way in which practitioners deliver the required outcomes. This will differ between settings within a country as well as between countries. The following describes a typical Finnish approach.

Based on Vygotsky's (1978) concept of the Zone of Proximal Development, practitioners in Finland engage in and encourage numerous play opportunities through which young children can learn. In addition to this, it is accepted that children will also learn through moving, exploring, working with others and expressing themselves artistically. A constructivist understanding of learning is commonplace and this encourages an understanding and appreciation of what the child already knows and what they have already experienced, which is then used as the starting point for further learning. Children are encouraged to find joy in and celebrate their successes. The young child's safety and well-being are at the forefront of practice and they are encouraged and supported to develop important life skills such as getting dressed, eating meals, managing basic hygiene and taking care of personal possessions. These and similar skills are given more importance in the Early Years than those of reading, writing and mathematics. The learning environment supports physically active play and children's natural curiosity and desire to learn. Many activities are structured to enable young children to explore the world with their senses and entire body. Children and personnel are encouraged to be physically active both indoors and outdoors. Moreover, children are guided to avoid sitting for long periods. Children's holistic well-being is promoted by providing them with an opportunity for calming down and resting during the day as well as versatile, healthy and sufficient nutrition.

Facilities provide opportunities for physical activity and development

Finnish childcare centres are typically built with large outdoor playing areas. Finland has a strong Scandinavian outdoor culture, and almost every childcare centre has their own little forest area for children to play in. The benefits of outdoor play are identified in Chapter 13 and research by Fjortoft (2004) identifies that a forest environment inspires children's imagination, encourages them to play in heterogeneous groups (boys and girls of different ages) and supports their motor development. In addition, playing outdoors supports overall physical development because it is more challenging for the senses, muscles and joints than more predictable or indoor environments. It was also found that children who play outdoors and in forests have better cardiorespiratory systems than children playing elsewhere (Fjortoft, 2001). The pictures (Figures 5.1 and 5.2) show a typical outdoor area and a forest space used by a day care centre in Finland.

FIGURE 5.1 A typical outdoor space in a Finnish day care centre.

FIGURE 5.2 A typical woodland space available to children in Finnish day care centres.

Clothing is appropriate for the outdoors

Finland is a Nordic country with four different seasons and the difference in temperature between the seasons can be remarkable with temperatures often reaching as low as −25 degrees in the winter and frequently hitting 25 degrees in the summer. This large variation means that children need to have appropriate clothing for the varying weather conditions. Bad weather is not generally seen as a reason or given as an excuse to stay inside but it is widely acknowledged that appropriate clothing is essential. Indeed, the weather has to be very bad before Finnish children are allowed to stay indoors (between −15 and −20, depending on the wind strength). Parental attitude towards providing appropriate clothing and tolerating dirt is generally very positive, and parents typically dress their children in clothes that are comfortable and stretchy/loose enough for active play. The clothing is practical and allows for playing both indoors and outdoors in almost all weather conditions. Parents often bring spare clothing should their child need to change or if weather conditions change, and space is provided in day care centres for children to store their spare clothes. Space is even provided for ice-skates and skis during the winter! The following pictures illustrate this approach in practice (see Figures 5.3–5.7)

FIGURE 5.3 Finnish children play outside whatever the weather; thus, appropriate clothing is essential!

FIGURE 5.4 Day care centres provide appropriate storage facilities for outdoor clothing.

FIGURE 5.5 Winter provides new and exciting opportunities for being outside; it is not a barrier!

FIGURE 5.6 Children in day care centres are provided with opportunities to ski and develop their balance.

FIGURE 5.7 Time is spent in the natural environment, and the forest is a favourite place for many.

Physical activity and physical development are a requirement

One of five curriculum areas in the Finnish curriculum includes PE and health and is titled: I grow, move and develop. The goal of this area is to encourage children to be physically active in versatile ways and to experience the joy of physical activity, and "learning by doing" should be integrated into each child's day. It is believed that regular and supervised exercise has a key role in children's holistic development, including the development of motor skills and fundamental movement skills. Teachers and practitioners are obligated to observe children's movement skills, to recognise those children who may need additional support and to provide support and supervision as appropriate. As a result, there are numerous opportunities for Finnish children to engage in physically active play, both indoors and outdoors, every day. The following list outlines a typical day:

- 6.30 am – day care centre opens (unstructured play inside)
- 8.00 am – breakfast
- 8.30 am – structured activities indoors
- 9.00 am – unstructured play outdoors
- 11.00 am – lunch
- 12.00 pm – rest (sleep, quiet activities, reading, calm play)
- 2.00 pm – snack
- 2.30 pm – unstructured play indoors
- 3.00 pm – unstructured play outdoors
- 5.00 pm – centre closes

From this, we can see that two hours in the morning and two hours in the afternoon are dedicated to unstructured outdoor play.

The following example, taken from a small research project conducted in three nurseries in the Midlands of England, using an ethnographic approach and observations (Stirrup, 2012), reflects a somewhat different approach:

- 9.30 am: registration
- 9.50 am: snack time (fruit, cheese and milk)
- 9.50 am–11.20 am: free time indoors (reading, dressing up, playing on computer, filling in progress books with a member of staff)
- 11.35–12:00 pm lunch
- 12 pm: home time (for some children).

A second example, taken from the same research project, portrays a more positive approach (certainly in terms of providing opportunities for young children to be physically active and to develop their gross motor skills):

- 9.30 am: "Gathering" – saying hi to all the children
- 9.50 am: free time. The majority of children choose to play outside (building blocks, soft-play, tricycles, running around)

- 10.10 am: some children return inside for snack time; fruit loaf and fruit
- 10.45 am–11.30 am: climbing frame activities for all
- 11.45 am: home time

Neither of the English examples followed the children into the afternoon. The first example illustrates how easy it is to provide nursery provision that does very little for a young child's physical development. The second nursery was part of the Forest School scheme (see Chapter 13) and provided weekly PE lessons for the oldest children in the setting (something that is not necessarily required of this age group but that was observed being quite successful by the researchers). Two very different approaches but both settings were following the same framework for the early years, perhaps suggesting that a lack of appropriate physical development opportunities may be, in part, due to the interpretations of the framework and the knowledge and understanding of the practitioners in these settings.

As detailed earlier and discussed further in Chapter 4, physical activity guidelines have been introduced to both the United Kingdom and Finland. Like Canada, Finland has 24-hour guidelines to acknowledge the important of sleep and rest (Ministry of Education and Culture, Finland, 2016). It is recommended that young children engage in at least three hours of physical activity and that one hour of this is vigorous in nature (e.g. playing tag, jumping on a trampoline, swimming or skiing). Brisk outdoor activities (trips to the woods, cycling and skating) and light physical activity (walking, throwing a ball, swinging on a swing and balancing) should make up the remaining two hours. To avoid sedentary activities, it is recommended that time is spent doing "unhurried daily chores" (playing with cars, building blocks or dolls, studying things, putting clothes on and eating).

As many young children are in Finnish nursery settings for most of their waking hours, five days a week, the role of the nursery in facilitating opportunities for these young children to be active for 180 minutes a day is clearly important. It has already been noted that many opportunities each day are provided for young children to be active both inside and outdoors, but what else is done by Finnish Practitioners to meet the physical development needs of young children and help them to reach their three-hour-a-day physical activity goal? The following are all examples of ways in which this has and can be achieved:

- Targeted physical activity interventions. Gordon, Tucker, Burke, and Carron (2013) found that short interventions lasting less than four weeks were most effective as children tended to need new stimuli after this time;
- Supporting parents to maximise physical activity opportunities for their children;
- Finding a balance between structured and unstructured physical activity opportunities:
  - On the one hand, unstructured activities are seen to be important, perhaps more so than more structured activities such as tag or throwing/

catching games because of the opportunities they offer young children to explore the environment and experiment with what their bodies are capable of in an autonomous and creative way. Likewise, unstructured physically active play is more effective for overall child development because it has the elements of fun, spontaneity and freedom and encourage curiosity, problem solving and imaginative play.

- Yet, on the other hand, studies (e.g. Iivonen & Sääkslahti, 2014; Ward, Vaughn, McWilliams, & Hales, 2010) have hinted at the benefits of more structured activities such as those more recognised as PE.
- Staff need to create "optimal environments" using different equipment and toys. Cardon, Van Cauwenberghe, Labarque, Haerens, and De Bourdeaudhuij (2008) and Cardon, Labarque, Smiths, and De Bourdeaudhuij (2009), for example, found that equipment such as climbing bars, swings, sandpits and slides were effective in increasing physical activity. Related research (Soini et al., 2016; Stratton & Leonard, 2002) illustrated how playground markings can also increase children's physical activity, albeit for short periods of time. In relation to this, Cardon et al. (2009) advise that interest in such markings can quickly be lost; thus, a recommendation for day care centres and nurseries might be to provide chalk for children to make their own markings as these are cheap and can easily be modified.
- Verbal encouragement from staff; this has been shown to be an effective way to increase young children's physical activity, but one study (Soini et al., 2014) highlighted that this approach was rare in Early Years settings.
- Just as the wider environment needs to encourage physical activity so too do the resources provided. Objects such as balls and wheels, large wheeled toys to push, pull and pedal, tyres and recycled materials all encourage physical activity. In addition, objects such as these will help develop strength, co-ordination and fine motor skills.
- Hnatiuk et al. (2018) underlined the importance of tailoring physical activities to the needs of the target group; thus, an understanding of community or cultural needs may be helpful.

Conclusion

A number of comparisons between Finland and the United Kingdom, in relation to physical development opportunities, PE and physical activity, have been outlined in this chapter. In providing an international comparison and highlighting the differences in practice between the systems in Finland and the United Kingdom, it is hoped that lessons can be learnt and examples of good practice be adopted. The point was made early on that, on measures of education and well-being, Finland scored better when compared to the United Kingdom. This was despite formal education starting later in Finland and the school day being shorter. Thus, key differences were explored and a number of practices put forward as being effective: the value of the outdoors as a play environment; the importance of good training for those in charge of the education and development of young children; strategies for coping with extremes of weather; having adequate indoor and outdoor facilities; and adopting pedagogies that enable staff to meet the physical development needs of young children.

Summary of key points

- Enable children to go outside every day and provide opportunities for them to encounter different surfaces, environments, textures and slopes.
- Provide equipment that will encourage physical activity through play and, at the same time, contribute towards physical development (boxes, wheels, boards, toys with wheels, etc.).
- Help children to play together and cooperate. Those who struggle with rules and being part of a team will find it hard to play organised games and, in turn, will be less likely to engage in these physical activities.
- Teach through play and multisensory activities. Children learn by doing, using their whole body and all of their senses. Sensory integration will be difficult without these opportunities.
- When children have difficulties concentrating and being still, they are not ready to be still – allow them to move instead.

Suggested further readings

Joy, play and doing together. Recommendations for physical activity in early childhood. Publications of the Ministry of Education and Culture, Finland 2016, 35. http://julkaisut.valtioneuvosto.fi/bitstream/handle/10024/78924/OKM35.pdf

National Core Curriculum for Early Childhood Education and Care. (2016). http://www.oph.fi/english/curricula_and_qualifications/early_childhood_education_and_care

---

References

Cardon, G., Labarque, V., Smiths, D., & De Bourdeaudhuij, I. (2009). Promoting physical activity at pre-school playground: The effects of providing markings and play equipment. *Preventive Medicine 48*, 335–340.

Cardon, G., Van Cauwenberghe, E., Labarque, V., Haerens, L., & De Bourdeaudhuij, I. (2008). The contribution of preschool playground factors in explaining children's physical activity during recess. *International Journal of Behavioural Nutrition and Physical Activity 5*, 11.

Curriculum, Appendix (The total amount of lessons during basic school). Retrieved from https://www.oph.fi/download/46678_pops_liite4.pdf

Department for Education (DfE). (2017). *Statutory framework for the early years foundation stage: Setting the standards for learning, development and care for children from birth to five.* London: Crown Copyright.

Donnelly, J. E., Hillman, C. H., Castelli, D., Etnier, J. L., Lee, S., Tomporowski, P., & Szabo-Reed, A. N. (2016). Physical activity, fitness, cognitive function, and academic achievement in children: A systematic review. *Medicine & Science in Sports & Exercise, 48*(6), 1197–1222.

Duncombe, R., Cale, L., & Harris, J. (2016). Strengthening 'the Foundations' of the primary school curriculum. *Education 3–13, 46*(1), 76–88.

Finland's report card on physical activity for children and youth. (2018). Retrieved from https://www.likes.fi/filebank/2800-Finland-reportcard2018-final-150.pdf

Finnish National Agency for Education. (2017). Retrieved from https://www.oph.fi/english/current_issues/101/0/teaching_continues_to_be_an_attractive_profession

Fjortoft, I. (2001). The natural environment as playground for children: The impact of outdoor play activities in pre-primary school children. *Early Childhood Education Journal, 29*(2), 111–117.

Fjortoft, I. (2004). Landscape as playscape: The effects of the natural environments on children's play and motor development. *Children, Youth and Environments, 14*(2), 21–44.

Gordon, E., Tucker, P., Burke, S., & Carron, A. (2013). Effectiveness of physical activity interventions for preschoolers: A meta-analysis. *Research Quarterly for Exercise and Sport, 84*(3), 287–294.

Griggs, G. (2007). Physical education: Primary matters, secondary importance. *Education 3–13, 35*(1), 59–69.

Haapala, E. A., Lintu, N., Eloranta, A. M., Venäläinen, T., Poikkeus, A. M., Ahonen, T., & Lakka, T. A. (2018). Mediating effects of motor performance, cardiorespiratory fitness, physical activity, and sedentary behaviour on the associations of adiposity and other cardiometabolic risk factors with academic achievement in children. *Journal of Sports Sciences, 36*(20), 2296–2303.

Hillman, C., Kalaja, S., & Liukkonen, J. (2015). The associations among fundamental movement skills, self-reported physical activity and academic performance during junior high school in Finland. *Journal of Sport Sciences, 33*(16), 1719–1729.

Hnatiuk, J. A., Brown, H. E., Downing, K. L., Hinkley, T., Salmon, J., & Hesketh, K. D. (2018). Intervention to increase physical activity in children 0–5-years old: A systematic review, meta-analysis and realist synthesis. *Obesity Reviews.* doi:10.1111/obr.12763

Iivonen, S. & Sääkslahti, A. (2014). Preschool children's fundamental motor skills: A review of significant determinants. *Early Child Development and Care, 184*(7), 1107–1126.

Mäki, P., Lehtinen-Jacks, S., Vuorela, N., Levälahti, E., Koskela, T., Saari, A., & Laatikainen, T. (2017). Lasten ylipainon valtakunnallinen seuranta [Children's overweight, National follow-up]. *Suomen Lääkärilehti, 72*, 4.

Ministry of Education and Culture. (2016). *Joy, play and doing together. Recommendations for physical activity in early childhood.* Publications of the Ministry of Education and Culture: Finland, 35.

National Core Curriculum for Early Childhood Education and Care. (2016). Finnish National Agency for Education.

Opintopolku. Retrieved from https://www.google.fi/url?sa=t&rct=j&q=&esrc=s&source=web&cd=1&cad=rja&uact=8&ved=2ahUKEwjz4Zm82PbdAhXLjy-wKHR5bD_oQFjAAegQICRAB&url=https%3A%2F%2Fopintopolku.fi%2Fwp%-2Fopo%2Ftilastot-opi-vipunen%2F&usg=AOvVaw1hRMjjcxO-savlTdYCFncO

Programme for International Students Assessment (PISA). (2015). *Results in Focus, OECD 2018*. Retrieved from https://www.oecd.org/pisa/pisa-2015-results-in-focus.pdf

Recommendations for physical activity in early childhood education. Helsinki, 2005. 44 pp. (Handbooks of the Ministry of Social Affairs and Health, ISSN 1236-116X; 2005:17), ISBN 952-00-1793-3 (print), ISBN 952-00-1794-1 (PDF).

Soini, A., Gubbels, J., Sääkslahti, A., Villberg, J., Kremers, S., Van Kann, D., & Poskiparta, M. (2016). A comparison of physical activity levels. *European Early Childhood Education Research, 24*(5), 775–786.

Soini, A., Villberg, J., Sääkslahti, A., Gubbels, J., Mehtälä, A., Kettunen, T., & Poskiparta, M. (2014). Directly observed physical activity among 3-year-olds in Finnish childcare. *International Journal of Early Childhood, 46*(2), 253–269.

Stirrup, J. (2012). *Physical activity and the importance of early years learning.* Institute of Youth Sport Conference 2012, Loughborough University.

Stratton, G., & Leonard, J. (2002). The effects of playground markings on the energy expenditure on 5–7-year-old school children. *Pediatric Exercise Science, 14*(2), 170–180.

Suomen Kuvalehti. (2018). *SK tutki: Näitä ammatteja arvostetaan.* Retrieved June 1, 2018, from https://suomenkuvalehti.fi/jutut/kotimaa/onko-ammattisi-nousussa-vai-laskussa-katso-mita-ammatteja-suomi-arvostaa-ja-mita-ei/

Townsend, N., Wickramasinghe, K., Williams, J., Bhatnagar, P., & Rayner, M. (2015). *Physical activity statistics 2015.* London: British Heart Foundation.

UNICEF Office of Research (2013). 'Child Well-being in Rich Countries: A comparative overview', *Innocenti Report Card 11*, UNICEF Office of Research, Florence (page 16).

Vygotsky, L.S. (1978). *Mind and society.* Cambridge, MA: Harvard University.

Ward, D. S., Vaughn, A., McWilliams, C., & Hales, D. (2010). Interventions for increasing physical activity at child care. *Medicine and Science in Sports and Exercise, 42*(3), 526–534.

6

NATURAL PHYSICAL DEVELOPMENT IN THE FIRST YEAR

Learning from the Pikler approach

Dorothy Marlen

Personal reflection

When my child was born by caesarean, I did not know about primitive reflexes or that difficult births may cause their retention and that this might be accompanied by subsequent physical awkwardness and possible learning difficulties in childhood and beyond. I was only aware that my child did not like sport and had difficulties with certain areas of learning. I carried questions for many years about physical movement progression in early childhood – what helps and also what hinders its full unfolding. These questions began to be answered when I trained in the Pikler approach at the Pikler Institute in Budapest, Hungary. The Institute has conducted over 60 years of observational research and demonstrated that children can develop a natural physical grace, co-ordination and healthy self confidence if given the freedom to self-initiate their own movement, in their own time, from birth. I learnt too that full movement progression (through rolling, crawling, sitting and coming up into standing) also re-quires a secure relationship with an adult/carer and a suitable environment. I brought these new understandings into the support groups I now run for parents and babies. Over nine years of running these groups, I have witnessed the exceptional physical fluidity and confidence in those children who have been able to experience non-assisted, self-initiated movement and play in the first year of life. I have also observed the many ways in which this can be hindered through birth, early difficulties and adult's well-intentioned assistance. I have also observed what can help. In this chapter I share some of what I have learnt about gross motor development from the Pikler Institute and what I have discovered from the groups that I run.

Introduction

Jane Swain, a paediatric physical therapist and associate director of the teacher education program at Sophia's Hearth Early Childhood Training Centre in the

United States, wrote about her visit to the residential children's nursery at the Pikler Institute in Budapest in 2007:

> I was in awe of the grace, beauty and efficiency of the infants' and tod-dlers' movements at Lóczy (The Pikler Institute, Budapest). Their balance, coordination and posture were extraordinary. Their movement possibili-ties were vast; they were very active and well-acquainted with transitional movements – that is, they did not remain in a few static positions, but instead moved in and out of positions easily. I did not see nearly the degree of drooling, low-tone trunks, wide-sprawling bases of support, compensa-tory high shoulders and stiffness, and other movement problems that I so often see in typically developing children in the U.S. Among the children at Lóczy, I also did not see abnormal retention of the primitive reflexes... When I inquired further of the staff about the lack of abnormal primitive reflex retention among the children at Lóczy, I was told that this is not an issue for them. Not an issue! There are paediatric therapists throughout the world who make a living treating children with abnormally retained re-flexes. For 28 years, I have witnessed increasing problems with proper inte-gration of the primitive reflexes in typically developing American children with no history of prematurity or birth trauma. Children in the orphanage at Lóczy come from situations in which they were abused, abandoned or neglected – yet they are developing beautifully.
>
> *(Swain, 2008)*

Freely expressed movement and play in the first year of life is foundational for the healthy development of physical, social and cognitive skills and a positive attitude to movement in later childhood (e.g. Brodie, 2018; O'Connor & Daly, 2016; White, 2015). Worryingly, recent studies have shown that more children are now starting school with neuro-motor immaturity, as well as lower levels of physical develop-ment than in previous decades (e.g. Goddard Blythe, 2005a, 2005b; Gieysztor et al., 2018; Duncombe & Preedy, 2018). With neuro-motor immaturity often the cause of later learning and behavioural difficulties (Goddard Blythe, 2005a, 2005b, 2011; Taylor, Houghton, & Chapman, 2004) and retained primitive reflexes being a likely contributory factor, the impact of inappropriate and inadequate movement opportunities in the early months of life is becoming worryingly apparent.

There are many ways in which young children become the unwitting victims of sedentary lifestyles, including a lack of play time (particularly outdoor time), regular use of screen technology and passive transport. Do current cultural life-styles potentially cause or exasperate early neuro-motor issues? There is very little research on what is the healthy amount of movement for children under three. However, one such piece of research concluded that

> contemporary lifestyles and environments appear to be preventing some young children from engaging in adequate levels of physical activity.

As the origins of an active lifestyle begin in the early years of life, physical inactivity during early childhood might have consequences for children's current and future health, behaviour, social and emotional development, and cognitive function.

(Cliff & Janssen, 2011)

My own training at the Pikler Institute and in the United Kingdom over the last ten years has equipped me with an understanding of natural "self-initiated natural motor progression" (how motor development naturally progresses when it is self-initiated and not assisted) and how young children are naturally active from birth. My work with parents and babies in groups highlights a number of barriers that may obstruct natural development and these will be outlined in a later part of this chapter. It is hoped that an understanding and awareness of the full natural movement progression and potential obstacles to this may provide parents, caregivers and other Early Years professionals with new tools to help infants experience full motor progression and the subsequent benefits. As stated in the introduction to the book "Unfolding of Infants' Natural Gross Motor Development," Dr Emmi Pikler

> ...demonstrated conclusively that a healthy infant, when raised in a stable, respectful relationship, has the inborn ability to learn to move, sit and walk without being taught. Furthermore, such infants move naturally with better co-ordination, more body awareness, a natural sense of uprightness and more grace than when they are assisted by propping, being held upright or otherwise helped to sit, stand, walk or climb.
>
> *(Resources for Infant Educarers, 2006, p. xi)*

Natural motor development and the Pikler principles

Dr Emmi Pikler (1902–1984) developed an original and successful approach to caring for young children, which she brought to her work as a paediatrician in Budapest in the 1930s and later at a residential nursery she founded in Budapest after the Second World War. This ran for 60 years caring for very young children (Sensory Awareness Foundation, 1994; The Signal, 2010; David & Appell, 2007). The residential nursery closed in 2011 and since then the institute (now called the Pikler House) has developed a day care centre, parent and child group classes and serves as a training, observation and research centre that attracts early childhood professionals from all over the world. The two main principles of the Pikler approach are:

1. The importance of a respectful relationship with a trusted carer especially during times of bodily care;
2. The importance of non-assisted, self-initiated gross and fine motor development in the early months and years.

(Tardos, 2010; Sensory Awareness Foundation, 1994)

These two primary principles are both essential and interdependent. The infant's ability to enjoy self-initiated movement and play is dependent on a foundation of a caring and respectful relationship with an adult. The calm presence and unhurried time of care with the adult (particularly during times of bodily care such as nappy changing, feeding and bathing) are internalised and provide the infant with a secure, trusting core from which to explore themselves and their environment (Kallo & Balog, 2005; Pikler, 1971; The Signal, 2010). Through self-initiated movement and play, the child is able to follow their natural inner motivation and curiosity (which emerges when they feel secure) about themselves and their world. This fosters a healthy self confidence in their own abilities and promotes a natural independence. They can also follow their own sense of tempo and learn how to self-regulate themselves – when to stop and rest. Healthy infants have a natural motivation to explore and try new movements and they find deep pleasure in practising and finally mastering moves and developing new abilities. They do not need adults to assist this natural process.

What they do need is a carer who is aware of their intrinsic needs and can provide an appropriate environment with suitable play objects. An important aspect of the Pikler approach is how the adult responds and interacts during times of self-initiated play. Interference is kept to a minimum as it is recognised that infants need to find out about their body and surroundings themselves, including overcoming (small) frustrations, in order to integrate new learning and development. Rather, the carer needs to focus on how to facilitate safe and satisfying self-initiated exploration, only intervening when absolutely necessary (Kallo & Balog, 2005).

I will now focus on the second principle: the importance of self-initiated gross motor development and what can hamper its unfolding. The Pikler Institute also researched fine motor development and the development of play in great detail but space prevents a description of this. More information on these aspects can be found in the resource list at the end of the chapter.

Natural gross motor progression

There is a general consensus in the literature on early movement about the normal progression of gross motor development from birth to standing (e.g. Brodie, 2018; Connell & McCarthy, 2014; O'Connor, & Daly, 2016; White, 2015) and a description of this, in relation to play, is also given in Chapter 14 of this book. At the Pikler Institute, infants' natural motor progression has been studied in great depth over many years (for example Pikler, 1968) This description differs in some very important respects from what is commonly expected in early motor progression. In particular, this research provides us with a detailed description regarding the important 'transition positions' (RIE, 2006). The Pikler research also informs us that, given the opportunity and freedom, healthy infants and toddlers are active and self-regulating and will move position on average every two minutes (Pikler, 1971).

The following is a brief summary of the natural gross motor progression by Emmi Pikler (1968, 1971) and RIE (2006) which I have also repeatedly observed in the parent and baby groups that I run when infants move through each stage without adult assistance. There are only average timings below on developmental stages as the time spent at each stage can vary enormously (Pikler, 1971):

1. The new born is laid on the back on the floor when not being held. Gradually there is control of head, hands and later legs. Hands, and later feet, are played with. Turning to the side (usually from around 3 months but maybe much later) becomes more common to explore simple play objects laid beside the baby (see Figure 6.1).
2. Rolling onto the side and back onto the back repeatedly until confident.
3. Rolling onto the tummy (from around 6 months).
4. Rolling from the back onto the tummy and back. Gaining balance and strength in head, neck, arms, core middle realm muscles and legs through repeated practice. Moving through space by rolling or shuffling on the back.
5. Gradually being on the tummy takes precedence to being on the back. Arms and back are strengthened by lifting up arms whilst on the tummy.
6. Balancing and playing on the side and lying on the back to explore objects (the side balancing position is generally only seen when there is a natural progression: see Figure 6.2).
7. From being on the tummy, the baby learns to belly crawl, using arms and legs.

FIGURE 6.1 Baby with the first "toy" – a handkerchief.

FIGURE 6.2 Ten-month-old enjoying the side position.

8. The half sitting position is found, propping up sideways on one arm, often at the same time as beginning to belly crawl (From about 7 months onwards).
9. Climbing over and through pieces of low equipment is enjoyed.
10. The next stage is crawling. Crawling on hands and knees. Often this stage will coincide with coming into full sitting and beginning to climb.
11. Full sitting in various positions. Because the sitting position has been freely found when the child is developmentally ready, it is possible to move in and out of it with ease. Bum shuffling does not happen if the natural progression has been possible (usually from about 7 months onwards).
12. Finally, lifting into standing, initially moving whilst supporting balance on furniture. From here balance develops to stand alone and eventually confidently take the first steps.

For more details and full description including illustrations of natural gross motor development, see RIE (2006).

The motor progression described earlier may, at first reading, seem to be the same as generally described elsewhere. However, there are important differences:

1. The baby starts the process of movement progression from lying on the back. A baby left to find hands and feet on his or her back will roll and then turn over independently when he or she is ready. Lifting the legs on the back in

play strengthens the core stomach muscles and leg muscles which will help the baby to turn to the side and fully roll on to their tummy:

> Pikler stressed the fundamental importance of placing a very young infant on his back to sleep or to play. From this first position, a baby's intrinsic spontaneous movements enable him to turn himself over when he is developmentally ready to be in a new position. On his back, a healthy young infant is in a position of greater ease, mobility, and mastery, where his gross motor skills can develop naturally through his own self-directed explorations.
>
> *(Resources for Infant Educarers, 2006, Introduction, p. xi)*

2. Time balancing on the side is recognised as an important position for several reasons including developing core strength and balance. This position is not seen in babies who are frequently put on their tummies from birth (see Figure 6.2).
3. The important belly crawling stage (often missed by babies who have been propped up before they are ready to sit independently).
4. Non-assisted, half sitting up when the infant has mastered lying on the tummy, and is learning belly crawling. This happens naturally between about seven and ten months.
5. Non-assisted full sitting up as the child learns to crawl on hands and knees.

Generally, the literature on gross motor development assumes that some of the baby's motor progression needs to be assisted (for example, tummy time and supported sitting up). The Pikler approach shows that this is not necessary, and too much may even hinder full progression. For example, placing a baby on its tummy before he or she has rolled from the back onto the tummy is not necessary and may be counterproductive as the early and very important stages of laying on the back and side may be missed. There is a detailed paper on the dangers of tummy time written by Judi Falk, one of the research doctors at the Pikler Institute, which sheds a new light on this subject (Falk, 2011). Likewise, supported sitting and equipment which enables babies to sit up, stand or "walk" before they are developmentally ready are also seen to be counterproductive, may delay development and/or may worsen any primitive reflex retention issues. It may be that natural self-initiated progression ensures that primitive reflexes are more fully integrated; the later grace and self confidence of children who have experienced a natural movement progression certainly seem to indicate this.

The weekly parent and baby groups that I run last approximately 90 minutes. There are usually seven parents and their babies in each group and they range in age from two months to when the child is confidently toddling. The families stay in the groups between 6 and 18 months during which time infants are freely active by their own initiative and without unnecessary interventions, rules or restraints from an adult. We spend quiet time observing the infants moving and playing without assistance and practice respectful care. Although parents and carers of infants can be encouraged to allow plenty of time for self-initiated movements and play, I have found in my groups and through wider experiences that there can be various obstacles to natural motor progression.

Observed barriers to natural self-initiated physical development progression and some solutions

Baby gyms and mobiles

As an illustration of the use of baby gyms as a barrier to natural motor progression, the following is an observation from one of the mothers in my groups:

> We'd been given a baby gym for Dylan (8 weeks) to play under, which he did and appeared to really enjoy reaching and stretching upwards towards the toys. After learning about the Pikler approach and a more centred, embodied way of supporting Dylan to explore his environment we decided to remove the gym bars and just lay the toys either side of him. The difference was quite remarkable, he stretched outwards like a starfish and wriggled much more than he had done when he was only reaching upwards under the bars. He moved through all 3 planes of movement and he also began to attempt a little roll over to the right-hand side by lifting his legs and arms.

Baby gyms may prevent the natural rolling sequence and, as in the earlier observation, restrict the natural movement of arms and legs. Kallo & Balog (2005) also describe reasons why mobiles and toys hung in front of a baby can be over stimulating and frustrating for the baby as they cannot be held or explored.

Car seats, buggies, bumbo seats, etc.

Too much time in these pieces of equipment prevents the infant from being able to move freely and may, if used excessively, cause a disinclination to lie on the floor on their tummies or backs, and stages of the natural progression may be skipped, possibly exasperating reflex issues. Too much time in "containers" has been associated with flat head syndrome and other developmental issues. See, for example:

- https://www.moveforwardpt.com
- https://www.moms.com/container-baby-syndrome-10-things-doctors-say-cause-it-and-10-ways-to-avoid-it/
- https://www.janetlansbury.com/2009/09/set-me-free/

Assisted tummy time

Placing the baby on its tummy before the baby finds the position itself may cause body tension in the back, neck, arms and shoulders and, in some cases, if given too much tummy time, the skipping of essential steps in a baby's physical development journey (e.g. finding hands and feet, limited flexing of hips and legs, little practice rolling from back to front, not finding the side balancing position, not crawling on belly: Falk, 2011). I have observed that infants who do not have tummy time reach recognised motor milestones at the same time as those who do. I have not observed "flat head syndrome" (a common reason for advising tummy time) in infants who start the motor progression from their backs. The cause of flat heads may be more to do with excessive time in buggies and other sitting equipment where the baby cannot move.

Supported sitting

I have observed parents supporting their baby into a sitting position from as early as five months (naturally and freely achieved between seven and ten months). This can cause the infant to get stuck in the sitting position, bum shuffle and/ or miss out the very important belly crawling and all fours crawling stages. It is much more difficult for an infant to find the crawling position from an "assisted" sitting position, where the legs are straight and splayed out to the front. It is also a very unstable position where infants can often fall over, if they are not ready to find this position themselves.

Birth "difficulties"

Caesareans, premature births and fast births have all been associated with developmental delays and retained primitive reflexes (Gieysztor, Chianska, & Paproka, 2018). These babies often find it difficult to find the flow of the natural progression and can seem stuck and very uncomfortable when put on their backs. Early support from cranial chiropractors or osteopaths, along with gentle care and massage, can, over time, potentially restore in these infants the ability to move through the natural motor progression from their backs. This is illustrated by one of the mothers from my groups:

> Sam had a very difficult birth and we were both quite traumatised and wary of each other afterwards. Sam was fussy, rigid in his body and quickly developed a body rash. He did not like being on his back or his front. I started an elimination diet and by 7 months we found the food culprit, and the rash cleared. This helped Sam. Osteopathic treatment had a huge effect, and from hardly moving, Sam picked up the natural progression flow and went through all the stages from his back to crawling by 10 months. Without knowledge of the Pikler approach, I would have sat him up early as this was the easiest position to keep him happy in. I also learnt how to slow care times and we have a great relationship now.

Undetected tongue tie

Remarkably, this is an issue for approximately half of the babies in any of my groups and causes distress for both mother and baby. There can be difficulty in breastfeeding, and both mother and baby may feel very discouraged right from the beginning of the baby's life. The body tension that is caused by the distress makes it uncomfortable to be placed on the front or back. The baby is then generally held or propped up in baby seats and may miss many of the stages of natural movement progression. Early remedial intervention for the tongue tie and cranial osteopathic/chiropractic intervention and massage can help the infant back to a relaxed, happier state from which the natural movement progression can hopefully commence (e.g. https://milkmatters.or.uk).

Skin conditions

Conditions such as eczema can cause extreme bodily discomfort and consequently an unwillingness to be laid on the back on the floor. Mothers have found that restrictive diets can improve the condition considerably, and cranial osteopathic/chiropractic treatment, along with massage to release tension caused by the condition, can be beneficial. Then the infants are able to find the motor progression flow, starting on their backs.

Rough handling and an emotional environment

Rough handling and various emotional situations in the home and with either parent, like post-natal depression, may cause the baby to become anxious, untrusting and therefore chronically tense, stiff and unsettled. This will, in turn, cause difficulties in finding the natural progression of movement. The Pikler approach modelled in a parent and baby group can provide parents with new ways to be with their baby, using gentle handling and a co-operative caregiving approach. Over time, the gentle support of the group can promote more trust and enjoyment in both child and carer (David & Appell, 2007; Falk, 2006). The two Pikler principles (respectful care and self-initiated movement) balanced together can make parenting much easier and more enjoyable.

Bulky nappies and inappropriate clothing

Tight trousers or skirts and bulky nappies can hinder free movement. Nappies unfortunately have not been developed with infant's motor progression in mind. Therefore, an awareness is required to observe how an infant's movement may be inhibited by certain makes of nappies. Likewise, loose leggings and tops are advised rather than fashion jeans or baby dresses, and bare feet or soft shoes where possible.

Flooring

Infants find it much easier to move on solid floors rather than soft or cushioned surfaces. They also find it easier to creep, crawl, come up into standing or walk if the floor is not slippery.

The environment

To facilitate natural gross and fine motor progression, the environment needs to be appropriate. Gross natural motor development cannot be separated from the fine motor development which progresses in parallel. The first toy is the hands! At around three months, a simple handkerchief can be placed in reach. The infant, through its natural curiosity, is drawn to explore objects. Simple toys of various weights and shapes provide many opportunities for fine motor skills to be developed and for gross movement to be encouraged. The environment needs to be set up appropriately for this to happen. The adult needs to observe and see what is interesting the child and make sure that the child's explorations are encouraged. The Pikler Institute has advice on the type and number of toys to place near a child and at what age (Kallo & Balog, 2005). There are, for example, pieces of equipment which encourage free movement, balance and exploration indoors as the infant becomes mobile:

- A safe fenced off area for babies to be on backs and crawling if in a group setting;
- Platform, ramps and steps (see Figure 6.3);
- Tunnels;
- A frame ladder/Pikler Triangle (see Figure 6.4);
- Boxes and slides;
- The Pikler Institute has developed nappy changing tables which allow the child to move freely and safely in the special moments of relationship based physical care (see Figure 6.5).

FIGURE 6.3 An infant experimenting with positions on some steps and reaching for toys.

FIGURE 6.4 Pikler Triangle for children to climb up and over.

FIGURE 6.5 A "Pikler" style nappy changing table that enables safe and free movement.

Conclusion

In this chapter, I have described natural motor progression in the first year and have suggested that, if certain conditions and opportunities are provided to facilitate this, some common neuro-motor development issues may be lessened or avoided. Observations, such as the ones I have described in this chapter, will be the subject of a formal research project in the near future.

A final thought is whether children who have experienced the full progression in the first year or so of life can retain a core flexibility, grace and body confidence that can be returned to later in life, even if, through trauma or lack of movement opportunities, the early fluidity is lost. This is perhaps another question for further discussion and research. Lastly, I will leave you with this quote and photo (Figure 6.6) from Anna (one of the mothers from my groups):

> I attribute his awesome balance to being a "Pikler" baby. If anyone has doubts, trust you're doing the right thing here.
>
> *(Anna Brown, mother and chiropractor)*

FIGURE 6.6 28-month-old child demonstrating his body confidence and excellent balance.

Summary of key points

- Gross motor development, as mapped out by the Pikler Institute, should and will occur naturally if a healthy infant can experience self-initiated movement and play.
- There are a variety of barriers that prevent natural motor progression in the early months which may cause or exasperate primitive reflex issues.
- Physical movement development needs to be understood and practised in the context of a secure, respectful relationship with an adult, and an appropriate environment.

- Unhindered healthy physical movement is foundational and essential for healthy overall development, including speech, learning, core confidence and self-esteem.
- Early childhood professionals, practitioners, advisors and parents need to be given a more "complete" understanding of the process of physical development. This may, in turn, reduce later learning difficulties caused by motor delay and retained reflexes.

Suggested further reading

Resources for Infant Educarers. (2006) *Unfolding of Infants' natural gross motor development*. From the original publication, Terminology of Basic Body Postures and Positions (1978). By Pikler, E and Translated by Varosy Toth. Los Angeles: Resources for Infant Educators.
www.thepiklercollection.weebly.com
www.pikler.co.uk – on line book shop

References

Brodie, K. (2018). *The holistic care and development of children from birth to three*. London: Routledge.

Cliff, D., & Janssen, X. (2011). *Levels of habitual physical activity in early childhood*. University of Wollongong, Australia. Retrieved from http://www.child-encyclopedia.com/physical-activity/according-experts/levels-habitual-physical-activity-early-childhood

Connell, G., & McCarthy, C. (2014). *A moving child is a learning child*. Minneapolis, MN: Free Spirit Publishing.

David, M., & Appell, G. (2007). *Lóczy: An unusual approach to mothering*. Budapest: Pikler Lóczy Tarasag.

Duncombe, R., & Preedy, P. (2018). Movement for learning. In P. Preedy, K. Sanderson, & C. Ball (Eds.), *Early childhood redefined: Reflections and recommendations on the impact of start right*. Oxford: Routledge.

Falk, J. (2006). *Bathing the baby*. Budapest: Pikler Lóczy Tarasag.

Falk, J. (2011). Why should we lay the infant in prone position? *Child and Youth Medical Journal (Official Journal of the Hungarian Paediatrician Association)*. Supplementum. Le Provanade Bt.

Gieysztor, E., Chianksa, A., & Paproka, M. (2015). Persistence of primitive reflexes and associated motor problems in healthy preschool children. *Archives of Medical Science, 12*(1), 167–173. https://www.researchgate.net/publication/305567529_Persistence_of_primitive_reflexes_and_associated_motor_problems_in_healthy_preschool_children

Goddard Blythe, S. (2005a). *Reflexes, learning and behavior* (2nd ed.). Eugene, OR: Fern Ridge Press.

Goddard Blythe, S. (2005b). Releasing educational potential through movement. A summary of individual studies carried out using INPP tests. *Child Care in Practice, 11*(4), 415–432.

Goddard Blythe, S. (2011). *Genius of Natural Childhood*. Stroud: Hawthorn Press.

Kallo, E., & Balog, G. (2005). *The origins of free play*. Budapest: Pikler-Lóczy Táraság.

Money, R. (2006). *Forward to E. Pikler (ed) unfolding of infants' natural gross motor development from the original publication terminology of basic body postures and positions (1978) translated by Varosy Toth*. Los Angeles, CA: Resources for Infant Educators.

O'Connor, A., & Daly, A. (2016). *Understanding physical development in the early years*. London: Routledge.

Pikler, E. (1968). Some contributions to the study of the gross motor development of children. *Journal of Genetic Psychology, 113*(1), 27–39.

Pikler, E. (1971). Learning of motor skills on basis of self-induced movements. In J. Hellmuth (Ed.), *Exceptional infant: Studies in abnormality* (vol. 2, pp. 54–89). New York, NY: Brunner-Mazel.

Resources for Infant Educarers (2006). *Unfolding of infants' natural gross motor development. From the original publication: Terminology of basic body postures and positions (1978). By Pikler, E. and translated by Varosy Toth*. Los Angeles, CA: Resources for Infant Educators.

Sensory Awareness Foundation. (1994). Bulletin – *Emmi Pikler* (190201984). No.14.

Swain, J. (2008). Emmi Pikler's trust in the wise infant. In *A warm and nurturing welcome. The gateway series five* (pp. 19–27). New York, NY: WECAN Publications.

Tardos, A. (2010, July–December). Introducing the Piklerian developmental approach. *The Signal Newsletter of the World Association for Infant Mental Health, 18*(3–4), 1–4.

Taylor, M., Houghton, S., & Chapman, E. (2004). Primitive reflexes and attention-deficit activity disorder: Developmental origins of class room dysfunction. *International Journal of Special Education, 19*(1), 23–37.

Taylor, M., Houghton, S., & Chapman, E. (2004). Primitive reflexes and attention-deficit/hyperactivity. *Education, 19*(1), 23–37.

The Signal. (2010). *Newsletter of the World Association for Infant Mental Health, 18*, 3–4 (Issue devoted to Introducing the Piklerian developmental approach).

White, J. (2015) *Every Child a mover*. Watford, UK: British Association for Early Childhood Education.

Additional websites

https://www.moms.com/container-baby-syndrome-10-things-doctors-say-cause-it-and-10-ways-to-avoid-it/

https://www.moveforwardpt.com

https://www.janetlansbury.com/2009/09/set-me-free/

7

PRACTICAL APPROACHES FOR MEETING THE PHYSICAL DEVELOPMENT NEEDS OF BABIES AND TODDLERS

Sue Gascoyne

Personal reflection

Much has changed since my first visit to a UK nursery some 15 years ago. Having been told: "They're only babies so we don't do much, we just cuddle them!", I scooped up my nine-month-old daughter and left determined to find an early childcare centre that shared my view of babies as agentic and purposeful beings. Of course, babies and young children need warm attachment and safety to thrive, but they also need stimulating environments in which to explore and move, and so began my interest in how children learn, the importance of a strong foundation of attachment and the sorts of resources and environments which enrich children's well-being and agency. Watching my then 7-to-24-month-old daughter happily engaged for hours at a time, exploring the sensory-rich objects in her homemade treasure basket (an enticing collection of natural and household objects), was fascinating. Sometimes she spent an hour manipulating and mouthing a single object, such as a woven coaster, while, at other times, she explored two or more objects together, at first accidentally as one item banged against another creating a sound, then later intentionally. Her interest in this eclectic resource continued until aged two, and then was reignited (along with mine) as she watched her younger brother's own personal adventure with his treasure basket. He too began with single item exploration, manipulating and mouthing these as if to understand "what this object is?," "what is it like?" and "what can it do?" Intrigued by how long single, seemingly simple objects held his focus for, and noticing similar patterns over 15 years of observations, convinced me of the significance of these whole-bodied explorations. With increased strength and skills, he began engaging with several objects at a time, exploring a metal tin, large chunky choke chain, a short sturdy whisk and small metal container individually and together. He explored which objects fitted inside each other, how to build and knock towers down and mixed up some enticing "meals." The addition of sand, dried rice or water breathed new life into both children's play, cementing for me the value of "loose parts materials" (Nicholson, 1971) which urge children to use them flexibly in age-appropriate ways. Recognising the importance of these earliest years in giving children the best possible start in life, this chapter focusses the physical development lens on babies to three-year-olds, exploring the ramifications of children encountering plentiful and varied explorations with sensory-rich materials and the benefits these afford (Gibson, 1979; Heft, 2010) for meeting the physical development needs of young children.

Introduction

Throughout this book, concerns are raised over young children's declining levels of physical activity and development. We know, for example, that 3-, 4- and 5-year-old children in pre-schools spend 60% of their outdoor playtime in sedentary activities and only 11% in moderate-to-vigorous activities (Brown et al., 2009). Examining reasons for this rise in sedentary behaviours in young children, we are alerted to the prominence of Western-world equipment (such as car seats, baby bouncers and screen use) as well as changing lifestyles and cultural concerns which restrict movement (due to safety concerns, inactive travel and labour-saving devices). Focussing on the youngest children, this chapter explores some simple yet effective approaches for reversing these trends. Drawing on my work with treasure baskets and other sensory materials such as paint, sand and water, four "vignettes" are introduced to highlight everyday ways in which the physical development needs of babies and toddlers might be met and White's concept of "movement-rich environments" attained (White, 2013, p. 170).

A focus on gross and fine motor skills

Although an emphasis upon gross and fine motor skills is a helpful starting point when viewing children's actions through a movement lens, this oversimplification risks missing the large-scale and whole-bodied movement so typical of young children, as well as the complex array of finger movements evident in a child's manipulation of objects or materials. Gross motor skills involve the use of the large muscles in the arms, legs and torso to perform fundamental locomotor, non-locomotor and manipulative movement skills. Fine motor skills, in contrast, tend to be associated with a limited repertoire of pincer and palmar movements often linked to pencil control. As this observation of an eight-month-old child playing with a treasure basket reveals, fine motor skills are far from simple and cannot be isolated from the gross motor movements which underpin these:

> [Florence] empties objects one at a time until she finds the metal teaspoon. She starts mouthing this, then picks up the measuring spoon and starts

mouthing that. She shows the spoon to another staff member. Offers it to her, then takes it back laughing several times. She returns to emptying objects one at a time mouthing the metal objects. …She picks up the metal bucket. …starts balancing the handle on her fingers, babbling and looking inside. [A shallow tray of purple sand is offered next to the treasure basket], Florence starts spooning the sand using the teaspoon. She puts the handle end in her mouth and discovers that the sand is stuck to the wet part of the spoon and continues spooning sand and putting the handle end in her mouth.

(Gascoyne, 2012, pp. 90–91)

The sensory allure of this resource is clearly a powerful motivator for Florence's wide-ranging fine (and gross) motor movements. But the mass, surface texture and other "intrinsic properties" (Jones & Lederman, 2006, p. 108) of objects also influence how each object is grasped and explored and what coordination of forces are needed, so it stands to reason that more sensorially varied resources and environments will afford greater movements. Observations of children playing with collections of objects or sensory-rich materials (Gascoyne, 2014) revealed wide-ranging hand and finger movements in 0–3s, such as squeezing, scooping, stirring, whisking, mashing, grinding, smoothing, sieving, rolling, prodding, poking, moulding, shaping, pinching, stamping, twisting, turning, gripping and levering. With such a variety of hand skills practised through sensory-rich open-ended play, and only a limited range of movements associated with more restrictive resources, movement-enhancing environments are clearly essential for developing fine motor control.

Active manual exploration is also key for early categorisation in the brain, with different "exploratory procedures" (Lederman & Klatzky, 1987) yielding wide-ranging information that must be decoded. Indeed, a disproportionate amount of the sensory cortex in the brain is involved in receiving and interpreting sensory information from the hand and a large area of the motor cortex is devoted to the control of these. Made up of 27 small bones moved by 37 skeletal muscles connected to the bones by tendons, the human hand is a highly sophisticated sensory receptor and learning tool. With the opposing fingers and thumb introducing opportunities for mastery in tool use, you only need to watch a baby pick up, handle and invariably explore objects with their hands and mouth to understand the importance of both as tools for receiving and decoding sensory information.

When children's hand movements during play with treasure baskets and mud kitchens (White & Edwards, 2012) were explored through a developmental lens to identify the ages at which different skills were evident, the following tentative patterns of movement and exploratory procedures emerged (see Table 7.1):

TABLE 7.1 Hand movements developed through play and the approximate age at which they emerge

Hand movements/skill	Approximate age at which skill apparent	Potential links to exploratory procedures
Prodding and poking	0–8 months	Pressing with fingers to elicit hardness of an object
Stroking		Lateral motion with fingers to identify texture
Squeezing and gripping	9–16 months	Enclosing an object and following contours to identify overall and precise shape, hardness or temperature
Stroking		Lateral motion with fingers to identify texture
Gripping	17–22 months	Tool use and enclosing object with hand to identify geometric properties, materials and overall shape
Turning and twisting	23–30 months	Following contours with fingers to identify more exact shape
Gripping and squeezing		Enclosure to identify volume, global shape, weight and hardness.
Pinching and gripping	31–40 months	Global and contour following to identify exact shape and hardness
Turning and twisting		Tool use and identifying global and exact shape
Prodding and poking		Identifying pressure and hardness
Pinching, gripping and squeezing	41–60 months	Identifying global and exact shape, weight and hardness
Turning and twisting		Tool use and identifying global and exact shape
Prodding and poking		Identifying pressure and hardness

Source: Gascoyne and White (2014).

The data presented in Table 7.1 are based on retrospective analysis of 82 observations and, although the numbers in each age group and the type of activity were not standardised, these findings do suggest value in providing opportunities for wide-ranging hand movements to be developed and practised, rather than a narrower focus on pincer and palmar movements. With the gross motor skills in Florence's play less obvious, yet nevertheless essential, for enabling this eight-month-old to independently sit up, balance and purposefully reach and manipulate the objects, the interplay between gross and fine motor movements is clear. Prolonged periods of focus, exploration and manipulation of objects and other sensory-rich resources couldn't happen without the core, back and shoulder strength associated with gross motor movements. Developing in tandem with each other, it is only once the "big skills" are in place that fine motor skills are refined. This is apparent in many handwriting interventions (such as Jimbo Fun detailed in Chapter 15) where large letters are usefully drawn in the air (gross motor movements) before or alongside more precise handwriting skills (fine motor movements) being tackled.

Meeting the physical development needs of babies and toddlers: some practical suggestions

The following play vignettes provide examples of simple everyday activities, highlighting the physical development opportunities offered to young children and scope for movement-enhancing features to inspire movement. Often children's thoughts emanate from the movement rather than the brain instructing the movement; therefore splitting the child's movement from its contextual roots would impoverish the richness of encounters like these, where the child's body, mind and materials are in a constantly evolving relationship. The first three observations stem from my own research into children's play with treasure baskets and messy play resources; the fourth vignette is provided by Godfrey (2018).

Vignette 1: Treasure baskets

A treasure basket is a sensory-rich collection of natural and household objects within a sturdy wicker basket. Developed by Elinor Goldschmied in the 1940s (Goldschmied & Jackson, 1994) when she observed babies' fascination for playing with everyday objects, this has since been extended for use with considerably older children (Gascoyne, 2012). Ideally the basket should be round, at least 5 cm deep, with straight sides and contain about 50 treasures, each carefully picked for their sensory-rich appeal, quality and play potential. The avoidance of plastic objects and actual toys considerably increases its appeal. Depending upon children's developmental stage and interests, the open-ended objects will yield very different types of exploration and movement:

<u>6-month-old:</u> "She grabs hold of the natural woven coaster, turns it around and puts it to her mouth" (Gascoyne, 2012, p. 62).

<u>7-month-old:</u> He "babbles as he picks up the cylindrical tin with lid. He holds it with one hand and manoeuvres the top. He then uses his feet to turn the tin on end. The tin falls and his moving toes 'catch' the falling tin" (Gascoyne, 2012, p. 66).

<u>11-month-old:</u> She "places the flowerpot by her doll's mouth and makes a slurping noise. She then picks up her own beaker and drinks from it" (Gascoyne, 2012, p. 117).

<u>19-month-old:</u> "He picked up the metal objects from the basket one by one and put them on a nearby table. He then returned to the basket before repeating the same process several times" (Gascoyne, 2012, p. 42).

<u>25-month-old:</u> "He picks up objects one-at-a-time, looks at them, waves them and places them next to himself. He chats to himself while doing this … He picks up the pan, puts the metal whisk in the pan and then tries other metal objects together. He tries to put the wooden whisk into the pan: this doesn't fit" (Gascoyne, 2012, p. 92).

FIGURE 7.1 A quality treasure basket should offer babies and young children an irresistible sensory-rich experience. (copyright Sue Gascoyne)

Vignette 1: Key reflection points

- The basket helps frame focus and the variety of objects, with no obvious theme, increases the "thrown-togetherness" (Massey, 2005) appeal of the objects, adding to their interest and fascination for young children to explore.
- Treasures need to be safe and scaled to fit a child's hand to minimise the need for adult restrictions, encourage "security of exploration" (Grossmann, Grossmann, Kindler, & Zimmermann, 2008) and increase potential for mastery orientation.
- While fine motor movements predominate, these are underpinned by gross motor movements and core strength.
- An enticing selection of sensory-rich objects is a powerful motivator for exploration and movement, underlining the link between movement and context and importance of children having something worth moving for.
- Problem-solving and scientific inquiry to understand "What is this object like?" and "What can it do?" are drivers for movement, as well as the movement developing "thought-in-action" (Anderson & Harrison, 2010 in MacRae, Hackett, Holmes, & Jones, 2017).

Vignette 1: Movement-enhancing features

- Filled to the brim and arranged to give tantalising glimpses, each carefully selected treasure contributes quality, interest and a sensorially enticing mix of shapes, properties, textures, weights and colours which fascinate and spark movement. Encouraging infants (and older children) to reach for, manipulate and move towards objects, such as when a cylindrical tin falls, rolling beyond a baby's reach, some infants even excitedly twitch their hands and feet in anticipation of treasure basket play.
- By clearing the area of toys and distractions and offering the treasure basket on the floor, babies and children can comfortably and safely access this in a developmentally appropriate way, be it lying on their front, back or side, squatting, sitting or standing.
- The addition of open-ended sensory resources such as sand, water or dried rice significantly increases children's repertoire of gross and fine motor movements with treasure basket objects (see the Sensory Play Continuum, Gascoyne, 2012).

FIGURE 7.2 Sensory-rich objects invite a wealth of fine and gross motor movements as the child investigates and develops their thinking. (copyright Sue Gascoyne)

Vignette 2: Child with cling film-covered paint

Molly aged 15-months hesitantly presses her flat hand onto the paint, wiggling her toes on the red splodge. She remains looking down at the paint then around at caregivers, as if to find an explanation for why her toes are not wet and covered in paint. She totters to another paint splodge repeating the same process, then crouches down, extending her arm and outstretched fingers. Still crouching and balanced with a toy truck in her right hand, she twists her body, craning her head and neck to poke her index finger into a streak of blue paint. Wiggling her finger back and forth, she levers a layer of cling film loose, revealing the painted paper below! Still squatting with body twisted, she gently prods the blue paint. Rising to a semi-squat, she reaches out to touch a nearby area of red paint with her outstretched arm, as if comparing the two and testing her understanding.

She sits back with legs bent before her, looking at her now paint-speckled feet. Craning her neck and twisting her entire body she examines her feet more closely. Up-righting herself, she gazes at the paint while holding the toy truck with both hands. When an educator models "driving the truck" through the paint she watches intently before reaching (first with left then right hand) for the toy and moves it back and forth with her right hand. In a half-sitting position, she leans forward to another paint splodge and drives the car back and forth through this with her weight supported on one knee and one arm. Pausing momentarily, her attention is drawn to a patch of yellow paint. Reaching first with her right hand she points with her index finger fully extended. Discovering a tear in the paper (and gap in the covering clingfilm) she points at it looking to others, as if for them to share in her discovery.

FIGURE 7.3 This tempting paint provocation invites whole-bodied investigation. (copyright Sue Gascoyne)

Vignette 2: Key reflection points

- Artificially distinguishing between gross and fine motor skills is simplistic and unsatisfactory as the infant employs a natural and continuously evolving series of gross and fine motor movements, which organically flow from one movement sequence to another.
- This child's repertoire of movements cannot be separated from the context for movement and thought-in-action, in this case the allure of the paint, discombobulation of it initially not being wet, then surprise when it starts to leave marks.
- The materials are active agents in the child's movement responses.
- The child's intrinsic motivation to explore is nurtured by educator's provision of a stimulating provocation and through their "autonomy supporting" (Deci & Ryan, 2000) practices which give this young child permission to explore and provide gentle support and encouragement through attentive noticing and modelling.

Vignette 2: Movement-enhancing features

- The scale of the provocation encouraged both gross and fine motor movements.
- The positioning of the paper on the floor enabled the infants to naturally access the resource using developmentally appropriate movements.
- The availability of toy trucks introduced opportunities for movement while the arcing lines and splodges of paint were dynamic rather than static.

Vignette 3: Child with ice cube "lollies"

Leaning forward with both forearms on the table, Archie (aged 21 months) grasps a lolly stick with a pincer grip whilst his other hand steadies the tray. With one red fish ice cube released he moves his right hand to another lolly stick to prise this free too. Grasping a red lolly in each hand he prods the paper with first one then the other. His hand slips down the stick till it rests on top of the ice cube. Noticing another child reaching for a green lolly he returns one of the red lollies and is given a green lolly by the educator sat adjacent to him. Grasping the top of the stick with his left hand his right hand cups the ice cube, as if maximising the sensory experience, his tongue protruding as he does so. With tongue still out, he clasps the green ice cube with both hands.

He moves both of his hands to the handle end of the lolly and shows this to the receptive educator before reaching for one of "her" lolly sticks. With one stick in each hand, and arms poised as if ready to carve a joint of meat, he prods the white paper before dropping the red lolly to cup the green cube with both hands and tongue surfacing again. He transfers the red and green lollies to his left hand freeing him up to reach forward and grasp the educator's blue lolly. Grasping several sticks in one hand and the new blue one in the other, he pauses looking at the differently coloured and shaped ice cubes, as if noticing the differences. He releases the blue lolly, transfers the green lolly to his left hand, alternatively dabbing the red and green lollies on the paper.

FIGURE 7.4 The resources that we offer and ways in which we do so, helps shape children's movement potential. (copyright Sue Gascoyne)

Vignette 3: Key reflection points

- The environment provided a cue, in this case restricting children's repertoire of movements. Containment of this activity at a table with practitioners and peers close together naturally limited the range of gross motor movements to reaching, and manoeuvring-type movements. Similarly, the provision of the ice cubes on lolly sticks introduced a very different range of hand movements to offering the cubes on the floor without handles.
- Although the range of movements was limited by the greater containment, as with the paint example, an artificial distinction between gross and fine motor skills was not apparent as the child used his entire body to access the resources, be it standing, reaching with full stretch or prodding the paper.
- The colours, shapes and arrangement of the cubes invited exploration by these young children, and the links between the hands and mouth as exploratory tools were evident as several children mouthed the cubes, or tongues poked out – a sign of concentration.
- As with the other examples, although the observation focus was on the child, the materials are centre stage as active agents, sparking interest and inquiry, providing sensory experiences and introducing discombobulation, as the ice cubes melted.
- The adult's role was key in providing the movement-restricting resources, responding to children's desire to mouth the cubes, orchestrating sharing when the cubes were monopolised and acting as play partners.

Vignette 3: Movement-enhancing features

- The smaller scale of the provocation and positioning at a table, with children either stood or sat, restricts some gross motor movements. However, children did need to stretch to reach the ice cube trays in the centre of the table and employ gross motor skills as they levered, banged and prodded the cubes.
- The angled lolly sticks supported manoeuvrability, encouraging fine motor skills. However, if provided without sticks this may have introduced a wider range of exploration with fingers and hands.

Vignette 4: Children with water (Godfrey, 2018)

Chloe (aged two years and eight months) stands next to a water tray. She reaches accurately across the tray to the handle of a jug; carefully lifts it; and, feeling the extra weight through the muscles in her arm, momentarily shows surprise that it is heavier than expected as it already contains water. She adjusts her grip and lifts the jug, accidently splashing some water. She brings the jug closer to the brass goblet and so begins the filling and emptying of containers. Other children gather round, offering their goblets to be filled. Some tip the contents onto the ground, forming puddles in which they jump, giggling as the water splashes. They seem to revel in their ability to make things happen.

Crouching on his haunches to turn a tap on a water butt, Oscar (aged two years and two months) demonstrates his ability to squat (and stand again) without losing balance. He repeatedly turns the tricky tap on and off. Still squatting, he reaches for a bowl and places it beneath the flowing water.

Holding a jug of water in one hand, two-year-old Jo picks up a funnel and carefully pours water into it. Expecting the funnel to be filling-up, she tilts her head and peers into the funnel, visibly surprised at the lack of water. Jo refills her jug and repeats, pouring accurately. She watches the top of the funnel carefully; the water has disappeared. I wonder if she will feel that her foot is getting wet and make the connection. She lifts the funnel up, stretching her arm above her head and leans back to look underneath. Then her eye is caught by another child using a funnel to pour water from one container to another. Watching from a distance she notices the water leaving the funnel and makes the connection with her own experiment. She picks a bowl to lift onto the table and holding the funnel above it repeats, as though testing to see if her funnel works in the same way.

FIGURE 7.5 Simple resources like this 'container' increase the movement enhancing potential of environments and repertoire of children's physical movements. (copyright Sue Gascoyne)

Vignette 4: Key reflection points

- The "movement-rich qualities of water draw children into play-filled experiences" (Godfrey, 2018), inspiring children's movement.
- The provision of complementary equipment such as containers, funnels and guttering significantly increased the range and repetition of fine and gross motor skills.
- Science and problem-solving feature prominently, with challenges for understanding or mastery evident and yielding greater movements. This underlines the importance of context and resources that spark interest.
- Some of children's actions such as Chloe's repeated "self-driven activity of filling and emptying" (Godfrey, 2018) may reflect a child's schemas (Athey, 2007) or intuitive drive to inhibit reflexes.
- Gross and fine motor movements, as well as balance, control and hand eye coordination, blend seamlessly rather than being distinct.
- Adults provide a permissive environment in which children's sense of agency and personal inquiries could flourish.

Vignette 4: Movement-enhancing features

- The importance of children having time and opportunities to master actions and ideas, be it turning on the stiff tap and controlling the water flow, accurately pouring or solving the mystery of the funnel. As well as satisfying movement experiences they developed thought-in-action, underlying the link between a child's body and mind.
- The range of equipment gave multiple opportunities for repeated gross and fine motor muscle development.
- Placing the water tray outdoors limits restrictions on children's exploration, enabling children to engage in "more enthusiastic movements" (Godfrey, 2018). Similarly, "non-restrictive, waterproof clothing further reduces practitioner concerns, leaving children free to move in response to the demands of the water and containers as they stretch, tip, fill, empty, splash, throw, and repeat" (Godfrey, 2018).
- The fascination and appeal of the water were a driver to movement. Children were able to access this in developmentally appropriate ways, be it standing or squatting.
- Children had space, time and permission to become absorbed in self-directed inquiries.

Whole-body learning experiences

As the earlier vignettes demonstrate, "with little time or investment, environments can be adapted so that they don't just accommodate movement and flow but actively encourage this" (Gascoyne, 2019, p. 174). Thoughtful provision of resources as well as chances to freely explore them provide young children with ample opportunities to use and develop their whole bodies not just their fine or gross motor skills. Children are sensorially active beings, intuitively learning in whole and embodied ways (Jennings, 2011):

> Early reflexes, senses and movement are the young child's route to learning, which is through the body. Movement and sensory experiences are crucial for the child's social and emotional development, behaviour and learning. Movement stimulates the neurological system that fires and wires the brain, forming a multitude of connections that lay important foundations for the young child's future learning and development. In this way, movement play is more than physical activity.
>
> *(Archer & Siraj, 2015)*

Yet, in the Western world, cries of "Do not touch!" are commonplace and young children are "mainly authorised to use sight … to explore the world" (Irigaray, 2017, p. 19). Whether motivated by concerns over safety, lack of time or an adult's lens on children's actions, this can unhelpfully introduce a disconnect between what some adults might expect or want and what children are hard-wired to do. "For very young children, acceptance involves understanding their need to be constantly on the move, touching things and discovering the world with all their senses. This is an important process not to be rushed" (Gascoyne, 2019, p. 184). As adults we may not understand a child's need to stand still in a puddle of water for hours on end or their compulsion to jump, splash, lie semi-submerged in, pour or transport water (or another media), but every movement has an intention, be it simply for the pleasure of it, the joy of experiencing their body, the feeling of exhilaration, the view revealed, the sensation of being wet and clammy, the satisfaction of exploration and testing ideas, the release of feeling free or the joy of unbounded sensory fun.

Conclusion

Drawing from simple examples of play with sensory materials and treasure baskets, the links between children's movement and their exploration, play, communication and thinking are evident. As these children's play has demonstrated, providing movement-rich physical and emotional environments, and planning for whole-bodied learning are essential not just for developing young children's physical literacy (see Chapter 2) but also for a sense of well-being and self.

Summary of key points

- Young children learn best using their whole body and senses so activities and environments should be sensory-rich and provide plentiful opportunities for wide-ranging and repetitive fine and gross motor movements and whole-bodied movement.
- Context and motivation are key. Movement is a communication tool and essential component of developing well-being, self-exploration and understanding.
- Movement-rich environments are essential for stimulating, enticing and giving children permission to move.

Suggested further reading

Gascoyne, S. (2012). *Treasure Baskets and Beyond*. Maidenhead: Open University Press.

Gascoyne, S. (2014). *There's more to fingers than meets the eye. Understanding the potential of children's hands*. In *24th* 'US, THEM & ME: Universal, Targeted or Individuated Early Childhood Programmes', EECERA.

References

Archer, C., & Siraj, I. (2015). *Encouraging physical development through movement-play* (1st ed.). London: Sage.

Athey, C. (2007). *Extending thought in young children: A parent-teacher partnership*. London: PCP.

Brown, W. H., Pfeiffer, K. A., McIver, K. L., Dowda, M., Addy, C. L., & Pate, R. R. (2009). Social and environmental factors associated with pre-schoolers' non-sedentary physical activity. *Child Development, 80*(1), 45–58.

Deci, E. L., & Ryan, R. M. (2000). The "what" and "why" of goal pursuits: Human needs and the self determination of behaviour. *Psychological Inquiry, 11*(4), 227–268.

Gascoyne, S. (2012). *Treasure baskets and beyond: Realizing the potential of Sensory-rich play*. Maidenhead: Open University Press.

Gascoyne, S. (2014). *There's more to fingers than meets the eye. Understanding the Potential of Children's Hands*. In 24th 'US, THEM & ME: Universal, Targeted or Individuated Early Childhood Programmes', EECERA.

Gascoyne, S. (2019). *Messy play in the early years. Supporting learning through materials engagements*. Abingdon: Routledge.

Gascoyne, S., & White, J. (2014) in Gascoyne, S. *There's more to fingers than meets the eye – Understanding the Potential of Children's Hands*. Proceedings of the 24th EECERA Conference. Crete: EECERA.

Gibson, J. J. (1979). *The ecological approach to visual perception*. Mahwah, NJ: Lawrence Erlbaum Associates.

Godfrey, M. (2018). *Reflections on children's movement*. Unpublished.

Goldschmied, E., & Jackson, S. (1994). *People under three*. London: Routledge.

Grossmann, K., Grossmann, K. E., Kindler, H., & Zimmermann, P. (2008). A wider view of attachment and exploration: The influence of mothers and fathers on the development of psychological security from infancy to young adulthood. In J. Cassidy & P. R. Shaver (Eds.), *Handbook of attachment: Theory, research, and clinical applications* (2nd ed., pp. 857–879). New York, NY: Guilford Press.

Heft, H. (2010). Affordances and the perception of landscape: An inquiry into environmental perception and aesthetics. Innovative approaches to researching landscape and health. In C. W. Thompson, P. Aspinall, & S. Bell (Eds.), *Innovative Approaches to Researching Landscape and Health* (pp. 9–32). London: Routledge.

Irigaray, L. (2017). *To Be Born: Genesis of a new human being.* Cham: Palgrave Macmillan.

Jennings, S. (2011). *Healthy attachments and neuro-dramatic-play.* London: Jessica Kingsley.

Jones, L. A., & Lederman, S. J. (2006). *Human hand function.* New York: Oxford University Press.

Lederman, S. J.,& Klatzky, R. L., (1987) Hand movements: a window into haptic object recognition. *Cognitve Pscychology, 19,* 342–348.

MacRae, C., Hackett, A., Holmes, R., & Jones, L. (2017). Vibrancy, repetition and movement: Posthuman theories for reconceptualising young children in museums. *Children's Geographies.* doi:10.1080/14733285.2017.1409884

Massey, D. (2005). *For space.* London: Sage.

Nicholson, S. (1971). How NOT to cheat children: The theory of loose parts. *Landscape Architecture* (Quarterly), *62*(2), 30–34.

White, J. (2013). *Playing and learning outdoors: Making provision for high quality experiences in the outdoor environment with children* (pp. 3–7). London: Routledge.

White, J., & Edwards, E. (2012). *Making a mud kitchen.* Sheffield: Muddyfaces.

8

PHYSICAL DEVELOPMENT IN THE EARLY YEARS FOUNDATION STAGE (EYFS)

Rebecca Duncombe

Personal reflection

As a former Primary School teacher with responsibility for Physical Education (PE), a former researcher in the Institute of Youth Sport and a former member of the Physical Education and Sport Pedagogy group in the School of Sport, Exercise and Health Sciences at Loughborough University, it might be logical to assume that my past experiences, knowledge and interests would equip me well to bring up my three boys in a physically active environment that nurtured effective physical development. Indeed, much of my early research focussed on high quality teaching and learning in Primary School PE and later on ways in which to promote physical activity in schools and at home. It has, however, only been recently that my interests have turned to physical development and this has, in part, been necessitated by the movement difficulties my boys were facing in school. They have always been active children (I took the twin pushchair to the tip shortly after the boys' third birthday) and they have always participated in a range of sports clubs (gymnastics, music and movement classes, swimming, football, rugby, horse-riding) but, somehow, this was not enough. They were certainly doing a lot of exercise but, reflecting back, they were not doing the right types of activities at the right ages. Tummy time had been promoted as essential at one of the baby groups that I attended but, other than that, I don't really recall anyone stressing the importance of providing good quality physical development opportunities or highlighting what impact a lack of these may have at a later date. I have always been a little embarrassed that, despite my background with its strong emphasis on PE, I had three children who struggled with their physical skills. All three children went to nursery and all three children left the Early Years Foundation Stage (EYFS) without the underpinning physical skills to really succeed in school and in sporting activities.

More recently, the Movement for Learning research (Duncombe & Preedy, 2018) has confirmed that this is a common problem. Both my co-researcher and myself had anticipated low levels of physical development at the start and end of the reception year being poor but we were still surprised at just how poor children's physical development levels turned out to be. This led us to question whether the physical development needs of young children are being met in nurseries and Reception classes and, if not, what was going wrong and was there anything that could be done to put children back on track?

Introduction

Chapter 1 traces the origins and evolution of physical development in the early years and outlines the physical development strand of the EYFS. It is, however, helpful to remind the reader here of what this constitutes. Physical development is one of three core components of the EYFS (the other two being: communication and language; and personal, social and emotional development). Within this, "Moving and Handling" and "Health and Self-care" are further identified and described as follows:

Moving and Handling: "Children show good control and co-ordination in large and small movements. They move confidently in a range of ways, safely negotiating space. They handle equipment and tools effectively, including pencils for writing" (DfE, 2017a, p. 8).

Health and Self-care: "Children know the importance for good health of physical exercise, and a healthy diet, and talk about ways to keep healthy and safe. They manage their own basic hygiene and personal needs successfully, including dressing and going to the toilet independently" (DfE, 2017a, p. 8).

Whilst "health and self-care" are important and interlinked with physical development, it is the first of these two sub-sections, Moving and Handling, that this chapter will focus on. The EYFS itself does not explain beyond the previous two sentences what constitutes good physical development or how this can be developed in young children within nurseries and Reception classes. It is for this reason that "Development Matters" (Early Education, 2012) was produced to explore further, although arguably not sufficiently, what good physical development provision looks like in practice. This document identifies activities for children in a range of ages (birth to 11 months; 8–20 months; 16–26 months; 22–36 months; 30–50 months; and 40–60+ months), the latter two specifically relate to children in the EYFS age range and, thus, are outlined in the following. According to this document:

A child aged 30–50 months:
* Moves freely and with pleasure and confidence in a range of ways, such as slithering, shuffling, rolling, crawling, walking, running, jumping, skipping, sliding and hopping;

- Mounts stairs, steps or climbing equipment using alternate feet;
- Walks downstairs, two feet to each step while carrying a small object;
- Runs skilfully and negotiates space successfully, adjusting speed or direction to avoid obstacles;
- Can stand momentarily on one foot when shown;
- Can catch a large ball;
- Draws lines and circles using gross motor movements: uses one-handed tools and equipment, e.g. makes snips in paper with child scissors;
- Holds pencil between thumb and two fingers, no longer using whole-hand grasp;
- Holds pencil near point between first two fingers and thumb and uses it with good control;
- Can copy some letters, e.g. letters from their name.

(Early Education, 2012, p. 24)

A child aged 40–60+ months:
- Experiments with different ways of moving;
- Jumps off an object and lands appropriately;
- Negotiates space successfully when playing racing and chasing games with other children, adjusting speed or changing direction to avoid obstacles;
- Travels with confidence and skill around, under, over and through balancing and climbing equipment;
- Shows increasing control over an object in pushing, patting, throwing, catching or kicking it;
- Uses simple tools to effect changes to materials;
- Handles tools, objects, construction and malleable materials safely and with increasing control;
- Shows a preference for a dominant hand;
- Begins to use anticlockwise movement and retrace vertical lines;
- Begins to form recognisable letters;
- Uses a pencil and holds it effectively to form recognisable letters, most of which are correctly formed.

(Early Education, 2012, p. 24)

In addition to this, within each age range, advice is offered in relation to what adults could do and what adults could provide (to improve the physical development offer in the setting). For example, in the 30–60+ months age group, adults could: encourage children to move with controlled effort and use associated vocabulary, such as "strong," "firm," "gentle," "heavy," "stretch," "reach," "tense" and "floppy"; pose challenging questions such as "Can you get all the way round the climbing frame without your knees touching it?"; and show children how to collaborate in throwing, rolling, fetching and receiving games, encouraging them to play with one another once their skills are sufficient. Likewise, they could provide: time and space to enjoy energetic play daily; large portable equipment that children can move about safely and cooperatively to create their own structures, such as milk crates, tyres, large cardboard tubes; and activities that give children the opportunity and motivation to practise manipulative skills, e.g. cooking, painting, clay and playing instruments (Early Education, 2012, p. 24).

This advice is helpful for those delivering the physical development strand of the EYFS and certainly extends understanding and provision of physical development opportunities beyond that which is outlined in the EYFS, but does it go far enough? Does it, for example, explain what an "appropriate landing" looks like and how to teach it to a young child? Does it explain how to identify a child who is moving "with confidence?" There does also seem to be an assumption behind this guidance that children have successfully passed through previous and essential stages of physical development. Worryingly, the only real advice in this document for helping children who are struggling is that adults should "Support children with physical difficulties with nonslip mats, small trays for equipment, and triangular or thicker writing tools" (Early Education, 2012, p. 24). This may help some young children to better engage in the activities that are provided for them but seems based on a naïve assumption that physical development is fixed and that there is nothing we can do to improve it. Children who are struggling with gross and fine motor skills often don't need more practise at a particular skill; they need a second chance to pass through missed stages of development. Contrast, for example, an approach that forces young children to practise their handwriting (and repeatedly fail at it) with one that targets the development of gross motor skills and a strong pincer grip using age-appropriate resources and activities that help to refine fine motor skills (see Chapter 15).

Are children in and at the end of the EYFS achieving good levels of physical development?

According to the EYFS profile results in England (DfE, 2017b), just over 90 per cent of children were achieving at least the expected level of development by the end of the EYFS within the Moving and Handling aspect of the framework. Drawing on my own research, I would suggest that these data are optimistic. That is not to say that the numbers cited in these results are wrong but, as will be outlined later, other research is revealing a different picture. Thus, my suggestion for this discrepancy is either that the physical expectations within the EYFS are too low or, controversially, that expectations have been set low to enable more children to succeed and for current provision to be seen in a more positive light. In support of the first suggestion, I will now explore data that relates to school readiness and levels of physical development.

School readiness

An internationally accepted definition of school readiness is hard to establish but the definitions that do exist appear to consider the social, emotional and physical skills that need to be developed during the early years to equip young children with the skills they will need to cope and hopefully thrive in school. UNICEF (2012) identifies an important difference between the appropriateness of the terms "ready for school" and "ready to learn," and points out that children are born ready to learn! Thus, "ready for school" is seen as most appropriate. UNICEF (2012) further explains:

> a child who is ready for school has the basic minimum skills and knowledge in a variety of domains that will enable the child to be successful in school… Success in school is determined by a range of basic behaviours and abilities, including literacy, numeracy, ability to follow directions, working well with other children and engaging in learning activities.
>
> *(UNICEF, 2012, p. 9)*

Of relevance to the English context because it is directly linked to the EYFS framework is the following definition from Public Health England (2015):

> School readiness is a measure of how prepared a child is to succeed in school cognitively, socially and emotionally. The good level of development (GLD) is used to assess school readiness. Children are defined as having reached a GLD at the end of the Early Years Foundation Stage if they achieved at least the expected level in the early learning goals in the prime areas of learning (personal, social and emotional development, physical development and communication and language) and in the specific areas of mathematics and literacy.
>
> *(p. 4)*

Based on the two definitions given here, we can see that being ready for school would require a broad set of skills extending beyond academic competencies. Kagan, Moore and Bredenkamp (1995), for example, identify five "domains": physical well-being and motor development; social and emotional development; approaches to learning; language development; and cognition and general knowledge, including mathematics. These domains, despite being worded differently, do seem to capture many of the skills and attributes identified in the earlier quote. Regardless of the precise definition, a holistic view of the child is clearly important and should alert practitioners and parents to the types of opportunities that should be on offer to the children in their care in order to help them develop adequately in all of these domains (and, thus, to be ready for school).

Are children ready for school?

Establishing whether children are ready for school is challenging. First, because children do not start school at the same age in all countries (Chapter 5, for example, identifies that Finnish children do not start formal schooling until they are 7, whereas in the United Kingdom, children start formal schooling the academic year after they turn four). Second, the interrelated nature of each dimension makes it hard to give an overall picture (a child who is chatty, happy to be left at the school gates and able to work with others, but who struggles to do up his or her buttons and to use cutlery is ready in some ways but not others). That said, research has been conducted into this area, often with worrying findings:

- Research conducted by Teach First that analysed the Department for Education's EYFS statistics in 2015 and 2017 (Schools Week, 2018) identifies that nearly one in three children who start Primary School in England at the age of five are not "school ready."
- A survey of school leaders conducted by the National Association for Head Teachers and the Family and Childcare Trust (TES, 2017) identifies worrying numbers of reception children starting school "unable to speak effectively, use the toilet or make friends."
- Findings from a study conducted by researchers from University College, London's Institute of Health Equity were cited in The Telegraph (2014) with the headline that "almost half of children are not developed enough at the age of five to be ready for school." Just 52 per cent had reached a good level of development, "meaning they were able to accomplish tasks such as being able to count to 20 or write a letter to Father Christmas."

These findings reveal a concerning picture and identify a number of difficulties that young children may face if they start school before they are "school ready." The focus of this book and chapter is, however, on children's physical development and the discussion will now move from a more holistic view of school readiness to focus more specifically on young children's physical readiness for school (whilst reminding the reader that these dimensions are all interrelated).

Physical development and physical readiness for school

The EYFS and "Development Matters" start to provide us with an idea of what it means to be physically ready for school within the core area of "Moving and Handling" (see earlier). This is an area that, according to the EYFS profile results, has been successfully "navigated" or passed through by 90 per cent of young children moving on to start their first year of formal schooling. As I have already stated, this is surprising, especially given the statistics cited earlier in relation to the percentage of children identified as ready for school and the data from the pilot stage of the Movement for Learning research project (Duncombe & Preedy, 2018), which assessed the physical skills of 46 children in the September that they started reception and found that:

- Children's Physical Development upon entry to reception (i.e. after approximately one year within the EYFS) is 18 percentile points behind levels from a decade ago.

- According to the Movement Assessment Battery for Children (Movement ABC-2) that was used to assess physical development in this project (Barnett, Henderson, & Sugden, 2007), just less than 30 per cent of children starting reception scored below the 16th percentile and would have been identified as being at risk of or as having a movement difficulty.
- Children who follow the EYFS during the reception year make very little progress in terms of their physical development when compared to a group of children from the same school who participated in a daily movement programme (Movement for Learning):
  - 12.2 per cent of children in the Movement for Learning group improved their physical development scores enough to no longer be at risk of or identified as having a movement difficulty (30.4 per cent at the start of reception to 18.2 per cent at the end).
  - 4.5 per cent of the group who did not do movement for learning and who only followed the EYFS scored lower on the physical development tests than they had at the start of the reception year and became at risk of or were identified as having a movement difficulty (27.3 per cent at the start of reception to 31.8 per cent at the end).

The pilot research was further developed in a second year of research involving 120 children and the preliminary analysis reveals a very similar picture illustrating that children are both starting and leaving the reception phase of schooling with levels of physical development below what we want them to be and certainly below the levels children achieved a decade ago. The number of children identified with or at risk of a movement difficulty is also cause for concern.

Further support for this discussion comes from a survey in which 25 teachers participated. They were asked whether they felt that physical development levels had declined in recent years (the survey was administered in 2016) and, of the 25 Leicestershire reception teachers surveyed, 96 per cent stated that they felt there had been a decline. 58 per cent mentioned fine motor skills as one example of a decline in physical development with handwriting and poor pencil grips receiving the most "mentions." The following quotes, taken from this survey, help to further illustrate some of the issues that the teachers noted in their Reception classrooms:

> "The children are less coordinated and slouch rather than sit securely on the floor, they don't sit upright in their chairs, they are less aware of personal space".

> "Poor proprioception. Bizarre pencil grips. Poor core stability and floppy bodies".

> "Poorer co-ordination and core body strength. Get tired quicker. Poor fine motor control - pencil and crayon direction and marks plus perseverance to complete a task. Poorer gross motor skills-skipping, jumping and ball control".

"Lack of muscle tone and mobility in play. Lack of core strength. Lack of stamina in physical activity and complaints about tiredness and aching. Very few children with good fine motor for pencil and other tool control including cutlery".

"Seeing children still in pushchairs in the months leading up to starting school. Fine motor control, e.g., when forming letters is poor. An inability to hold a brush or a pencil. Children lacking the coordination skills to skip, hop from foot to foot and balance on one leg".

An additional indication that the physical development needs of young children are not being met in the EYFS comes from The "Big Moves" project in Leicestershire. Like Movement for Learning, the aim of this project was to allow children to re-visit key stages in physical development in order to improve both their fine and gross motor skills. The programme was designed as an intervention for those most in need of it but, due to the increasing numbers of children identified by teachers as having poor levels of physical development, the programme was often rolled out more widely in schools. The programme is aimed at Key stage 1 children (ages 5–7) but many schools have delivered it to Reception classes as well. "Big Moves" is delivered over six weeks with children practising coordinated movement patterns on the floor in the school hall every day for approximately 20 minutes. Exercises include slow rolling, commando crawling and rocking on all fours. The movements are progressive and increase in complexity: as a movement is mastered, it is "dropped," and a more complex movement is introduced. If, after the six weeks block, little progress has been made, a child will be given another six weeks. If, after this, no significant improvement has been made, referral to children's therapy services (Physiotherapy and Occupational Health) is recommended.

Baseline data were collected at the start of the project so that improvements by the end of the project could be ascertained. Historically, all but a small minority of children of this age would have been able to successfully complete these baseline assessment tasks, but data from the Big Moves project reveal that this is now far from being the case. Children were asked to demonstrate their physical ability across 12 specifically chosen developmental milestones that indicate postural stability, head control, balance, body awareness and co-ordination of limbs. The milestones are basic skills, such as balancing on one leg, holding an "on all fours" position, crawling and marching. To pass the marching test, for example, a child should be able to march with control over a short distance of approximately 10 m. Their arms should swing easily at the sides and the opposite knee should lift to around hip height as the arm swings. The body should be upright, relaxed and the eyes looking forward. The child is judged as failing the test if one or more of the following occurs:

- The arms and/or legs move in a random, disorganised way;
- The child moves one-sidedly – the arm and leg on the same side move together;
- The child rushes and cannot move with control;

- The legs are kept straight and stiff/the child cannot lift the knees up;
- The movement starts Ok but after a short while, the legs begin to drop and the knees are no longer lifted. The body "sags."

Over the last five years, very large numbers of reception and Year 1 children have consistently been failing these basic tests. Between 2012 and 2018, for example, 2,363 children from 78 Primary Schools across Leicestershire were assessed and 77.06 per cent were not able to successfully complete 5 or more of the 12 tests. A child should be able to successfully complete at least 9 out of the 12 movements assessments to pass. A score below this indicates that the child has yet to develop these skills and would benefit from the Big Moves programme *and* a more active lifestyle. A score below 5 indicates significant delay in the acquisition of sensory motor skills and that the child is in *definite* need of the movement programme.

Prior to delivering the "Big Moves" programme, teachers attend a training day and are provided with ongoing support. Of additional interest here are the numerous anecdotal reports from teachers on these training days regarding difficulties that children face in relation to maintaining an upright position in a chair, attention, listening, tool use, pencil grips and self-care. These reports are similar in nature to the quotations provided from the survey conducted with 25 teachers mentioned earlier. These, in combination with the baseline data from both the Movement for Learning Project and Big Moves research, support the case being made in this chapter that children's physical development in and at the end of reception is below what it should be.

It is, however, worth remembering that physical difficulties are unlikely to have been caused solely by deficiencies in the EYFS and, as outlined in Chapters 6, 7, 10 and 14, disruptions to a child's physical development journey may be caused by a number of factors outside of the control of nurseries and schools. Birth interventions, a lack of movement opportunities in the first few months, devices that "contain" children (e.g. pushchairs, baby walkers and bouncy seats), cultural shifts that see fewer opportunities for young children to play unsupervised outdoors, increasing screen use and a general lack of physical activity may all be contributing to the problem. If, as the Movement for Learning and Big Moves data suggest, there is an issue with young children's physical development within the EYFS then this needs to be acknowledged and practitioners armed with the "tools" (knowledge and understanding) to be able to effectively respond to the situation.

Conclusion

An overview of the physical development requirements of the EYFS has been provided within this chapter and an argument constructed to address whether the physical development needs of young children are, indeed, being met by this. Although official figures suggest that approximately 90 per cent of children leaving reception have achieved the expected levels of development within the "moving and handling" component of the EYFS, data were presented to challenge this. Multiple studies are in contradiction with these findings and suggest a much smaller percentage are leaving reception with adequate levels of physical development. Given what we know about the link between good levels of physical development and later success in the classroom as well as engagement in PE, physical activity and sport, we would be wise to consider what needs to change. The following, for example, are offered as potential ways that might help to reverse the current situation:

- Better/more training for practitioners and teachers in the area of physical development;
- Update official guidance to better support practitioners in the provision of appropriate physical development opportunities (replacing or revising "Development Matters," for example);
- A stronger focus on physical development in training courses (for EYFS practitioners and teachers) to enable a better acknowledgement, awareness and understanding of the relationship between good physical development and behavioural/learning difficulties;
- Raise expectations of what children should be able to do at ages three and four;
- Improve understanding from policy makers and Ofsted inspectors of the physical development needs of young children;
- Re-visit official screening tests that were once administered upon school entry (these were routinely administered by a school medical officer until the 1980s).

In relation to this final point, the suggestion is not necessarily that the official tests should be reintroduced but that an understanding of what was expected in the past may help to raise the expectations that we have of children today.

Summary of key points

- Physical development is a core component (prime area) of the EYFS with the sub-section of "moving and handling" covering the development of fine and gross motor skills.
- "Development Matters" was produced in 2012 to help practitioners deliver the EYFS but this chapter has questioned whether it goes far enough to enable practitioners to plan and implement appropriate Physical Development opportunities for the children in their care.
- Official findings from the EYFS profile results in England (DfE, 2017b) show that approximately 90 per cent of children achieved at least the expected level of development by the end of the EYFS within the Moving and Handling aspect of the framework. This finding was challenged and research data presented to illustrate that many children were starting and leaving the EYFS with levels of physical development lower than desirable and lower than ten years ago.

- Low expectations, in terms of young children's physical development, were put forward as a potential reason for the discrepancy between official figures and data from other research projects.
- A number of suggested changes to help meet the physical development needs of young children were identified.

Suggested further readings

Duncombe, R., & Preedy, P. (2018), Movement for learning. In P. Preedy, K. Sanderson, & C. Ball (Eds.), *Early childhood redefined: Reflections and recommendations on the impact of start right*. Oxford: Routledge.

UNICEF. (2012). *School readiness: A conceptual framework*. New York, NY: United Nations Children's Fund.

References

Barnett, A., Henderson, S. E., & Sugden, D. A. (2007). Movement assessment battery for children – Second edition (Movement ABC-2). London: Pearson.

DfE. (2017a). *Statutory framework for the early years foundation stage. Setting the standards for learning, development and care for children from birth to five*. London: DfE.

DfE. (2017b). *Early Years Foundation Stage profile results in England*. Darlington: DfE. Retrieved from https://assets.publishing.service.gov.uk/government/uploads/system/uploads/attachment_data/file/652602/SFR60_2017_Text.pdf

Duncombe, R., & Preedy, P. (2018). Movement for learning. In P. Preedy, K. Sanderson, & C. Ball (Eds.), *Early childhood redefined: Reflections and recommendations on the impact of start right*. Oxford: Routledge.

Early Education. (2012). *Development matters in the Early Years Foundation Stage (EYFS)*. London: Early Education. Retrieved from https://foundationyears.org.uk/files/2012/03/Development-Matters-FINAL-PRINT-AMENDED.pdf

Kagan, S. L., Moore, E., & Bredenkamp, S. (1995). *Reconsidering children's early development and learning: Toward common views and vocabulary*. Report of the National Education Goals Panel, Goal 1 Technical Planning Group, U.S. Government Printing Office, Washington, DC.

Public Health England. (2015). *Improving school readiness: Creating a better start for London*. London: Public Health England. Retrieved from https://assets.publishing.service.gov.uk/government/uploads/system/uploads/attachment_data/file/459828/School_readiness_10_Sep_15.pdf

Schools Week. (2018). *One in three reception children aren't 'school ready', warns Teach First*. Article published in Schools Week. Retrieved from https://schoolsweek.co.uk/one-in-three-reception-children-arent-school-ready-warns-teach-first/

TES. (2017). *Rise in number of children 'not ready' to start school*. Retrieved from https://www.tes.com/news/rise-number-children-not-ready-start-school

The Telegraph. (2014). *Half of children are not ready to start school*. Retrieved from https://www.telegraph.co.uk/news/uknews/11113837/Half-of-children-are-not-ready-to-start-school.html

UNICEF. (2012). *School readiness: A conceptual framework*. New York, NY: United Nations Children's Fund.

9

PHYSICAL DEVELOPMENT AND PHYSICAL EDUCATION FOR 5–7-YEAR-OLDS

Vicky Randall and Gerald Griggs

Personal reflection

Recently, I was working with Key Stage 1 children in their Physical Education lesson. They were taking part in a task that required them to hunt for pirate clues in order to solve a nautical puzzle. The lesson was based upon the pedagogical principles of cooperation and required the children to develop the skill of running while maintaining a steady pace. Each child worked in a small group of three travelling from one clue to the next. At the end of the lesson, I overheard one of the children (Bella), say to her group, "I like running. It takes me places." In this moment, a passing comment from a five-year-old child captured what PE means to me. If we can equip young people with the skills and confidence to experience the world around them, then in return, the world will open up for them. Bella was beginning to understand this too. As educators, we hope that Bella and her classmates will go on to lead healthy and active lives, but more importantly, physical activity and health will be the outcome of whatever they enjoy participating in. During that lesson, Bella was curious, socially engaged and reflective. She, like many others her age, exhibited a natural enthusiasm for moving. They had begun their PE journey.

Introduction

The opportunities that movement affords young people are vast. The education of the physical self can create spaces where children learn about themselves, how to be healthy and invite social interaction. When taught well, PE can spark opportunity for creativity, challenge and curiosity and, with this, harness the potential for meaningful learning (Ní Chróinín, Fletcher, & O'Sullivan, 2018). From our own experiences of teaching PE, we have witnessed all too often a polarised love and loathing of the subject. For some people, they find a joy of movement from a young age that leads to a future of sports participation, leisure or community activities. For others, experiences have led to a belief that PE is only for the "sporty."

In this chapter we will provide an overview of the PE curriculum at Key Stage 1, with practical examples to support curriculum planning for physical development. We also wish to highlight some of the contemporary challenges facing teachers in meeting the subject's expectations. As we write, our motivation is to inspire other educators to see that PE is a worthwhile time investment and an important feature of a broad and balanced curriculum. Key Stage 1 frames a child's first formal experience of the National Curriculum and of PE and must, therefore, set the tone and ambition of what it means to be physically educated.

The National Curriculum for Key Stage 1

In England, Primary Education relates to the first seven years of compulsory schooling (ages 5–11). During this time, the subject aims for PE are typically met through two key stages: Key Stage 1 (ages 5–7) and Key Stage 2 (ages 7–11). With a specific remit for developing physical competence and confidence, PE holds a unique place in a child's education. Children do not enter Key Stage 1 as a blank movement canvas; some will already have had diverse and rich physical experiences, while others more impoverished. However, as a prime area of learning in the Early Years Foundation Stage (EYFS) (see Chapter 8), all children should have at least experienced regular learning associated with movement and handling and health and self-care (DfE, 2017). These early experiences may start to resemble National Curriculum for Physical Education as well as provide opportunities for structured and unstructured play.

The National Curriculum sets out the aims and purpose of each subject (DfE, 2013a). The aim of which is to provide coherence, entitlement and understanding for those who teach it. For PE it states that:

> A high-quality physical education curriculum inspires all pupils to succeed and excel in competitive sport and other physically-demanding activities. It should provide opportunities for pupils to become physically confident in a way which supports their health and fitness. Opportunities to compete in sport and other activities build character and help to embed values such as fairness and respect.
>
> *(DfE, 2013a, p. 198)*

In meeting this expectation, the aims of PE are there to ensure that all pupils:

*   Develop competence to excel in a broad range of physical activities;
*   Are physically active for sustained periods of time;
*   Engage in competitive sports and activities;
*   Lead healthy, active lives.

(DfE, 2013a, p. 198)

As we become more entrenched in a global concern over child health (physical and mental) and a nation that is passionate about the pursuit of sporting excellence, debate continues about what the subject's role and purpose should be (Bailey, 2018; Coulter & Ní Chróinín, 2013; Penney, 2008). Currently the aims of PE value the development of children's health and physical skill within social, competitive and cooperative contexts. While we recognise that sport participation and improved health are noble aims, we also believe PE has much more to offer. In a systematic review of the literature, Bailey et al. (2009) highlighted evidence to support how PE can also contribute to cognitive, social and affective development. However, success in PE relies on children starting this phase of education with adequate levels of physical development. Mere participation will not necessarily result in these outcomes being met.

By the end of Key Stage 1, pupils should typically make progress towards the curriculum's age-related expectations. Teachers are required to teach and monitor key areas of learning across each subject through ongoing assessment. For example, by the end of Key Stage 1, the National Curriculum states that:

> Pupils should develop fundamental movement skills, become increasingly competent and confident and access a broad range of opportunities to extend their agility, balance and coordination, individually and with others. They should be able to engage in competitive (both against self and against others) and co-operative physical activities, in a range of increasingly challenging situations.
>
> *(DfE, 2013a, p. 199)*

The National Curriculum provides an overarching framework of statutory learning within PE curriculum time. What it does not do is provide teachers with all the content and skills of what should be taught and how it should be delivered. The curriculum expectations are a minimum entitlement only and alone do not capture the richness of good quality PE experiences. Schools are, therefore, encouraged to devise programmes that are aspirational, locally devised and based on the needs of their pupils. Figure 9.1 summarises the key areas of learning from the Key Stage 1 attainment statement, as presented by the Physical Education Expert Subject Advisory Group (ESAG) (2017).

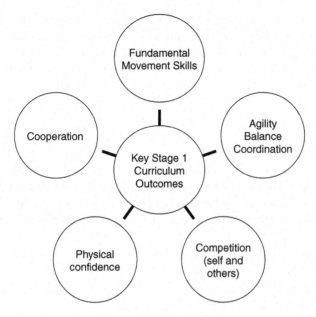

FIGURE 9.1 Key areas of learning for Physical Education in Key Stage 1.

Each of the circles in Figure 9.1 offers a different type of learning experience. For example, the development of cooperation requires each child to engage and navigate social aspects of their learning, such as turn-taking, fairness, helping others and working together, whereas fundamental movement skills require an explicit focus on the development of movement itself (Gallahue & Ozmun, 2011; Graham, Holt-Hale, & Parker, 2012; Pickup & Price, 2007). These skills are essentially the basis of all physical activities and can be understood as the accuracy or precision (skill) of an organised series of basic movements that involve the combination of two or more body segments (Gallahue & Ozmun, 2011; Malina, Bouchard, & Bar-Or, 2004) – see Chapter 3. Collectively they underpin good physical development and support children to become physically confident and competent.

Key Stage 1 Physical Education in practice

In the reflection at the start of this chapter, we described a lesson where Key Stage 1 children were involved in a pirate themed treasure hunt, finding and solving clues in small groups. You might have thought, what makes this lesson PE specifically? If you did, then you were thinking critically about teaching and learning and what makes a subject unique. You may be forgiven for thinking that the clue was in the description of children moving. While this is a noteworthy observation, children being physically active will not necessarily determine that learning directly relates to a PE outcome.

Doherty and Brennan (2014) explain that children can be educated *in, through and about movement* and therefore, movement experiences may also be a feature of other curriculum subjects. Thus, PE will, at various times, develop learning in, through and about movement to support wider curriculum areas too. For example, movement could be used to explore mathematical concepts: using the body to explore the number 10 – how many ways can we make 10 using the people in the class, or setting out a number line of cones where children hop forwards alongside each cone to represent +1 and backwards one hop to represent −1.

To arrive at a well-planned lesson, we have suggested so far that the overarching principle is that the content should be built upon what children will learn, not just do. Using the pirate themed example given at the start of this chapter, use the following questions to unpick how such a lesson might have been planned:

• In what way will physical development be experienced (through the social, cognitive or affective domain)?
• What specific learning aims did the lesson set out to achieve (what was the knowledge, skills or understanding being taught)?
• What type of learning environment helped the children to become successful in achieving the desired outcome (how did the teacher present the learning)?

The first question refers to the purpose of the lesson – the learning context. At this stage of planning, the teacher considers the needs of the class and the curriculum aims. The second question refers to the specific knowledge, skills and understanding that shape the learning tasks for that lesson, as found in the subject's Key Stage 1 attainment statement. This is where the learning objective for the lesson is formed. The third question requires teachers to think about the type of environment they wish to establish. Here we refer to environment, not in terms of the lesson's location – a building, a school field or the swimming pool – but the climate and expectation of what has been set. We suggest that the pedagogy of how content is presented is as important as the content itself.

Table 9.1 presents example core learning outcomes for Years 1 and 2. Each learning outcome can be linked back to the National Curriculum attainment statement for Key Stage 1. From this table, select one outcome and consider a learning objective that could be developed from it. At this stage try and focus on the learning first and not the activity. Tasks can be devised at a later point to suit the teaching approach, context and needs of the children. Each outcome should be context free and be able to sit within different activity settings. For example, in order for a child to meet the learning outcome of "explore and copy a range of movement actions," the teacher might establish a learning objective of "jumping for height." The opportunity to develop this skill might then be applied in activities such as games to catch a ball; swimming to enter the water; or gymnastics to exit a piece of apparatus.

The learning outcomes in Table 9.1 can be associated with physical development in a range of different ways (social, cognitive and affective). A physical outcome such as "understand how to change movement through the use of space, relationships and effort" will require a child to explore physical skills within different movement concepts. Graham et al. (2012) explain that if a movement skill describes what the body is doing (e.g. running, jumping, kicking, catching, rolling), then a movement concept describes how the skills are being performed. In order to achieve "movement competency," each skill must be performed not only technically well but also in a variety of ways. The "Movement Concept Wheel" (see Graham et al., 2012, p. 32) is a practical tool to help teachers and pupils explore the interaction between the movement skills and movement concepts. The individual skills within the skill themes of locomotor (travel), manipulation (object control) and non-manipulation (stability/balance) are placed at the centre of the wheel and can each be rotated around the movement concepts, in turn, to allow children to explore each movement skill in a unique and different way. Table 9.2 explores the ideas presented in the Movement Concept Wheel through an example of the locomotor skill of jumping. This is by no means an exhaustive list, and children may enjoy coming up with their own words to explore the movement further, e.g. fizzy, pop, swirl, strong, jagged, floaty, etc., to create a rich movement vocabulary.

TABLE 9.1 Core bank of generic learning outcomes for Key Stage 1

Examples of core learning outcomes for Key Stage 1 physical education

Core learning outcomes Year 1	Core learning outcomes Year 2
• Explore and copy a range of movement actions in isolation	• Explore and perform a range of travel, balance and object control skills
• Be able to select actions using different movements of the body, for different purposes	• Be able to work with others to create different ideas
• Respond imaginatively with movement to words, images, sounds and objects	• Use vocabulary to create expressive movement phrases
• Explore how to change movement actions through speed and space	• Understand how to change movement through use of space, relationships and effort
• Link simple actions to create short phrases of movement	• Be able to comment on how their body feels and changes during different activities
• Be able to work independently and in cooperation with others	• Describe what they can do well and how they could improve
• Be able to describe what they like and what they don't like	• Be able to lead and copy a range of movement actions
• Explain how their body feels when taking part in activities	• Know how to express an idea through movement
• Understand how to move in safe spaces	• Understand gesture and how to apply it in a movement context
• Be able to travel over, under and through objects with control	

TABLE 9.2 The development of jumping through the movement concepts, adapted from the Movement Concept Wheel (Graham et al., 2012)

Fundamental movement skill	Movement concept	Example
Jumping (locomotor skill)	Space (extensions)	Large/small Near/far
	Space (location)	In self-space or general space
	Space (levels)	High, medium, low From low to high Form low to high
	Space (pathways)	In a curve In a zig-zag In a straight line
	Space (direction)	Forwards, backwards, sideways, with a half turn, with a full turn
	Effort (speed)	Fast and slow
	Effort (force)	Strong and light
	Effort (flow)	Free, bound, locked
	Relationship (body parts)	Start on 2 feet and land on two Start on 1 foot and land on two Start on 2 feet and land on one Start on 1 foot and land on the other (leap) Start on 1 foot and land on the same (hop) Jump twisted, wide, straight, tucked
	Relationship (people)	With a partner, jump in unison, cannon, back to back, sideways, mirroring, one in front of the other
	Relationship (objects)	On and off apparatus, with a skipping rope, through a hoop, over a line

As children progress towards the end of Key Stage 1, some will be ready to challenge their physical skills in more specialised ways (Gallahue & Ozmun, 2011). Applying rules of games, for example, gives children the opportunity to make their movement learning more complex. When a child has mastered the skill of jumping (see Table 9.2), they can then be challenged to link it with other skills to create a movement phrase: for example run, jump, catch, land and throw. An alternative challenge might be to add a time rule, for example, perform a sequence of skip, jump, roll and balance within 15 seconds, or repeat this sequence twice through. For those at an early stage of skill learning, a sudden increase in challenge may result in limited success and frustration. As an aim of the National Curriculum for Physical Education, children are required to engage in competitive activities from as early as Key Stage 1; therefore consideration must be given at all times to the child's underpinning levels of physical development, their relative stage of skill learning and their readiness to tackle more difficult tasks. The environment and context for learning will shape the child's movement experience, which at this stage should be characterised by mastery, opportunity, exploration and practice (Gallahue & Ozmun, 2011; Graham et al., 2012).

The place of competition in Key Stage 1

Competition has been the subject of fierce debate over the years with polarised views being expressed (Layne, 2014; Leah & Capel, 2000). Taken in the context of defeating others, this translation into Primary PE can result in teaching approaches associated with "winning or losing" or "wining at all costs" (Layne, 2014). However, the Latin derivation of the word, "competre" meaning to "strive together" (Leah & Capel, 2000), might offer an alternative perspective on what it means to be competitive, placing an emphasis on social understanding and character.

In the most recent iteration of the Primary National Curriculum (DfE, 2013a), competition has, for the first time, been placed at the heart of the subject's aims and attainment statement. This has required teachers to reflect upon what "competitive activities" looks like in practice. Pickup and Price (2007) suggest that age appropriateness needs to be considered when planning Primary PE. Placing the activity's needs ahead of the child will result, at best, in limited progress and, at worst, in injury or long term disengagement. For example, a child in Key Stage 1, who is still yet to show control in skills such as running and stopping, will only be placed under increased risk (both emotionally and physically) if asked to perform these skills competitively at speed and against others. The danger of this type of activity can result in the focus being on the outcome of the performance rather than the focus on skill development.

Howells (2015) suggests that when done well, competition can be used in a constructive way to support a child's development. A teacher's own definition and understanding of what competition is, is likely to influence what children then experience. When adopting competitive activities within teaching, the Physical Education ESAG advises teachers to:

- Check that the task is appropriate to the developmental stage of the child;
- Ensure competitive tasks are not performed in isolation (i.e. they should also be accompanied with feedback and/or praise);
- Choose tasks that motivate and develops skills;
- Differentiate activities to suit individual needs;
- Make sure activities are inclusive and do not exclude children.

Creating an age appropriate and competitive environment in Key Stage 1 does not have to be complicated. Simple tasks can be effective to engage learners. The key principle is that lessons should focus on what the child can do, not what they can't do. Howells, Carney, Castle and Little (2018) highlight that this can be achieved by simply challenging an individual or group to achieve a personal best or working towards a shared challenge.

Whilst competition can no doubt create exciting and motivating opportunities for children, it should not be the sole purpose of any PE curriculum or lesson. Layne (2014) explains that if competitive experiences are going to exist, then the teacher must ensure this is done appropriately and the children have the correct pre-requisite skills. As children develop their skill, confidence, understanding and knowledge of the activity, competition can then be used as a tool to challenge learning even further.

The current challenge for Primary Physical Education

So far in this chapter, we have outlined the key areas for learning in the Key Stage 1. In recent years, reports by OFSTED (2009, 2013, 2014) have highlighted concerns regarding teachers' ability to implement the Primary PE curriculum competently and confidently. Historically, reasons for this have been attributed to the lack of time dedicated on programmes for initial teacher education, with many university providers offering as little as 0–5 hours (Blair & Capel, 2011; Elliot, Atencio, Campbell, & Jess, 2013). A more recent study by Randall, Richardson, Swaithes and Adams (2016) suggested that the issue with teacher confidence and competence may not solely be the fault of the initial teacher education system. A national sample of 1,118 training teachers highlighted that, while most were willing to teach PE, nearly 50 per cent had no opportunity to do so when on an assessed school placement (Randall, 2017). Furthermore, trainee teachers reported that the biggest barrier to their development was the employment of external providers such as sports coaches, who replaced the teacher as the core deliverer of PE for their class.

Changes in government policy might give some indication as to why teachers have become removed from the delivery of PE in Primary Schools. First, in order to meet ambitious public service agreement targets, engaging children in two hours of high quality PE and school sport each week, the Physical Education School Sport and Club Links (PESSCL) strategy (DfES/DCMS, 2003), which was later raised to five hours in the Physical Education and Sport Strategy for Young People (PESSYP) (DCSF, 2008), cited outside providers, such as sports coaches, as being used to support schools in meeting targets (Griggs & Randall, 2018; Lavin, 2008). Second, the implementation of the "National Agreement for Raising Standards and Tackling Workload" (DfES, 2003) began to remodel and broaden the school workforce in England and was "designed to tackle the problem of workload, and the crisis in teacher recruitment and retention" (Gunter, 2007, p. 1). Consequently, since 1 September 2005, all teachers have had an entitlement to a guaranteed minimum of 10 per cent of their timetabled teaching commitment for planning, preparation and assessment. Research indicates that in a bid to cover the 10 per cent shortfall in staffing, many schools opted to employ poorly qualified, low cost sports coaches to deliver PE lessons (Griggs, 2010). Over time, their employment has increasingly removed responsibility for the delivery of PE from the class teacher to a school sports coaching programme, resulting in teachers becoming progressively and further deskilled (Keay & Spence, 2012).

Despite views that the use of non-teaching staff is having a positive impact within schools (Callanan, Fry, Plunkett, Chanfreau, & Tanner, 2015; Evans & Davies, 2010; Parnell, Cope, Bailey, & Widdop, 2017; Smith, 2015), the Post London 2012 Olympic and Paralympic promise of ring-fenced funding, in the form of the Primary PE and Sport Premium (DfE, 2013b), has expanded the outsourcing of PE exponentially (see Griggs, 2016). As a consequence, many Primary Schools have locked themselves into an increasingly "privatised" model of PE provision (Smith, 2015). The implications for Key Stage 1 have not yet been documented; however, if the funding were to stop, generalist Primary teachers may well be required to return to teaching PE having spent as much as five years away. We would argue that it is a strength, not a weakness, of the generalist teacher that they have more knowledge of the child than the activity areas they are teaching to.

Conclusion

The aim of this chapter has been to provide an overview of the National Curriculum for Physical Education at Key Stage 1 and its contribution to a child's physical development. Our argument has been framed around the development of the child first, ahead of the needs of the activity areas. While the curriculum programme of study provides a minimum statutory requirement for pupils, on its own, it lacks the richness and detail of what it is to be physically educated. Schools must reflect upon the place and purpose of PE as part of their broader curriculum aims and what it means to develop physically competent children. While many challenges still confront the profession, including limited time at initial teacher education, policy directives and continued pressures on curricular and teacher workload, the importance of high quality physical learning and development remains as important as ever. When taught well, learning in, through and about movement can support not only a child's physical health, but their social, cognitive and affective learning too.

Summary of key points

- PE has a broad contribution to children's development. It does, however, rely to some extent on the physical development levels of the young children it was designed for. As a result, an understanding of the impact of poor physical development on achievement and enjoyment of PE is important and needs to be recognised.

- The Key Stage 1 National Curriculum is a statutory entitlement for all children and outlines the minimum entitlement that schools should provide.
- The environment for teaching PE involves more than just the location of where a lesson takes place. It includes the climate that a teacher establishes and the pedagogical approaches they choose to take.
- To ensure learning in PE is purposeful and relevant, the needs of the child must be placed ahead of the needs of the activity.
- Competition is more than just the outcome of performance. When the process of learning competitively is valued, children can also develop skills of character and attitude.
- Pressures of the wider curriculum on teachers often mean it is not always possible to teach PE in a way that best serves the children.

Suggested further reading

Doherty, J., & Brennan, P. (2014). *Physical education 5–11: A guide for teachers.* London: Routledge.

Griggs, G. (2012). *An introduction to primary physical education.* London: Routledge.

References

Bailey, R. (2018). Sport, physical education and educational worth. *Educational Review, 70,* 51–66.

Bailey, R., Armour, K., Kirk, D., Jess, M., Pickup, I., & Sandford, R. (2009). The educational benefits claimed for physical education and school sport: An academic review. *Research Papers in Education, 24,* 1–27.

Blair, R., & Capel, S. (2011). Primary physical education, coaches and continuing professional development. *Sport, Education and Society, 16,* 485–505.

Callanan, M., Fry, A., Plunkett, M., Chanfreau, J., & Tanner, E. (2015). *The PE and sport premium: An investigation in primary schools.* London: NatCen Social Research.

Coulter, M., & Ní Chróinín, D. (2013). What is PE? *Sport, Education and Society, 18,* 825–841.

Department for Culture, Media and Sport (DCSF). (2008). *Physical education and sport strategy for young people.* London: Author.

Department for Education (DfE). (2013a). *The National Curriculum in England: Key stages 1 and 2 framework document.* London: Crown Copyright.

DfE. (2013b). *£150m Olympic legacy boost for primary school sport in England.* Retrieved 3 April 2016, from https://www.gov.uk/government/news/150-million-to-boost-primary-school-sport

DfE. (2017). *Statutory framework for the Early Years Foundation Stage: Setting the standards for learning, development and care for children from birth to five.* London: Crown Copyright.

DfES. (2003). *Raising standards and tackling workload: A national agreement*. London: Author.

DfES/DCMS. (2003). *Learning through physical education and sport: A guide to the physical education, school sport and club links strategy*. London: Author.

Doherty, J., & Brennan, P. (2014) *Physical Education 5–11: A guide for teachers*. London: Routledge.

Elliot, D. L., Atencio, M., Campbell, T., & Jess, M. (2013). From PE experiences to PE teaching practices? Insights from Scottish primary teachers' experiences of PE, teacher education, school entry and professional development. *Sport, Education and Society, 18*, 749–766.

Evans, J., & Davies, B. (2010). Family, class and embodiment: Why school physical education makes so little difference to post-school participation patterns in physical activity. *International Journal of Qualitative Studies in Education, 23*, 765–784.

Expert Subject Advisory Group. (2014). Glossary of key words in the National Curriculum [Online]. Worcester: AfPE. Retrieved 13 September 2015, from http://www.afpe.org.uk/physical-education/glossary-of-terms/

Gallahue, D. L., & Ozmun, J. C. (2011). *Understanding motor development: Infants, children, adolescents, adults*. London: McGraw-Hill.

Graham, G., Holt-Hale, S. A., & Parker, M. (2012). *Children moving: A reflective approach to teaching physical education*. New York, NY: McGraw-Hill.

Griggs, G. (2010). For sale – primary physical education £20 per hour or nearest offer. *Education 3–13: International Journal of Primary, Elementary and Early Years Education, 38*, 39–46.

Griggs, G. (2016). Spending the primary physical education and sport premium: A West Midlands case study. *Education 3–13: International Journal of Primary, Elementary and Early Years Education, 44*(5), 547–555.

Griggs, G., & Randall, V. (2018). Primary physical education subject leadership: along the road from in-house solutions to outsourcing. *Education 3–13 13*. doi: 10.1080/03004279.2018.1520277

Gunter, H. (2007). Remodelling the school workforce in England: A study in tyranny. *Journal for Critical Education Policy Studies, 5*(1), 1–11.

Howells, K. (2015). Physical education planning. In K. Sewell (Ed.), *Planning the primary national curriculum: A complete guide for trainees and teachers*. London: Sage.

Howells, K., Carney, A., Castle, N., & Little, R. (2018). *Mastering primary physical education*. London: Bloomsbury.

Keay, J., & Spence, J. (2012). Addressing training and development needs in primary physical education. In G. Griggs (Ed.), *An introduction to primary physical education*. London: Routledge.

Lavin, J. (2008). *Creative approaches to physical education*. London: Routledge.

Layne, T. E. (2014). Competition within physical education: Using sport education and other recommendations to create a productive, competitive environment. *Strategies, 27*(6), 3–7.

Leah, J., & Capel, S. (2000). Competition and cooperation in physical education. In S. Capel & S. Pitrowski (Eds.), *Issues in physical education*. London: Routledge/Falmer Press.

Malina, R. M., Bouchard, C., & Bar-Or, O. (2004). *Growth, maturation and physical activity*. Champaign, IL: Human Kinetics.

Ní Chróinín, D., Fletcher, T., & O'Sullivan, M. (2018). Pedagogical principles of learning to teach meaningful physical education. *Physical Education and Sport Pedagogy, 23*(2), 117–133.

OFSTED. (2009). *Improving primary teachers' subject knowledge across the curriculum*. London: Crown Copyright.

OFSTED. (2013). *Beyond 2012 – outstanding physical education for all.* London: Crown Copyright.

OFSTED. (2014). *The PE and sport premium for primary schools: Good practice to maximise effective use of the funding.* London: Crown Copyright.

Parnell, D., Cope, E., Bailey, R., & Widdop, P. (2017). Sport policy and English primary physical education: The role of professional football clubs in outsourcing. *Sport in Society, 20*(2), 292–302.

Penney, D. (2008). Playing a political game and play for position: Policy and curriculum development in health and PE. *European Physical Education Review, 4*, 33–49.

Pickup, I., & Price, L. (2007). *Teaching physical education in the primary school: A developmental approach.* London: Continuum.

Randall, V. (2017). Preparing our next generation of primary physical educators. *Physical Education Matters,* 12.

Randall, V., Richardson, A., Swaithes, W., & Adams, S. (2016). *Generation next: The preparation of pre-service teachers in primary physical education.* Winchester: University of Winchester.

Smith, A. (2015). Primary school physical education and sports coaches: Evidence from a study of School Sport Partnerships in north-west England. *Sport, Education and Society, 20*, 872–888.

10

UNLOCKING PHYSICAL POTENTIAL

Putting right what has "gone wrong"

Rebecca Duncombe and Sally Goddard Blythe

Personal reflection (Rebecca Duncombe)

It dawned on me only recently that I have been teaching about "inclusive pedagogies" to our first- and second-year university students for 16 years. Every year, somebody comes to speak to the students about how to adapt Physical Education (PE) lessons to suit the needs of every learner. They tell (and sometimes show) our students how to adapt the game, how to adapt the equipment, how to adapt the environment, how to differentiate lessons and never once, it seems, has anyone considered that we might actually be able to adapt the children to suit the activities. Clearly, this is a controversial suggestion and one that wouldn't be feasible in many situations but, if we don't have high expectations of our children in PE, will they reach their physical potential? If we consider what might be causing a lack of ability in PE, we might be tempted to blame poor physical development but what led to poor physical development in the first place and can we do anything to improve it?

In answer to these questions, I would like to present a short case study of my own experience with my eldest son. When he started school, he was clumsy, uncoordinated, fell over and off his chair for no reason, attempted to fit through gaps that did not exist and could not engage successfully in any sporting activity. He would stand in the middle of a football pitch and, at best, turn to face the ball as his teammates charged up and down past him (they quickly learnt to never pass him the ball). On sports day, he was the only one turning his arms backwards in the skipping race (and was obviously getting nowhere). He struggled to catch a ball, it often hit him on the head as if he'd not seen it coming and his throwing was never in the direction he intended it to be. His class teacher once commented, "he's not good at PE is he?" Most of his family, on both sides, could list quite impressive sporting achievements. Something did not add up!

Following an 18-month daily primitive reflex inhibition programme (based on the principles of neuroplasticity) from the Institute of Neuro Physiological Psychology (INPP), his physical abilities are now, at the age of 12, unrecognisable. Figure 10.1 indicates how much his balance improved following the reflex inhibition programme. Thus, this chapter will further explore the role of reflex inhibition in helping to unlock physical potential and, consequently, improve the physical capabilities of young children.

FIGURE 10.1 Improved balance following completion of a reflex inhibition programme.

Introduction

I am guessing that my description earlier could be used to describe many young children and, those reading this chapter may even recognise some of these symptoms in their own children, the children who are in their care or whom they teach (possibly even in themselves or in the school friends who they grew up with). Clumsy and uncoordinated children may eventually find themselves with a diagnosis of Developmental Coordination Disorder (DCD) although this seems to be dependent, amongst other things, on the severity of symptoms, the pushiness of the parents and the particular school that they attend. Children with DCD have throughout the years been referred to in a number of different ways (Sugden & Wright, 1998), for example: as clumsy children; as dyspraxic; or as having movement, motor or coordination difficulties. The current version of the

Diagnostic and Statistics Manual of Mental Disorders (DSM-5) refers to this condition as DCD and this term will, therefore, be adopted throughout this chapter. The other terms are, however, helpful in providing clues as to what the condition entails. Sugden and Wright (1998) provide further explanation:

> The overall picture of a child who has DCD shows that to a degree, the basic fundamental skills of reaching, grasping, sitting, standing, walking and running have emerged. However, the necessary development into competent functional skills, which enable children to manipulate and control their environments has not occurred (Henderson, 1992). This lack of development means that, by comparison, children with DCD fall behind their peers in all of these functional skills, resulting in a detrimental effect on their progress at school.

The diagnostic criteria for DCD are described as follows in DSM-5:

- Motor performance that is substantially below expected levels, given the person's chronological age and previous opportunities for skill acquisition. Poor motor performance may manifest as coordination problems, poor balance, clumsiness, dropping or bumping into things; marked delays in achieving developmental motor milestones (e.g., walking, crawling, sitting) or in the acquisition of basic motor skills (e.g., catching, throwing, kicking, running, jumping, hopping, cutting, colouring, printing, writing).
- The disturbance in Criterion A, without accommodations, significantly and persistently interferes with activities of daily living or academic achievement.
- Onset of symptoms is in the early developmental period.
- The motor skill deficits are not better explained by intellectual disability (intellectual development disorder) or visual impairment and are not attributable to a neurological condition affecting movement (e.g., cerebral palsy, muscular dystrophy, degenerative disorder).

The main purpose of this chapter is to explore whether and how children, either diagnosed with or suffering from symptoms of DCD, might be enabled to engage successfully in physical activities, sport and PE; children whose physical development has been interrupted, delayed or is not yet complete. We know from other chapters in this book (see Chapters 6 and 14) how important each stage of development is but what can we do to help children for whom this has "gone wrong?"

Helping children to reach their physical development potential

The expression "walking before you can run" is especially pertinent to this discussion as it calls on us to consider what skills we need in place before more advanced skills can be developed. It also encourages us to consider an approach that takes children backwards (in terms of their development) to enable them to go forwards. Many physical development and movement programmes exist that utilise this approach and some are outlined in this book (see Chapters 8 and 15). Movement for Learning (M4L), for example, gives reception children repeated opportunities over a four-week period to practise very basic skills over and over again and enables them to fill some of the gaps in their physical development journey. Impact data reveal improvements in physical development scores but, even at the end of a year's engagement with this programme, many children's physical development lagged behind that of children in previous years and was below a level desirable for both academic success and ability in PE. I didn't test my son's physical development scores before and after the reflex-inhibition programme that we put him on but the changes in his ability and behaviour exceeded our hopes and expectations. Shortly before seeking help for this I had never heard of primitive reflexes but, the more I learnt, the harder it was to ignore them, both in my own children and the children I later worked with in a professional capacity.

What are retained primitive reflexes?

All typically developing babies are born with a number of primitive reflexes to enable them to survive the first few months of life. They help to facilitate feeding in the first weeks of life (rooting and sucking reflexes); it is also believed that some of these reflexes help with the movements that are required of the baby during the birth process (Goddard Blythe, 2009). These reflexes should be present for up to six months but should start gradually declining from birth and be replaced by postural reflexes, which should be fully developed by the age of three and a half (Goddard Blythe, 2009). Where this is not the case, neurodevelopmental delay (NDD) or immaturity in the central nervous system is signified. The terms neuromotor immaturity (NMI) and NDD encompass many of the difficulties faced by children diagnosed with or suffering from symptoms of DCD but are often, albeit sometimes partially, underlying factors in other related conditions such as Dyslexia, Attention Deficit Disorder (ADD) and Asperger's Syndrome. They may also be linked to issues related to poor auditory or visual processing, poor balance or proprioception, anxiety and panic disorders, general behavioural concerns and underachievement in the classroom. Taylor, Houghton & Chapman (2004), for example, noted that, "in general, boys diagnosed with Attention Deficit Hyperactivity Disorder (ADHD) had significantly higher levels of reflex retention than non-diagnosed boys" (p. 23). In addition, Jordan-Black (2005) found that one reflex the asymmetrical tonic neck reflex (ATNR) (detailed in the following section) was significantly associated with lower levels of attainment in reading, spelling and mathematics, and McPhillips and Jordan-Black (2007) identified that a retained ATNR was associated with poorer attainment levels in core literacy skills in young children. Likewise, in a study conducted in Germany and reported in Goddard Blythe (2005a), 100 per cent of children aged 7–8 who were in a special class for children with speech impairment displayed residual primitive reflexes. In another study, Goddard Blythe (2001) assessed 54 children, with an independent diagnosis of dyslexia, for abnormal primitive reflexes and found the following (further details of each reflex follows in the next section):

- 44/54 (81 per cent) had a retained Moro;
- 51/54 (94 per cent) had a retained tonic labyrinthine reflex (TLR) in extension;
- 44/54 (81 per cent) had a retained TLR in flexion;
- 52/54 (96 per cent) had a retained ATNR to the left;
- 54/54 (100 per cent) had a retained ATNR to the right;
- 39/54 (72 per cent) had a retained symmetrical tonic neck reflex (STNR).

In 2011, Goddard Blythe presented a summary of several small-scale studies that had been carried out in Northumberland and Berkshire, investigating the incidence of NMI in children in mainstream schools and the impact on both behaviour and specific learning outcomes of the INPP developmental movement programme for schools. Although the numbers were not sufficient for statistical analysis, a small number of children who had been referred for behavioural support prior to participating in the movement programme were removed from the waiting list for support by the end of the first term without having received behavioural support in the interim.

In exploring some of these reflexes in more detail, it is possible to see why they may affect coordination and how inhibiting (or putting to sleep) these primitive reflexes may help children to better engage in and enjoy PE, sports and physical activity. The information that follows is taken from Goddard Blythe (2005b, 2009).

The Moro reflex

The Moro reflex should be present at birth and be inhibited in the first four months of life. Its purpose in the newborn and in the first few months of life is to act as a primitive startle reaction to any sudden unexpected stimulus for which the baby has no adequate defence. Triggering the Moro at birth through sudden movement, sound, change of light, temperature or position elicits abduction of the arms and legs into a posture of surrender, a rapid intake of breath, momentary freeze followed by adduction of the arms and legs and exhalation usually accompanied by crying. Children with a retained Moro tend to be hypersensitive and overreact to a range of sensory stimuli (sights, sounds, touch and movements), thus, hearing, vision and posture may be affected. Eventually, this may lead to oversensitivity to the anticipation of an event that a child has learnt will elicit an unpleasant response (i.e. the Moro). Whilst we are unaware of any research that looks at the relationship between a retained Moro and ability in/ attitudes towards PE, sport and physical activity, it is not hard to see why a child who fears movement or robust touch, or who finds it difficult to visually follow rapidly moving objects (sometimes a product of several immature reflexes), may try to avoid many sporting activities. In addition, children with a retained Moro do tend to have poor balance and coordination, difficulty catching a ball and are susceptible to adrenal fatigue (due to the release of adrenaline each time the Moro is triggered).

The Tonic Labyrinthine Reflex (TLR)

The TLR is triggered by flexion or extension of the head beyond the mid-plane (i.e. as the head lowers forward or extends back beyond the level of the spine). It results in a change in muscle tone depending on the direction the head has moved. If the head moves backwards (TLR in extension), the arms and legs extend and become stiff. If the head moves forward (TLR in flexion), the arms and legs fold in. A baby in the womb is in a constant state of flexion but, in order to pass through the birth canal, the baby must make two 90-degree turns requiring the baby to flex, extend and rotate. It is, therefore, believed that the TLR may assist in the birth process. Once the baby has been born, the TLR helps the baby to cope with the new found demands of gravity by changing muscle tone as a response to head movements. The TLR should be fully inhibited by the age of three and a half when head control has been gained and the head righting reflexes (more mature postural reflexes) have developed. A retained TLR beyond this age may cause problems with balance, posture, muscle tone, coordination and visual functioning. As with the Moro, it is not difficult to see why this reflex, when retained beyond three and a half months, may interfere with sporting success and enjoyment.

The Asymmetrical Tonic Neck Reflex (ATNR)

The ATNR develops in the womb and enables the baby to adjust its position and may also play a part in the birth process. The ATNR is triggered when the head is rotated to one side or the other; the resulting response is extension of the arm and leg in the side the head has turned to and bending of the other arm and leg (see Figure 10.2). Of relevance to later reading, writing and catching, the ATNR is believed to encourage good hand-eye coordination in the first weeks of life because the eyes move with the head and follow the extending arm, helping to extend focussing distance from near-point to arm's length and back again, and train the system to shift from central to peripheral vision, and vice versa. The ATNR should be inhibited between four and six months but, if it remains beyond this time and into early childhood, it can affect balance, the ability to cross the midline, hand-eye coordination and muscle tone. An inability to cross the midline (an imaginary division running down the middle of the body separating left and right) will affect handwriting because the hand has to cross the midline in order to write from left to right, and reading because the eyes have to track from one side to the other and back again. A retained ATNR, therefore, can influence both gross and fine motor skills, make catching, striking, kicking and throwing difficult (because the legs, arms and eyes will need to cross the midline to do this well) and impact balance. Again, it is easy to see why a retained ATNR may reduce sporting capacity and potential.

FIGURE 10.2   ATNR in infant under six months of age. (copyright Goddard Blythe, S.A., Personal collection)

The Symmetrical Tonic Neck Reflex (STNR)

The STNR should be present for a short time at birth, recede, then reappear shortly before an infant is ready to get up on all fours for crawling, and be inhibited by the age of about 11 months. The reflex is, again, triggered by head movements: in four-point kneeling (crawling position), as the head looks up (extends), the arms also extend and the bottom collapses back down onto the feet; as the head looks down (flexes), the arms also flex and the bottom raises up in the air (see Figures 10.3 and 10.4). The STNR is believed to: help align the spine in the quadruped position in preparation for upright posture; play a part in training visual skills to adjust when shifting focus from far to near distance, as is required when copying from the board; and help the child pull up to standing (as he or she looks down, the hips and knees push up to standing). A retained STNR may affect standing and sitting posture (picture the child who sits in his or her chair with his or her legs up tucked beneath them and the child who sits in a W-position on the floor). As the STNR produces such a dramatic response in either the upper or lower half of the body, many gross motor skills may be affected and children with a retained STNR will often find it hard to learn to swim, participate in gymnastics activities and ride a bike. Swimming, for example, can be affected because, as the head lifts up, the legs want to drop down and many children with a retained STNR will prefer to swim underwater as the weight of the water counteracts this response. If a retained STNR has prevented crawling from occurring, specific visual skills are unlikely to have been practised, potentially affecting developmentally later activities that require the ability to shift focus from near to far distance, or to follow something moving at speed (e.g. a ball).

FIGURE 10.3 Child demonstrating the STNR in extension.

FIGURE 10.4 Child demonstrating the STNR in flexion (for illustrative purposes only; it would be rare to see this extreme position in a child of this age).

A "cluster" of retained reflexes

Whilst it is not always the case, children who present with one retained primitive reflex are likely to have retained a number of them. Clearly, the impact of more than one reflex on both academic and sporting ability will be more problematic than the retention of one reflex alone.

Postural reflexes

As the primitive reflexes start to subside, they should start to be replaced by postural reflexes, a process that should be fully complete by the age of three and a half. The development of the postural reflexes reflects maturation in the functioning of the central nervous system. One type of postural reflex, the head righting reflexes "enable the child to maintain his head and trunk in a specific position when the body position is altered in any way" (Goddard Blythe, 2005b, p. 27). The absence of these may be linked to poor posture and immature eye movements, with possible impact on visual-perception.

A brief overview of four primitive reflexes has been given previously and the impact of their retention, in combination with underdeveloped postural reflexes, on a child's ability in sport, PE and physical activity outlined. The point was made early in the chapter that we shouldn't always accept a child's physical ability as "fixed," so what might be done to help children who are struggling to reach their physical potential? An understanding of why primitive reflexes are retained in the first place as well as an explanation of how they might be inhibited is helpful here and will follow in the next two sections.

Why are primitive reflexes sometimes retained?

There is no single or proven reason for why primitive reflexes are retained in some children in the absence of identified pathology, but it is believed that a combination of factors may contribute towards preventing their inhibition and/or integration. These include:

- Complications in the womb;
- Difficult births;
- A lack of movement or opportunities to move in the first few months.

As birth interventions (caesareans, ventouse/forcep delivery) become more commonplace and lifestyles become more sedentary, it is possible to start to understand why some children do not complete the reflex inhibition process. In Chapter 6, Dorothy describes the Pikler approach, which allows and enables babies to pass through each stage of physical development at their own pace and in their own time by offering plenty of opportunities for time spent flat on the floor, first on the back and then on the stomach. Contrast this to a situation that many babies find themselves in where they have been strapped into various devices (baby bouncers, bumbo seats, car seats and push chairs) to enable parents and care givers to participate in modern life, but which both restrict movement and force the baby into what is known as a C-shape (rather than them being allowed to spend time flat on their backs, which was common when old fashioned prams and carry cots were used).

How can primitive reflexes be inhibited?

Clearly prevention is better than cure but if something has "gone wrong" during the inhibition process, possibly as a result of the factors identified in the earlier section, what might be done? Indeed, is there anything that we can do for young children displaying movement difficulties to help them to better participate in sport, PE and physical activity? The argument from the start of this chapter has been that we can and should help young children to reach their physical development potential and that we should not accept poor physical abilities as "fixed." It was also pointed out in the personal reflection that it is often the sport or the equipment or the rules that are adapted to meet the needs of children; it is hoped that what follows may start to challenge this way of thinking.

The reflex inhibition programme devised by the INPP is a developmental movement programme that offers children a "second chance" to pass through the reflex integration process. The programme takes an average of 12 months and involves daily exercises lasting approximately 10 minutes. The exercises mimic many of the movements that a child should have made as a baby and, through doing these exercises, neural pathways are formed and strengthened – a process which Goddard Blythe (2004) likens to "making motorways for the mind and body". The actual process is understandably complex, certainly more complex than is described here, but hopefully enough detail has been provided to give a taste of what is involved. The INPP offers individual clients a personalised programme, but a school programme has also been adapted from the original exercises. Some of the research findings from the school programme will now be highlighted in the following.

Goddard Blythe (2005a) outlines the findings from a study in Northern Ireland that examined the reflexes of the following children:

- 339 children (aged 5–6), none of whom participated in the INPP developmental movement programme;
- 324 children (aged 8–9), of whom 168 children participated in the INPP developmental movement programme and 156 who did not.

At the start of the research, 48 per cent of the children aged 5–6 and 35 per cent of the children aged 8–9 showed elevated levels of retained reflexes. Other findings of interest include:

- Elevated levels of retained reflexes are correlated with poor educational achievement at baseline;
- Children who undertook the exercise programme showed a statistically significant greater decrease in retained reflexes than children who did not undertake the exercises;
- Children who undertook the exercise programme showed a highly significant improvement in balance and coordination, and a small but statistically significant increase in a measure of cognitive development over children who did not undertake the exercises (Goddard Blythe, 2005a, p. 426).

These studies were published in 2005. The M4L research project, which is detailed in Chapter 15, illustrates that the situation is potentially even worse just 12 years later, with data revealing that out of 46 children in the pilot phase of the project, 75 per cent had a TLR retained at 50 per cent or more, 89 per cent had an ATNR retained at 50 per cent or more and 83 per cent had an STNR retained at 50 per cent or more (Duncombe & Preedy, 2018). The M4L programme was never designed to be a reflex inhibition programme but some of the exercises do replicate developmental movements and did appear to have a small inhibitory effect on the primitive reflexes of the children in the intervention group (compared to a comparison group who did not participate in the programme and whose reflexes appeared to worsen). This pilot phase of the research included a small sample of children; data are currently being analysed for an extension of the project that tested 120 children and preliminary findings show a similar trend to those found in the pilot phase.

Conclusion

This chapter has put forward the argument that children's levels of physical development may affect their participation in sport, PE and physical activity but that these levels are not necessarily "fixed." It was outlined at the start that some children with movement and coordination difficulties may be diagnosed with DCD and that some may be undiagnosed but present with similar symptoms. Likewise, children labelled with other neurological disorders such as ADD, dyslexia and Asperger's may also have overlapping symptoms. Retained primitive reflexes were then put forward as a possible reason for these difficulties and four of the key primitive reflexes were described and explanations given for why their retention may negatively affect ability in sport, PE and physical activity. Finally, implementing developmental movement programmes, such as the one designed by the INPP, was identified as one possible solution. It is likely that the physical development needs of some children were not met when they were babies and toddlers and, where this is the case, providing a second chance for these children to pass successfully through the reflex inhibition process and necessary physical development stages may be of benefit.

Summary of key points

- Children diagnosed with DCD or displaying similar symptoms have yet to reach their physical development potential.
- Retained primitive reflexes may be an underlying issue in neurological disorders such as DCD and other related conditions like dyslexia, ADD and Asperger's.
- Developmental exercise programmes, such as the one devised by the INPP, exist and may help to reduce retained primitive reflexes in young children and, in turn, improve motor function.
- The potential link between retained primitive reflexes, poor movement skills and low ability in PE, sport and physical activity has been outlined.
- Further research into the effect of retained primitive reflexes and ability in/attitudes towards PE, sport and physical activity is required, as is more research demonstrating the impact of developmental movement programmes designed to inhibit retained primitive reflexes.

Suggested further reading

Goddard Blythe, S. (2009). *Attention, balance and coordination: The ABC of learning success.* Chichester: Wiley-Blackwell.

Cheatum, B. A., & Hammond, A. A. (2000). *Physical activities for improving children's learning and behaviour: A guide to sensory motor development.* Leeds: Human Kinetics.

References

Duncombe, R., & Preedy, P. (2018). Movement for learning. In P. Preedy, K. Sanderson, & C. Ball (Eds.), *Early childhood redefined: Reflections and recommendations on the impact of start right.* Oxford: Routledge.

Goddard Blythe, S.A. (2001, April). *Neurological dysfunction as a significant factor in children diagnosed with dyslexia.* Proceedings of the British Dyslexia Association International Conference, University of York.

Goddard Blythe, S. A. (2004). *The well balanced child.* Stroud: Hawthorn Press.

Goddard Blythe, S. A. (2005a). Releasing educational potential through movement: A summary of individual studies carried out using the INPP test battery and developmental exercise programme for use in schools with children with special needs. *Child Care in Practice*, 11(4), 415–432.

Goddard Blythe, S. A. (2005b). *Reflexes, learning and behaviour: A window into the child's mind.* Eugene, OR: Fern Ridge Press.

Goddard Blythe, S. A. (2009). *Attention, balance and coordination: The ABC of learning success.* Chichester: Wiley-Blackwell.

Goddard Blythe, S.A. (2011). Neuromotor immaturity as an indicator of developmental readiness for education. In Eva Maria Kulesza (Ed.), *Movement, vision, hearing – The basis of learning.* Warszawa: Wydawnictwo Akademii Pedagogiki Specjalnej im Marii Grzegorzewskiej.

Jordan-Black, J.-A. (2005). The effects of the Primary Movement programme on the academic performance of children attending ordinary primary school. *Journal of Research in Special Educational Needs, 5*(3), 101–111.

McPhillips, M., & Jordan-Black, J.-A. (2007). Primary reflex persistence in children with reading difficulties (dyslexia): A cross-sectional study. *Neuropsychologia, 45,* 748–754.

Sugden, D. A., & Wright, H. C. (1998). *Motor coordination disorders in children.* London: Sage.

Taylor, M., Houghton, S., & Chapman, E. (2004). Primitive reflexes and attention deficit hyperactivity disorder: Developmental origins of classroom dysfunction. *International Journal of Special Education, 19*(1), 23–37.

11

ADAPTING SPORTS FOR YOUNG CHILDREN

Carolynne Mason

Personal reflection

I am wearing two hats as I write this chapter. The first hat is that of an academic researcher who has researched young people's experiences of sport and physical activity for more than 15 years. Through these experiences, I have seen the potential benefits of sport in the lives of many children and their families. However, the same experience has made me very aware that some children do not experience – or have access to – positive experiences of sport in childhood. Positive experiences of adapted sport in the Early Years can make a broad and valuable contribution to children's Early Years experiences and also contribute to children having – and continuing to have – active lives. In contrast, when children do not have access to positive experiences of adapted sport in the Early Years, this may contribute to children being inactive within the Early Years and beyond.

The other hat I am wearing is that of a parent to children who experienced many adapted versions of sport in their Early Years. Writing this chapter has made me reflect on my own motivations for encouraging them to engage in sport from an early age. Through this reflection, I identified that these motivations varied depending on the child, the sport, the provider and the setting and these motivations changed over time. The expectations placed on adapted versions of sport in the Early Years are complex but based on my academic and personal experiences, I would like to argue that sport in the Early Years should be simple – it should be about all children and their families engaging in safe and enjoyable, age-appropriate activities that they enjoy and that can contribute to their physical development.

Introduction

Sport is a specific form of physical activity which involves a complex set of skills and abilities which are acquired in a progressive manner both within and beyond sport. The foundations for being good at sport develop from birth with appropriate movement and play experiences. Fundamental Movement Skills (see Chapter 3) can then develop from firm physical underpinnings and eventually translate into participation in more formalised sports. Referring specifically to children's experiences of sport, Côté, Lidor, and Hackfort (2009, p. 7) state that sport requires "the integration of several human abilities and processes," including fundamental movement skills (e.g. running, throwing, kicking and catching) and more complex sport-specific skills (e.g. serving in tennis). They further argue that participation in sport requires a high degree of cognitive-perceptive ability (e.g. noticing stimuli, decision-making), affective abilities (e.g. staying motivated) and the ability to interact with coaches, parents and peers. This characterisation of sport suggests that children are only ready to engage in formalised sport at the point at which they have developed sufficient physical, social and emotional skills.

Whilst there is no definitive age at which children become "sport ready," the age of six appears to be commonly accepted as a minimum age for children to begin to take part in sport. Canadian based "Sport for Life" is an organisation that aims to improve the quality of sport and physical activity in Canada and this advocates that children are ready to participate in sport beyond the age of six but only if their experiences in the Early Years provide an "Active Start" where children:

- Develop general movement skills;
- Undertake daily physical activity with an emphasis on fun and are not sedentary for more than 60 minutes except when sleeping;
- Engage in some organised physical activity;
- Explore risk and limits in safe environments;
- Participate in an active movement environment.

Sport for Life also advocates that the "Active Start" phase should include well-structured gymnastics and swimming opportunities.

In contrast, in the United Kingdom, the Primary School Physical Literacy Framework was recently developed by the Youth Sport Trust (YST) in partnership with Sport England (SE), the County Sport Partnership Network (CSPn), the Association of Physical Education (afPE), Sports Coach UK (scUK) and 23 National Governing Bodies of Sport (NGBs) (Sport England, n.d.). The framework indicates that sport specific activities should not be introduced until children reach upper Key Stage 2 (ages 9+) because it is only at this point that children will have developed sufficiently to be able to engage in traditional sport. Thus, there seems to be an argument for formal sport being introduced at an age that is outside of the scope of this book and this is why the inclusion of sport in the Early Years needs careful thought, consideration and, in most cases, adapting to meet the needs of younger children.

This chapter provides an examination of the role of adapted sport in the lives of young children. It begins by exploring why participation in sport in the Early

Years may be relevant. It then highlights some ways in which sports may be adapted to be more applicable to young children and, finally, it outlines a selection of examples of adapted sports.

Why might participation in sport be important in the Early Years?

Although it has been suggested that formal sports should not be provided until children reach the age of 6 and even 9, the case will be made here for the inclusion of adapted sports into the "physical diet" of younger children. It is recognised within this chapter that appropriate movement opportunities in the very Early Years are essential but that, as children reach a certain level of development, having passed through these essential stages, they may be ready for a challenge that stretches them beyond simple throwing, catching, striking and running activities.

Positive early experiences of sport have been shown to impact participation in sport in adolescence and beyond. For example, research conducted with almost 1,400 UK children indicated that young people who played a range of different sports in childhood continued to play sport in later life. By participating in different sports, both team and individual, children were able to draw on these experiences at a later date (Roberts & Brodie, 1992). However, it is important to note that negative experiences of sport in childhood may, conversely, decrease the likelihood of participation in sport in adulthood (Gilbert, 2001). This highlights the importance of children's early experiences being enjoyable and appropriate. In addition, young children are less likely to compare themselves to others and tend to believe that ability is related to effort (Lee, Carter, & Xiang, 1995). Thus, early childhood may be a good time to learn new skills as younger children don't tend to equate success and failure with effort.

Participation in sport in early childhood is also perceived to be beneficial in providing a foundation for children to progress on a pathway towards becoming elite athletes. This association was examined by Côté et al. (2009) who explored the relationship between early sport experiences and elite performance by specifically examining two pathways to elite success: "early sampling" and "early specialisation." Early sampling in this context referred to children taking part in a number of different sports and early specialisation involved a strong focus on participating in one sport. Côté et al. (2009) concluded that early sampling enabled children to learn emotional, cognitive and motor skills that would facilitate their involvement in sport in later life regardless of the level of their participation. Early sampling and deliberate play were described as "building blocks for self-regulated investment in elite sport during adolescence and adulthood" (Côté et al., 2009, p. 9). The risks of early sport specialisation have been well documented elsewhere (injury, burn-out, drop-out, etc.) and, therefore, the focus for young children should be on wider learning and development outcomes rather than sport specific skills. In support of this, a related study found that early specialisation may result in young people being lost to sport prematurely (MacPhail, Gorely, & Kirk, 2003).

How might sport be provided for children in the Early Years

The case has so far been made for the inclusion of a wide range of sporting opportunities for young children but what might these opportunities look like in practice? The research by Côté et al. (2009) implies that a wide range of sports should be offered (such as the multi-sport approach). Further advice can be found within the Early Years Physical Literacy Framework (YST, 2017), which states that, between the ages of 30 and 50 months, children should experience new movements and new activities involving adults and peers where they can extend their movement vocabulary, learn to follow instructions and increase ways of travelling (galloping, jumping and landing, rolling, climbing). Furthermore, it is suggested within this framework that children will also benefit from opportunities to repeat and practise activities, manipulate, balance and control objects with their hands and feet (passing hand to hand around body, rolling, dropping and picking up, bouncing, kicking, aiming and retrieving with a range of objects). Children should also develop balance, participate in adult-led water play and engage in a variety of actions and sequences of actions, stimulated through music, story and rhyme.

Sport is more visible within the Primary School Physical Literacy Framework (Sport England, n.d.) which outlines that young children need to engage in structured and free play opportunities in environments which introduce and develop control and co-ordination in large and small movements. Sport is initially featured in the framework in Key Stage 1 but in relation to skills that many sports require. As a result, it is suggested that adapted versions of sport might take place in multi-skills clubs that involve play, reinforce the importance of being physically active and provide opportunities for children to develop their social skills.

In order to provide further clarification, the following two sections will provide examples of how specific sports may be adapted to meet the needs of children in the Early Years. First, tennis will be used as a case study example and then a number of other sports will be overviewed (in relation to the ways in which they have been adapted for the Early Years).

Adapting sport for the Early Years: a case study of tennis

In 2013, researchers from Loughborough University and Youth Sport Direct[1] worked in collaboration with The Tennis Foundation and the Lawn Tennis Association (LTA) to examine ways in which more young children (aged 2–4) could access an adapted version of tennis in the Early Years (Youth Sport Direct et al., 2013). The research included:

- Online surveys;
- Site visits to Early Years settings;
- Interviews with staff, parents/carers, Early Years practitioners;
- Interviews with coaches who had experience of delivering adapted versions of tennis to children aged 2–4 years.

This section draws on this research and, in particular, the experiences of the coaches who had successfully adapted tennis-based sessions to meet the needs of young children.

The coaches within the study all had experience of engaging young children aged 2–4 in adapted tennis sessions. They indicated that children varied in the age at which they became ready to engage in more formalised sports coaching with 3 and half being considered the minimum age at which children could begin to engage in more structured coaching (note this is considerably younger than the 6 and 9 age recommendation stated earlier). When asked to describe a typical session, coaches responded that sessions were often broken down into small blocks of time in order for activities to be changed frequently to keep the children engaged and enjoying the sessions. Other key features that were typical responses from the coaches included:

- Skill development including throwing, catching and hitting a ball, achieved through game playing (e.g. hot potato where the children throw bean bags, relay races and slaloms through cones);
- Activities such as singing and stories to help ensure that the children enjoyed their experiences;
- The sessions often concluded with a fun group game (e.g. dodgeball);
- Some coaches used activity stations for the children to progress through during the session.

A range of different equipment was identified as being used during these sessions and included a variety of balls (tennis, foam, football, large, small), bean bags, hoops, spots, Zsig (tennis brand) equipment, cones, directional arrows, hand and feet, small nets, throw down lines, parachute, ladders and foam/small rackets. Most coaches commented that, within an adapted sport session, the equipment needed to be appealing to young children and this included being brightly coloured. Balloons were considered to be a useful alternative to balls because they have the advantage of moving slower which enabled the children to play with them more effectively.

The coaches also outlined the techniques they used in order to ensure the sessions provided young children with positive experiences. Some coaches stated that young children enjoy repetition, so they know what to expect each week in terms of structure and expectations placed on them; however, all coaches agreed that it was important that the adapted tennis sessions were fun and enjoyable. The ability of the coach to communicate and engage with young children was also an important aspect of making the adapted tennis sessions successful. Likewise, understanding the needs of young children was noted as being vital to the success of the session, and this included coaches being able to communicate well with children, to be encouraging and supportive, to ensure success and to minimise the chances of failure for children.

The coaches identified that the main challenges for delivering adapted tennis in the Early Years were: the children's limited attention span; developing the communication and social skills of young children; keeping children engaged and on task; health and safety issues; and managing parental expectations. The coaches were asked what they felt were parents' expectations of Early Years tennis and, in response, they suggested that parents have a variety of reasons for encouraging their children to become involved in tennis. For example, some parents hoped that Early Years tennis would be a route to future tennis participation, whilst other parents saw their child's engagement in tennis to be primarily motivated by the opportunity to have an enjoyable experience as illustrated by the following quote from a coach:

> I think that's a real mix, you get a real mixed bag on that, we have some parents who genuinely are interested in their child becoming a tennis player. Some of them think that they want their child there just for the fun and social aspect. You've got the odd parent who then wants them there just because their friend's there and then you can even have a case where it can even be just a babysitting service with them on a Saturday. So there's real different interests from parents but if you were looking at the ones who are more focussed they're looking for their children's skills to be developed at an early age so it will help them through their sporting career I guess rather than just specific to tennis.

In the same study, Early Years practitioners and foundation stage teachers were asked about the role of adapted sports in terms of making a contribution to fulfilling the Early Years Foundation Stage (EYFS) Physical Development requirements. The Early Years practitioners and foundation stage teachers indicated that they believed that adapted tennis could contribute to enhancing children's Physical development and to their personal, social and emotional development. The provision of tennis was seen by most as something that would allow young children to improve their hand-eye co-ordination, their gross motor skills, their throwing and catching, their spatial awareness and their general co-ordination. Interviewees indicated that these benefits would only be realised with an adapted version of tennis and not in sessions that were predominantly skills-based because children would not enjoy or engage with these sessions.

An LTA coach who had delivered tennis sessions for small groups of young children as an extra opportunity attached to nursery provision in two different settings was interviewed about her experiences. Parents did not attend the sessions in either context but, in one context, the coach was supported by nursery practitioners. Each of the tennis sessions included around 12 children of different ages (3–4s and 4–5s) and they lasted for 30 minutes. The coach suggested that some of the children who had just turned three had problems concentrating within the session. The coach described the way in which she delivered the sessions:

> We didn't always often get the rackets out, because rackets in those little hands it's an added liability. We do a lot of ball, a lot of jumping, hopping, being able to jump, land, two feet in a hoop, all of that kind of stuff, taking turns, making lines, trying a little bit to work together, like rolling a ball

to a friend... They are such a mix ... I like them to have lots of fun and lots of success, so it's easy and often it is quite repetitive... but the biggest challenge is simplistic instructions. Just being able to get them to sit and listen ... they can't form a queue, they can't go into a line and stay like that.

Other examples of adapted Early Years sports programmes

Swimming and gymnastics within the Early Years have both been identified in the chapter as sports that can benefit children in developing an active life and help to provide a strong foundation for children to continue to be active. Whilst it is possible for parents and carers to provide opportunities at home for children to engage in these activities, there are also a growing number of providers that offer adapted versions of these sports. Providers include commercial organisations, local authorities, leisure trusts, county sports partnerships and charities. Some adapted versions are endorsed or supported by the national governing body (NGB) whilst others are independent of NGBs. There are also a growing number of branded offers that often operate under a franchise system which are focussed around a particular sport but also offer a fundamental skills approach. These offers are designed to encourage progression through a number of stages and typically include a range of different activities to encourage a wide range of developmental outcomes including physical, social and emotional. Examples of adapted sport are discussed in the following: The British Gymnastics FUNdamentals programme, Turtle Tots, Tumble Tots, Rugbytots, Little kickers and Socatots. There are many others that could have been included but there was not capacity within this chapter.

The British Gymnastics FUNdamentals

The British Gymnastics FUNdamentals programme aims to support children aged under 6 years to acquire essential physical, social and emotional life skills (e.g. strength, endurance, agility, balance, flexibility, co-ordination, concentration and team working). A wide range of physical and musical activities are offered within 16 themes, such as "healthy eating," with each theme being delivered over six sessions, each lasting 45 minutes. A cat mascot and his friends feature in the programme delivery with each cat focussing on a particular skill, for example, "springy cat" enjoys jumping about. Progression is recognised through awarding badges, certificates and medals and these rewards also evidence participation and learning.

Turtle Tots

Turtle Tots is a water-based programme which aims to provide "fun, social and stimulating classes" (https://www.turtletots.com). In addition to aqua-natal classes for expectant mothers, Turtle Tots provides progressive classes for babies and toddlers to learn water safety and learn to swim with the support of a parent or carer who can also benefit from the class by burning up to 250 calories. The classes are delivered by teachers who have lifeguard qualifications and are trained in accordance with the Amateur Swimming Association (ASA) or Swimming Teacher's Association (STA) standards including the STA's baby and preschool qualification. This programme aims to provide a range of benefits for both the adult and the child attending the classes. Physical development opportunities for children who swim regularly include cardio-vascular development, strength building, improved co-ordination and associated motor skills.

Tumble Tots

Not all Early Years adapted sports offers are associated with NGBs: for example, Tumble Tots was established in 1979 (www.tumbletots.com) and is designed to provide children with physical skills of agility, balance, co-ordination and climbing as well as confidence and self-esteem. There are two programmes that are available according to the age of the child. Tumble Tots is the name given to the classes for children aged up to five years and these are split into the following age groups: 6 months to walking, walking to 2 years, 2 to 3 years, 3 years to school age and walking to 5 years. The first stage is designed to stimulate and encourage babies to use all their senses through social play and exploration to crawl and learn together. The focus of the next stage (walking to 2 years) is on developing motor and social skills, encouraging independence and providing new challenges to keep children self-motivated. This stage is followed by a flexible play programme where children explore and gain physical confidence (and physical literacy) and improve their social and language skills. Gymbobs is aimed at children who are school age to 7 years and this programme is more challenging in order to develop children's physical skills, confidence and teamwork skills.

Rugbytots

Rugbytots was established in 2006 (www.rugbytots.co.uk). The Rugbytots programme was designed to develop children's physical, psychological and social attributes whilst also encouraging rugby specific skills. In common with the other examples the programme is divided into three groups based on the age of the children: Junior Rugbytots is a 30-minute session for children aged 2–3.5 years and is designed to encourage the use of core skills such as balance, agility and co-ordination in children. Social skills are also promoted through encouraging sharing, taking turns and working together. Senior Rugbytots is a 45-minute session for children aged 3.5–5 years and aims to build on the basic motor skills already learnt along with more specific rugby skills. Advanced Rugbytots is targeted at children aged 5–7 years and claims to adopt the same fun first approach for children who have already participated in Rugbytots.

Little Kickers

Little Kickers was launched in 2002 and now operates across four continents (www.littlekickers.co.uk). Little Kickers is described as a positive, fun-filled preschool football programme which aims to teach fundamental football techniques and elementary life skills in a vibrant, group play environment along with social skills. The programme also aims to promote balance, agility and co-ordination. This programme separates children into four distinct age groups starting with Little Kickers: 1.5–2 years; Junior Kickers: 2–3.5 years; Mighty Kickers: 3.5–5 years; and Mega Kickers: 5–7 years.

Socatots

Socatots (www.socatots.co.uk) is the world's leading football based developmental activity programme specifically designed for children (girls and boys) aged 6 months–5 years old. It offers a unique approach designed around systematic training sessions involving parents' active participation. Designed specifically for children, Socatots activities are full of fun, age-appropriate challenges, working to utilise and manage all parts of the child's agility, balance and co-ordination as well as their social skills. This creates a fun and fast paced setting, ensuring children are kept active throughout.

The adapted versions of sport outlined earlier are all opportunities that are available to parents who have the means to afford them as all incur a charge (see enrichment activities in Chapter 4). Some organisations including Local Authorities, County Sports Partnerships and charities also provide opportunities for Early Years children to engage in adapted versions of sport on a subsidised basis. Typically, these adapted sport sessions take place at leisure centres, sports halls, community centres or Sure Start Centres.[2] These are aligned with priorities identified by the organisation responsible and they are often supported by external funding. For this reason, the organisations may choose to prioritise areas of socio-economic disadvantage or areas where there is little or no alternative provision for this age group. Alternatively, they may provide a more commercial alternative in more affluent areas in order to cross subsidise other provision.

Early Years settings potentially provide an ideal setting in which adapted sport can be offered to young children regardless of the socio-economic status of the family. However, there are many barriers that exist which make this universal provision aspirational. Survey findings with Early Years practitioners in the tennis study earlier (Youth Sport Direct et al., 2013) indicated that there was a recognition that physical activity and sport within Early Years settings were something that children would be able to engage in and something they would enjoy. Nursery staff disagreed or strongly disagreed that the physical ability of children aged 2–5 (76 per cent) or children not enjoying physical activity (88 per cent) was a barrier to delivering physical activity and sport within Early Years settings. However, there were a number of barriers that were identified by nursery practitioners to delivering physical activity and sport of which the most commonly cited were: limited space (64 per cent), cost (52 per cent) and lack of practitioner knowledge (51 per cent). The environmental challenges and constraints that exist in some Early Years settings are illustrated in Figures 11.1 and 11.2.

FIGURE 11.1 Indoor space in a Sure Start Centre set up for physically active play.

FIGURE 11.2 Space used at a nursery for tennis (note the rubber matting which was curling up at the edges).

Foundation stage teachers also highlighted a number of barriers to delivering physical activity and sport within their own settings and these included: timetabling issues which meant the foundation stage children were not always given priority (in terms of access to indoor and outdoor physical activity space); a lack of intra-school competitions for children of this age; inadequate staff: pupil ratios; a lack of teacher knowledge about different sports; and time pressures.

Whilst the predominant focus of this chapter has been on ways in which sport can be adapted to suit the Early Years context, it is important to acknowledge that not all sport offers for the Early Years require children to attend classes. Sport in the form of deliberate play can be instigated and adapted by children without adult intervention. Children can also take part in informal adapted sport activities with parents and carers at home and beyond. These informal activities have not been subject to extensive academic scrutiny, but their importance was recognised by Judy Murray, who, in 2012, launched "Set4Sport" with the specific aims of convincing more families to participate in physical activity in ways that may also enable children to become participants in sport in the longer term. As part of this initiative, Murray provided examples of games that she adapted at home for her sons, Andy and Jamie Murray, when they were very young (Murray, 2013). In addition to their tennis success, Murray also noted that both Andy and Jamie were very successful in other sports which she attributes, in part, to the early foundation that they gained at home.

Conclusion

This chapter has demonstrated that, whilst sport is generally considered to be something that is only to be encouraged in children after the age of 6, the Early Years can provide a valuable opportunity in which young children and their families can engage in sporting activities that are adapted to meet their needs. Much of this book has been concerned with ways in which the physical development needs of young children can be met. In order to engage in sport, even adapted sports such as those described earlier, young children need a well-developed physical foundation. Likewise, once the physical foundations are in place, young children need opportunities to develop their fundamental movement skills without the additional challenge of aspects more typically associated with participation in sport (such as teamwork, rules, strategy, good spatial awareness and competition).

Despite this, it has been argued earlier that sport does have a part to play in the lives of young children but that this must be carefully planned for. Adapted sporting opportunities can provide a means through which fundamental movement skills might be practised, but they also enable opportunities for social, emotional and cognitive outcomes. It has also been shown that early exposure to a range of sports may help encourage future participation and an active lifestyle throughout the teenage years and into adulthood. The power of sport in early childhood should not be underestimated but its provision needs careful thought, planning and adapting to ensure it is appropriate for the needs of the children it is provided for.

Summary of key points

- Adapted sports provide an opportunity to contribute to children's broad development and to develop sport specific skills which are associated with participation in sport in later years.
- Positive experiences of early engagement in adapted sport are associated with participation in sport in later childhood and as an adult.
- Sampling a range of sports in early childhood has been shown to provide more positive experiences of sport than early specialisation.
- Opportunities to engage in adapted sport exist both formally and informally but there may be inequality in access to adapted sport opportunities.
- Children need good levels of physical development and a grasp of basic fundamental movement skills before more formal sporting opportunities are offered (although some adapted sports may offer the chance for FMS to be practised).

Suggested further reading

Sport England. (n.d.). *Primary school physical literacy framework*. Retrieved from https://www.sportengland.org/media/1075/physical-literacy-framework.pdf
YST. (2017). *Early years physical literacy framework*. Retrieved from https://www.london.gov.uk/sites/default/files/early_years_physical_literacy_framework.pdf

---

Notes

1 Youth Sport Direct is the commercial arm of the Youth Sport Trust, an independent charity devoted to changing young people's lives through sport.
2 Sure Start centres provide families with advice on health, parenting, money, training and employment. Early learning and full day care for pre-school children are available at some Sure Start centres.

References

Côté, J., Lidor, R., & Hackfort, D. (2009). ISSP position stand: To sample or to specialize? Seven postulates about youth sport activities that lead to continued participation and elite performance. *International Journal of Sport and Exercise Psychology*, 7(1), 7–17.
Gilbert, E. D. 2001. Towards a richer understanding of girls' sport experiences. *Women in Sport and Physical Activity Journal*, 10, 117–143.
Lee, A., Carter, J. A., & Xiang, P. (1995). Children's conceptions of ability in physical education. *Journal of Teaching and Coaching Physical Education*, 14(4), 384–393.

Murray, J. (2013). Games that helped make Murray a champion. *BBC*. Retrieved from https://www.bbc.co.uk/sport/get-inspired/23342076

MacPhail, A., Gorely, T., & Kirk, D. (2003). Young people's socialisation into sport: A case study of an Athletics Club. *Sport, Education and Society, 8*(2), 251–267.

Roberts, K., & Brodie, D. (1992). *Inner-city sport*. Culemborg: *Giordano Bruno*.

Sport England. (n.d.). *Primary school physical literacy framework*. Retrieved from https://www.sportengland.org/media/1075/physical-literacy-framework.pdf

Youth Sport Direct, Duncombe, R., Mason, C., Morris, J., Brown, S., & Nevill, M. (2013). *Researching the development of an early years tennis programme*. Unpublished Research Report.

YST. (2017). *Early years physical literacy framework*. Retrieved from https://www.london.gov.uk/sites/default/files/early_years_physical_literacy_framework.pdf

12

ADAPTING THE ENVIRONMENT FOR THE EARLY YEARS

Carol Archer

Personal reflection

My interest and dedication to young children's physical development and move-ment have been inspired by my own experience of being physically active as a young child as well as my teaching experience in the classroom, and later as an Early Years advisor in an inner London borough where our unique focus on this area of the curriculum since 2005 has had a profound impact on practice and children's experiences.

Fired by my own experience of playful outdoor activity as a young child brought up at a time during a "cultural right to roam," I played out in our garden in inner London and beyond. Climbing trees in the garden, swinging on the old swing, digging mud (and eating it too), dad hosing us down with water as we played in the hot summer sun. At about six years of age, beyond the garden gate I skated up and down the road, knocked on the doors of Stephen and Neil to come and be playmates running around our street, which inclined quite steeply uphill where we rode hand me down bikes and later rode to the high street to collect provisions for our parents.

As my skills developed, the garage walls provided just the right place to skil-fully throw two balls in quick succession as I chanted a rhyme in the same beat as the balls hit the wall. This was where hand stands were practiced, failed, re-hearsed never giving up until perfected. The cricket path nearby led to places afar for us as seven- and eight-year-olds, where we picked wild flowers along the way, scrumping apples from overhanging trees, in search of new horizons that seemed quite far from home. We didn't have a TV, we played games and did endless drawings that, over time, became more detailed as fine skills matured. "Come home when you're hungry," I remember my mum telling us, relieved that she could do all the work in the home without us "under her feet."

My own experiences as a child were facilitated by a positive and enabling environment, and it is the provision of such an environment, albeit not as "free" as my own, that can and does facilitate opportunities to be active and to move in ways that ultimately benefit children's physical development, health and learning.

Introduction

Having reflected on my own experiences and considered how free I was to move, it is hard not to make comparisons to the situation that young children find themselves in today. I was free to roam unsupervised for long periods of time; I was left to sort out my own conflicts, to decide what I wanted to do and where I wanted to play. There was a definite lack of structure to what I was doing but it was an excellent environment within which to develop and refine my emerging and rapidly improving motor skills. Arguably, the environment in which I grew up in and was allowed to play in enabled me to be active and a number of factors played a part in this. For example, my parents allowed me to spend time in this way; it was acceptable for children to play out in the street without parental supervision; and there was a lack of "devices" enticing me back into the home to engage in more sedentary behaviours. A cultural "right to roam" has, over the last few decades, been supplanted by increasing restrictions on children's opportunities to wander independently beyond the garden gate, if they have one (Derbyshire, 2007). Over the last few decades, increasing car use has rendered local roads and streets unsafe places to play, rising numbers of play spaces have been lost to urban builds, and the pull of screens and electronic devices have all contributed to young children spending more time being sedentary indoors and less time physically active outdoors than their parents and grandparents used to be. The consequences for children are profound in terms of their health and well-being as all these factors have impacted on increasing numbers of children being identified as overweight, obese or having not reached their physical development potential by the time they reach reception age. More young children are spending time playing on their own and consequently less time interacting with their peers, adversely affecting development of their social skills and well-being. Yet, if children got out into the countryside, parks and gardens, they would be healthier and better adjusted. The benefits for children participating in activities in green surroundings have been identified as improved concentration, motor ability and increased social play (Pretty et al., 2009).

With this in mind, as well as my own observations of the more physically restricted environments that young children are increasingly starting to grow up in, I developed, in collaboration with a colleague, the Movement Environment Rating Scale (MOVERS) (Archer & Siraj, 2017). This chapter will address the physical development needs of children aged 0–6 (although it is important to note that the MOVERS focusses on 2–6-year-olds but can be applied to environments for children aged 7–8 years). The MOVERS has been developed for use in early childhood education settings that are interested in raising quality in the vital curriculum area of physical development. The MOVERS can be used for self-evaluation and improvement in order to provide more enabling places for children to move and learn. This is important information in the light of the Effective Provision of Pre-school and Education (EPPE) (Sylva et al., 2004) and later longitudinal research following these children's achievements into and through Secondary School (Sylva, Melhuish, Sammons, Siraj-Blatchford, & Taggart, 2012). It is recommended that the MOVERS is used in conjunction with "Encouraging Physical Development through Movement-Play" (Archer & Siraj, 2015a) as this acknowledges the relationship between movement and appropriate child development as well as the UK physical activity guidelines (see Chapter 4). The importance of the MOVERS lies in its focus on physical development, movement and practice when supporting children's health, well-being, learning and development.

Physical development is an important but often overlooked area, yet it is one of the three key interrelated developmental domains for children aged up to six years of age (Archer & Siraj, 2015b). Attention up until recently focussed on cognitive and social-emotional domains omitting physical development and the MOVERS fills this gap. It is important to understand, however, that all three domains overlap and are interrelated. The MOVERS was, therefore, developed to enable practitioners to better understand this vital area and, hopefully, in turn, to help improve the quality of young children's movement experiences, the environment and pedagogy in early childhood education settings and the early primary years. The content of the MOVERS includes four sub-scales which cover:

1. The curriculum, environment and resources for physical development:
    - Item 1: Arranging environmental space to promote physical activity;
    - Item 2: Providing resources including portable and/or fixed equipment;
    - Item 3: Gross motor skills;
    - Item 4: Body movement to support fine motor skills.
2. Pedagogy for physical development
    - Item 5: Staff engaging in movement with children indoors and outdoors;
    - Item 6: Observation and assessment of children's physical development indoors and outdoors;
    - Item 7: Planning for physical development indoors and outdoors.
3. Supporting physical activity and critical thinking
    - Item 8: Supporting and extending children's movement vocabulary;
    - Item 9: Encouraging sustained shared thinking by communicating and interacting through physical activity;
    - Item 10: Supporting children's curiosity and problem solving indoors and outdoors.
4. Parents/carers and staff
    - Item 11: Staff inform families about children's physical development and the benefits to their learning, development and health.

These 11 items are broken down into smaller steps that identify *indicators* of quality. These items and indicators can be used by settings to assess current levels of progress as well as identifying areas for development. Some of these items will be outlined in more detail within the context of the following four sub-scales.

MOVERS Sub-scale 1: Curriculum environment and resources for physical development

The curriculum

The curriculum for young children refers to the Early Years Foundation Stage (EYFS), as outlined in Chapter 8, and the Key Stage 1 curriculum, as outlined in Chapter 9. As such, there is no need to re-visit the content of these but what is relevant here is that the MOVERS is appropriate for the curriculum requirements of pre- and early Primary Schools providing these settings with a means to assess their environments and pedagogy within the context of physical development.

The environment

In the majority of settings, the physical environment should include space indoors and outdoors for physical activity. Space is routinely assigned to most curriculum areas in nursery and Reception classes; however, provision for physical development is not always considered nor made accessible in the indoor environment. This area of learning is often perceived to be achieved through outdoor activities; therefore, little attention is given to the space indoors for movement. The focus of this section will look first at ways in which the indoor environment can be adapted to meet the needs of young children and, second, at the outdoor environment, taking different ages and stages of development, in turn.

Turning our attention first of all to an enabling indoor environment for infants, the provision of adequate floor space cannot be overstated for this age group. Babies' natural play space is the floor where they can comfortably lay on their backs, reach for a toy, stretch to roll over onto their tummy and roll back again, and eventually crawl along the floor on their tummy, then on hands and knees, climb, and in time pull themselves up to standing, and cruise along furniture. There are a multitude of benefits of these early movement patterns for children (Goddard Blythe, 2005; Lamont, 2001). For example, a young baby starting to crawl will need to exercise their visual tracking skills (looking forwards and backwards and from side to side) as they start to explore their environment; these skills are essential for later reading, writing and copying from the board. Likewise, while crawling on the floor, the hands are forced to open out more fully, a noticeable development from the palmar grasp visible in the newborn infant (a retained palmar grasp often contributes to an immature pencil grip and difficulties with handwriting and other fine motor skills). Strength in the hands, arms and shoulders also develops when crawling and this provides an underpinning foundation for fine motor skills. Balance is first tested when a young baby no longer has a large surface area in contact with the floor (i.e. when they are on their back or front) and thus crawling and sitting challenge and develop their growing sense of balance and vestibular control. If children have problems with balance, they may have difficulty standing, walking, running or climbing the stairs without falling or bumping into things. Resolving balance problems can bring about a significant improvement to the overall quality of a child's life and his or her ability to play and learn (Macintyre & McVitty, 2004). Infants learn to sit up when their back muscles are strong enough. This is important information because when children are older they need to have a stable posture in order to sit upright and write, copy from a board, type or listen to the teacher. Thus, the importance of a safe, secure and suitable indoor space for an infant to move in developmentally appropriate ways cannot be stressed enough.

The MOVERS includes the two-year-old age group, most of whom will now be stable on their feet and walking independently. Many two-year-olds are eager to run, climb, jump and experiment with new ways of moving on their own or with their peers. Even indoors these explorers feel the need to climb and we would be wise to find creative ways to enable them to do so safely (onto sofas, for example, where they can fall from and roll onto soft mats and cushions). Jumping from a stationary position at ground level or from an appropriate height in safe indoor surroundings may prepare a toddler for more exploratory leaping outdoors when they are ready. These creative young children love to dance and to be watched with attention or to dance with their peers and/or carers. Two-year-olds also need to repeat the early movement patterns of the infant such as tummy crawling, crawling on all fours and rolling. As with infants, all of these movements demand floor space for the young child to do what their bodies tell them to as they play on the floor with creative or construction materials, trains and tracks, for example. Adults may want to sit in chairs but young children become more sedentary by doing so and instead are more likely to move their bodies more freely when floor based. Two ways of enabling this to happen are to define an area for movement indoors daily, or regularly, with soft mats and a variety of easily accessible materials as well as ensuring that activities are placed on the floor for toddlers to access them while moving on their hands and knees or on their tummies to reach and play with them. Opening up the environment to floor space by removing tables and chairs may seem like a challenge but the floor is where these young children move and learn (see Figure 12.1). The routines of the day also need to be flexible enough to allow for uninterrupted time for children to engage in movement indoors some of the time.

Lastly, within this section, the focus will turn to preschool and primary aged children. Children aged from 3 to 6 (and up to eight years) need also to return to early movement patterns (Lamont, 2001). We may not know if they have missed these significant movements through their Early Years or if parents are able to remember their child's movement history. Nonetheless, the benefits of these movement patterns for children's learning and development and behaviour

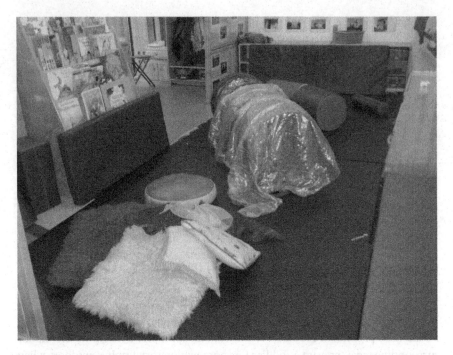

FIGURE 12.1 Setting up the indoor floor space to allow children to move and develop their physical skills.

cannot be overemphasised and, therefore, interesting and relevant activities need to be planned for them. An endless variety of movements are more likely to be created by preschool and early primary aged children when they are provided with open ended provision. Large soft PE mats placed simply in an area inviting children to move will draw out creative expressive unique movements and amazing physical feats of balance alone or with their peers. A-frames and ladders or poles can be erected indoors (or outdoors) in a range of ways enticing children to accomplish a variety of ways to use their bodies. Wooden boxes to jump from onto a mat which may include a number ladder on which to land. Cardboard boxes of various sizes offer many opportunities for hiding inside or when joined together for crawling through; or ones large enough to stand in while the adult blows bubbles for the children to jump and catch.

As has been demonstrated previously, the potential of the indoor environment to meet the physical development needs of young children should not be overlooked and requires thought and planning. The outdoor space, however, possibly springs to mind as a more obvious environment for children to move and be active but it still requires attention. The MOVERS items 3 and 4 cover gross motor skills and body movement to support fine motor skills, respectively. The organisation of space and resources should promote physical activity and enable young children to experiment, be creative and explore their body potential. Early movement patterns such as tummy time and crawling on all fours can be practiced, rehearsed and accomplished outdoors where different terrains, equipment and the weather offer a variety of challenges and sensory experiences. For young children to stimulate their sensory systems, equipment of varying challenges should be provided to keep children interested and motivated. Equipment needs to be suitable for the age and stage of the children at the setting though it is important not to underestimate a young child's desire to be challenged when sliding down a long, bendy slide, or climbing a frame with footholds, spinning in a cone, climbing a tree or balancing on a plank. Preschool and early primary aged children can be set a challenge to build a structure for themselves to travel along on their tummies or to balance along. For example, a fairly simple structure consisting of a chair, a plank and a crate can be erected by children into a slide which they can slither down on their tummy or use to construct into a structure that they can balance along.

The body needs to be stable before the hands can be free to focus on specific fine motor skills. Growth and development over time gradually enable the young child to engage in more challenging physical activities, such as pulling up to walking, hanging by their hands from monkey bars and using hands to pull up on ropes and climbing walls. These physical feats of accomplishment help to build stability and strength in the young child's body and dexterity in their hands and fingers and it is in these ways that fine motor skills are developed and before young children are expected to hold a pencil and write using a mature pincer grip (MOVERS, 2017, p. 35). It takes time and skill for a young child to dress in preparation to go outside to play in the cold, wet, snowy weather. Putting coats on, doing up buttons and pulling on extra layers of socks and waterproof clothes, boots, hats and gloves are all dependent upon the nimbleness of young fingers. It is through much experience of whole-body movement and physical activity that the development of fine motor skills depends. Thus, organising an environment consisting of portable and fixed equipment to enable children to be both creative and physically active is essential (see Figures 12.2 and 12.3). The following could be considered:

- Tunnels to crawl through;
- Ropes attached to trees to pull up on and climb or swing from;
- Climbing walls and frames offering diverse challenges demanding many bodily movements and adjustment to move up, down and through;
- Slides to whizz down on;
- Large mats for children to move on and explore their body potential;
- Equipment to spin in or on top of;
- Opportunities to play in puddles and snow;
- Water to transport using a variety of containers, filled from taps and hoses and used in a variety of ways (e.g. to make soup or mix with sand to make a wall).

FIGURE 12.2 Fixed and portable equipment set up to enable physically active play outdoors.

FIGURE 12.3 Garden area set up with a range of physical development opportunities in mind (the slope in the background encourages children to run up, roll down and enjoy the challenge of pushing wheelbarrows up a gradient; the wooden crates and the small climbing frame at the bottom of the slope encourage exploration; and plants in the foreground enhance the attractiveness of the area).

Children should feel the breeze on their skin, the sun warming their body, hands freezing cold in the snow, running and playing to keep warm, or being still to calm and cool down swinging slowly in a hammock or laying inside a Tepee. Thus, the physical environment should cater to these needs: a canopy can protect from the rain and sun, and clothing appropriate for changeable weather conditions will enable infants and young children to be outdoors in rain, snow, sunshine or on a windy day. All of this physical work takes time and effort as a multitude of tiny steps in growth and development takes place to further support children's posture, co-ordination, spatial orientation, vision and balance, which will be with them for the rest of their lives (Macintyre & McVitty, 2004).

Resources

Just as the environment is important, so too are the resources housed within them. The following resources are suggested to help meet the physical development needs of young children:

- **Indoor resources for infants:**
  Mats; soft beautiful rugs; toys made of natural materials; body balls; small softy balls; cushions; soft-play shapes; rolling cushion; mirrors; rocking cone; aesthetically pleasing materials; tunnels; builder's trays; messy play materials; water; sand; sofa; small gym.
- **Indoor resources for two-year-olds:**
  Lots of soft mats; cardboard boxes; lycra material; chiffon scarves; carnival sticks; rolling cushions; aesthetically pleasing materials; large body balls; large bean filled cushions; equipment for playing music; musical instruments; creative materials; small world play; construction.
- **Indoor resources for preschool and primary aged children:**
  Cardboard boxes of various sizes; bubbles, variety of balls; bean bags; large bean filled cushions; large PE mats; A-frames and ladders and poles; boxes to jump off; number lines; ascetically pleasing materials; parachute; ribbon sticks; chiffon scarves.
- **Outdoor resources for all young children:**
  A variety of textures to crawl on, such as grass; wood chippings; wooden bridges; a range of surfaces such as hills, steps, even and uneven; dens to build and play inside; hammocks to swing on; climbing frames of various shapes and challenges; containers for growing and harvesting herbs and food; chicken pen with chickens to look after and collect eggs from; bikes with carriers; sledges; swings; pulleys; mud to dig; sand and water; taps and hoses to access water; receptacles to transport water, sand and mud; places for solitary time and places to share with a friend; spinning cones and tops; balance equipment; wheeled toys; wheelbarrows; mats; ropes to pull up on; tyres; structures to jump off; logs/planks to walk along and balance on; A-frames and ladders; climbing walls; slides; monkey bars; sand pits; trees to climb.

MOVERS Sub-scale 2: Pedagogy for physical development; (item 5: Staff engaging in movement with children)

The pedagogical role of adults in the Early Years has been influenced by Vygotsky (1978) who recognised the significance of the adult in the child's zone of proximal development (ZPD). The ZPD defined by Vygotsky is "The distance between the actual developmental level as determined by independent problem solving and the level of potential development as determined through problem solving under adult guidance or in collaboration with more competent peers" (1978, p. 86). Put simply, the child's ability to progress from what they can do alone to taking on new and extended experiences is dependent upon the educator's effective practice in encouraging and directing the child in their playful explorations, thus enhancing their learning (Siraj-Blatchford, 2009). This can also be achieved between peers. Siraj-Blatchford (2009, p. 85) points out that "left to their own devices we know that the play of children often becomes repetitive, and effective educators, therefore, should encourage children to take on new and extended experiences." It is a skilful educator who is able to find a balance between leaving children to play creatively and intervening to guide them. Child development builds on the mutual interaction and communication between teacher and child. Educators, therefore, have an important role to play as the child pursues new experiences by supporting them through careful observation and consequent interpretation, careful questioning and interacting with the child in the zone of their potential development. The skilful and knowledgeable adult gets to know the children in their care, their interests and capabilities, planning ahead, initiating activities that they will enjoy and benefit from (Siraj-Blatchford, 2009, p. 10). In this way, the effective educator monitors the child's activities assessing their development and possible potential, thus initiating or maintaining learning processes (Siraj-Blatchford, 2009).

Research has clearly shown us that practitioners' knowledge and understanding are vital (Siraj-Blatchford, Sylva, Muttock, Gilden, & Bell, 2002). If Early Years educators are to be effective educators of young children, they need to have a good grasp of pedagogical content knowledge (Sylva et al., 2004). Nonetheless, "enhancing young children's development is skilful work and for educators to do it well, they need training and support" (Evangelou, Sylva, Kyriacou, Wild, & Glenny, 2009, p. 5). A small-scale study (Archer & Siraj, 2015b) carried out in an inner London borough found that an intervention resulted in staff more confident in implementing a movement curriculum, which, in turn, enhanced children's movement experiences. Staff should, therefore, be appropriately trained and then provided with ongoing support to extend their knowledge and understanding as they progress through their careers. In this way, a "pedagogy for physical development" could become an effective reality.

MOVERS Sub-scale 3: Supporting physical activity and critical thinking

Sub-scale 3 of the MOVERS addresses the ways in which adults can support young children in their physical activity and critical thinking. Language plays an essential part in helping young children to meet their physical development needs. Language, in this context, refers to what is said as well as non-verbal interactions and, as such, is more complex than just speaking to children. Item 8 of the MOVERS identifies a range of vocabulary associated with body movement (Archer & Siraj, 2017); this includes:

- The sounds that may accompany movement, such as "whoosh" when coming down a slide or "whee" when swinging on a swing;
- Naming body parts;
- Prepositions, verbs and adverbs to enable children to describe what they are doing and to help them to follow instructions (e.g. can you quickly run and jump over that crate? Or how slowly can you crawl under that box?);
- Words associated with the expressive arts;
- Words to describe and explain performance (e.g. height, distance, time, speed).

Children may choose to move alone or with others, adults or peers, and on occasions their interactions may be non-verbal. They may sustain their movement interactions by responding to one another in non-verbal physical bodily movement. There are other times when thinking is sustained through language as "two or more individuals work together as they attempt to solve a problem, or clarify a concept, evaluate activities, or extend a narrative" (Siraj-Blatchford et al., 2002, p. 1). This is also applicable to those times when child-adult or child-child are involved in solving a problem related to physical activity and contribute to the thinking together, developing and extending their ideas. Sustaining movement conversations through language relevant to the child's movement explorations should include feelings, thoughts and emotions that go with it. Items 8, 9 and 10 in the MOVERS show a gradual progression towards excellent practice when staff respond with relevant and appropriate language; encourage children to communicate with each other; and support and sustain shared thinking (SST) while helping children to explore ideas, solve problems and make links in their learning.

MOVERS Sub-scale 4: Parents/carers and staff (Item 11: Staff inform families about children's physical development and the benefits to their learning, development and health)

Parents, carers, family members and Early Years practitioners play a key role in ensuring children's physical development needs are met. As was discussed in an earlier section, providing appropriate indoor and outdoor environments for young children to play and, in turn, to develop is important. Sub-scale 4 of the

MOVERS draws attention to more precise ways in which the adults responsible for the care of young children could help them achieve their physical development potential. Melhuish, Sylva, Sammons, Siraj-Blatchford, and Taggart (2001) and Melhuish et al. (2008) identify the home learning environment as having one of the greatest impacts on young children's development and it is, therefore, imperative that parents and carers are aware of this and of appropriate ways to support their children. Family members and carers could, for example, join young children in physical activities such as rough and tumble play, digging and planting flowers/vegetables, going on a bike ride, building sandcastles or taking them swimming. Such activities provide encouragement and stimulation for children's imagination and contribute to overall physical fitness and strength (Archer & Siraj, 2015a). When parents join children in these activities, opportunities arise to enjoy playful times together and strengthen bonds between them. Moreover, Macket (2004) identifies that enabling children to play outdoors is one of the best things that can be done for their health, well-being and future life chances, something that is explored further in Chapter 13, on Forest Schools. Early childhood settings have been identified as one "vehicle" through which information (regarding young children's physical development needs and appropriate ways of meeting these) could be conveyed to parents/carers (Desforges & Abouchaar, 2003; Siraj-Blatchford & Siraj-Blatchford, 2009; Sylva et al., 2004).

Thus, in assessing whether a childcare setting is sharing information with parents about their child's progress in this curriculum area and the benefits of appropriate and adequate physical development opportunities to their child's learning, development and health, the MOVERS seeks to address the following questions:

1. Are parents aware of the setting's educational aims and practices in this curriculum area?
2. Do staff feel sufficiently knowledgeable to talk to parents and advise them about encouraging their children to be more physically active at home, or to hold meetings with parents to discuss this area of their children's learning and development?
3. Are parents' views sought about the physical activity programme developed by the setting?
4. What do staff do to encourage parental involvement in physical development at the setting and at home?
5. Are they invited into the settings to see children engaging in movement activity and/or to organise physical activity fun days?

Conclusion

This chapter has outlined the importance of providing an environment that meets the physical development needs of young children. It has highlighted both the indoor and outdoor environment that is available for children to play and develop, and identified a range of age appropriate resources that could be provided. It was argued early on that modern societal norms have meant that children have less opportunities to be active and to engage in unsupervised, outdoor play than in the past and that this has partially necessitated a need for preschool provisions to fill a gap that historically was met more "naturally" for most children. The MOVERS draws attention to: the need for appropriate pedagogies; opportunities for expression; adequate training and continuous professional development (for practitioners); and good communication and sharing of knowledge between settings and parents/carers. It highlights what a setting is doing well as well as identifying what could be improved, and provides a tool for reflection and progress. For a child to develop socially, emotionally, cognitively and physically, they need effective Early Years pedagogues whose training and continuing professional development have equipped them with the necessary theory, knowledge, understanding and ability to put this into effective practice. Rising levels of mental health problems, obesity and declining levels of physical development among children today are the responsibility of us all. We need to ensure that children are provided with high quality environments and pedagogical practice. With increasing emphasis on measured outcomes and focussed targets on Literacy and maths, Early Years pedagogues are being pulled away from direct work with children. We must not lose sight of a secure knowledge base of child development, understanding and engagement in learning and retain an effective play-based approach to Early Years education. It is, therefore, imperative that we give attention to the body and its capabilities and influences on the brain. The brain and the body are inextricably linked and the experiences of the body shape the mind. As Goddard Blythe (2005, p. xv) warns, "A society that does not promote the sensory development of its younger generation is at the same time diminishing its overall intellectual capacity."

Summary of key points

- Young children need to move – it is vital to their health, well-being, learning and development.
- The indoor environment is as important as the outdoors when planning for movement and physical activity.
- Good quality training and professional development in PD are key to high quality pedagogical practice.
- The MOVERS can be used to evaluate settings and plan progressive steps towards improvement in this vital curriculum area prior to inspection.
- To support ongoing development in this curriculum area, refer to the book "Encouraging Physical Development through Movement-play" (Archer & Siraj, 2015a) for theory, implementation and Chief Medical Officers guidance.

Suggested further reading

Claxton, G. (2015). *Intelligence in the flesh. Why you mind need your body more than it thinks.* New Haven and London: Yale University Press.

Hannaford, C. (1995). *Smart moves. Why learning is not all in your head.* Arlington, VA: Great Ocean.

Kranowitz, C. S. (2005). *The out-of-sync child. Recognising and coping with sensory processing disorder.* New York, NY: A Skylight Press Book/A Perigee Book. Penguin.

Pre-school Learning Alliance. (2018). *Moving right from the start. The importance of physicality in the early years.* London: Pre-school Learning Alliance.

References

Archer, C., & Siraj, I. (2015a). *Encouraging physical development through movement-play.* Sage: London.

Archer, C., & Siraj, I. (2015b). Measuring the quality of movement-play in early childhood settings: Linking movement-play and neuroscience. *European Early Childhood Education Research Journal, 23*(1), 21–24.

Archer, C., & Siraj, I. (2017). *Movement environment rating scale (MOVERS) for 2–6-year-olds provision. Improving physical development through movement and physical activity.* London: Sage.

Derbyshire, D. (2007). How children lost the right to roam in four generations. *MailOnline.* Retrieved from https://www.dailymail.co.uk/news/article-462091/How-children-lost-right-roam-generations.html

Desforges, C, & Abouchaar, A. (2003). *The impact of parental involvement, parental support family education on pupil achievement and adjustment: A literature review.* Research Brief no: 433. Retrieved from http://www.fug.no/getfile.php/1203224.1542.ruequyevas/Forelderinvolvering+av+Charles+Deforges.pdf

Evangelou, M., Sylva, K., Kyriacou, M., Wild, M., & Glenny, G. (2009). *Early years learning and development: Literature review.* Research Report DCSF-RR176. London: Department for Children, Schools and Families.

Goddard Blythe, S. (2005). *The Well Balanced Child. Movement and early learning.* Stroud: Hawthorn Press.

Lamont, B. (2001). *Babies Naturally.* Retrieved from https://neurologicalreorganization.org/category/articles/page/2/

Macintyre, C., & McVitty, K. (2004). *Movement and learning in the early years: Supporting dyspraxia and other difficulties.* Sage: London.

Mackett, R. (2004). *Making children's lives more active.* London: Centre for Transport Studies, University College.

Melhuish, E. C., Sylva, K., Sammons, P., Siraj-Blatchford, I., & Taggart, B. (2001). *The Effective provision of pre-school education (EPPE) project*: Technical paper 7: Social/behavioural and cognitive development at 3–4 years in relation to family background. London: Institute of Education, University of London and DfEE.

Melhuish, E. C., Sylva, K., Sammons, P., Siraj-Blatchford, I., Taggart, P. & Phan, M. (2008). Effects of the home learning environment and pre-school centre experience upon literacy and numeracy development in early primary school. *Journal of Social Issues, 64,* 157–88.

Pretty, J., Angus, C., Bain, M., Barton, J., Gladwell, V., Hine, R., Sellens, M. (2009). *Nature, childhood, health and life pathways. Interdisciplinary.* Centre for Environment and Society (iCES) Occasional Paper 2009-2, University of Essex. Retrieved from http://www.essex.ac.uk/ces/esu/occ-papers.shtm

Siraj-Blatchford, I. (2009) Conceptualising progression in the pedagogy of play and sustained shared thinking in early childhood education: A Vygotskian perspective. *Education and Child Psychology, 26*(2), 77–89.

Siraj-Blatchford, I., & Siraj-Blatchford, J. (2009). *Improving children's attainment through a better quality of family-based support for early learning.* Early Years Research Review 2. London: Centre for Excellence and Outcomes in Children and Young People's Services (C4EO).

Siraj-Blatchford, I., Sylva, K., Muttock, R., Gilden, R., & Bell, D. (2002). *Researching effective pedagogy in the early years* (REPEY). Department for Education and Skills Research Report 356. HMSO: Norwich.

Sylva, K., Melhuish, E. C., Sammons, P., Siraj-Blatchford, I., & Taggart, B. (2012) *'Effective Pre-school, primary and secondary education project (EPPSE 3–14): Influences on students' development from age 11–14'.* Research Brief DFE-RB202. London: Department for Education.

Sylva, K., Melhuish, E., Sammons, P., Siraj-Blatchford, I., Taggart, B., & Elliot, K. (2004). *The effective provision of pre-school education (EPPE) project: Findings from pre-school to end of key stage 1.* Institute of Education, University of London, University of Oxford, Birkbeck, University of London and Sure Start for the Department for Education and Skills. Nottingham: DfES Publications.

Vygotsky, L. S. (1978). *Mind in society.* Cambridge, MA: Harvard University Press.

13

PHYSICAL DEVELOPMENT THROUGH OUTDOOR PLAY

The example of Forest School

Janine Coates

Personal reflection

I have spent much of the last decade working with children in various educational settings, whether as a practitioner or as researcher and, through this, I have learned a lot about early childhood. It wasn't until I had my own child four years ago, though, that I really started to think about what it means to be a child and about what makes childhood so great. Thinking back to my own childhood, I began to realise that what made my childhood great was being outdoors. I spent every minute I could adventuring into unchartered territory (at least to my mind, it was uncharted) and these are the times I remember most favourably. This made me think about the experiences of the many children I had worked with over the years, and how much of their physical activity came from Physical Education (PE) classes, and how so little of it came from exploring the world outside.

It was around this time that I came across a news article about Forest School. Reading about how children were climbing trees, building fires and running a-mock in the woods took me right back to my own childhood. Being an academic, I wanted to learn more about how playing in the woods might benefit children, and the rest, as they say, is history. This chapter presents some of what I've learned about Forest School over the last few years, presented, specifically, with physical development in mind.

Introduction

When we think about outdoor play amongst young children in educational settings, quite often our minds drift towards images of children playing in a playground with toys and on outdoor equipment such as climbing frames and slides. These kinds of play experiences are valuable to children, providing them with opportunity to negotiate new and sometimes challenging environments, and to play in meaningful ways with peers with little adult direction. However, for many children, outdoor play is limited to engagement with these sorts of "manufactured" environments. While any outdoor play is beneficial for children, research has shown that play in natural environments, such as those with green spaces, plant life, sand, water and animal habitats, is not only preferred by children (Taylor, Wiley, Kuo, & Sullivan, 1998) but also benefits children in a range of ways, including by reducing stress (Wells & Evans, 2003), improving mental well-being (Whitebread, 2017), promoting prosocial behaviour (Moore & Wong, 1997) and encouraging a range of different forms of play (Hughes, 2009). A study by Faber Taylor and Kuo (2011) even showed that playing in green spaces can help reduce symptoms related to attention-deficit hyperactivity disorder, especially when those spaces are open, like a meadow or woodland. Further, studies have shown that engagement in outdoor play is a consistent predictor of children's physical activity, particularly when they are engaged in unstructured free-play (Burdette, Whitaker & Daniels, 2004; Sallis, Prochaska, & Taylor, 2000).

In addition to this, a recent systematic literature review showed that certain types of outdoor play can be particularly beneficial to children. Brussoni et al. (2015) considered the relationship between risky outdoor play and children's health. Risky outdoor play refers to play which includes an element of risk or danger to the child, such as the risk of injury. These forms of play are often engaged in by children during unsupervised play, and can include activities like climbing trees, using tools, and unsupervised exploration of an environment, where there is a risk of becoming lost. This play often raises alarm bells for adults who are responsible for young children, and so, tends to be prevented. Brussoni et al. (2015), however, showed that risky outdoor play benefits children's emotional resilience, social functioning and physical health and well-being. They go on to argue that the provision of opportunities which encourage this kind of play should be promoted in settings which cater to young children.

Despite this, recent research has shown that children are playing outdoors much less than previous generations (Clements, 2004; Gray, 2011; Stone & Faulkner, 2014). This has been attributed to: changes in educational policy, which place more emphasis on academic skill development (Powell, 2009); increased use of digital technology (Clements, 2004); adult concern over children's safety (Valentine & McKendrick, 1997; Veitch, Bagley, Ball, & Salmon, 2006); and a reduction in the availability of outdoor spaces for children to play in (Veitch, Salmon & Ball, 2007). Therefore, settings which cater to young children are ideally placed to develop new opportunities which promote outdoor play, in various forms.

This chapter will provide an overview of an outdoor education initiative which focusses on play in natural environments: Forest School. It will discuss how Forest School, and similar enterprises, can help initiate opportunities for children to engage in physically active play to meet their physical development needs across a range of ages and enable them to confidently navigate challenging spaces and refine their gross and fine motor skills.

What is Forest School?

Forest School is an outdoor learning initiative which engages children in the natural environment through a range of practical activities. The Forest School process was first developed in the early 1990s when a group of early years educators at Bridgewater College in Somerset, the United Kingdom, observed early years provision while on a trip to Denmark and were struck by how the underlying Scandinavian philosophy of *Frulitsliv* or "free air life" was applied in these settings. In particular, they were interested in the focus on outdoor, child-centred learning through play. Using these principles, the team developed a BTech in Forest School, which was offered from 1995, and was predominantly targeted at early years practitioners; although Forest Schools currently span the age ranges, with most seen in early years and primary education settings. Since the Bridgewater training was developed, a number of new training providers offering Forest School practitioner training have been developed, all of which teach the same core values. These are outlined by the Forest School Association (FSA) – the professional body for Forest School practitioners. According to the FSA, the core principles of Forest School are that it:

• Is led by a qualified (Level 3) Forest School practitioner (see https://www. forestschoolassociation.org for information about Forest School training);
• Is a long-term process which includes contact with a woodland environment (preferably spanning different seasons);
• Follows a child-centred pedagogy where children learn about and manage risk;
• Integrates care for the natural environment;
• Has a high adult: child ratio and includes observations of learners to enable scaffolding of learning.

It is worth pointing out here that while traditionally a Forest School would include access to a woodland environment, many Forest Schools, particularly those in urban settings, do not. Indeed, several settings do not have access to a woodland space and instead use the available space they do have to develop a suitable Forest School setting. In many of the schools I have visited, this has included using space on school grounds where there are some trees, around which activities can be set out. Further, while prolonged engagement in the Forest School is encouraged, many providers are unable to access spaces year long, and so several forest schools run for between 6 and 12 weeks, where children will attend for a half or full day each week. In her book, *Forest School in Practice*, Sarah Knight presents a number of case studies demonstrating how Forest Schools might work in different environments, which gives a good overview of how different settings might adapt Forest School provision to meet their specific needs.

Using the principles set out earlier, Forest School aims to teach children a range of problem-solving and cooperation abilities as well as developing their confidence, motivation and self-esteem through a range of play-based learning opportunities (e.g. tree-climbing, den building, fire lighting, tool use, crafting using natural materials, free-play, etc.) (Knight, 2009; O'Brien, 2009). Fundamentally, Forest Schools provide children with the opportunity to engage in physically active, experiential learning in outdoor settings (O'Brien & Murray, 2007). This is underpinned by a play-pedagogy, where children engage in a range of adult- and child-initiated activity, but where they are encouraged to participate in ways which are meaningful and appropriate for their needs (Knight, 2009). Thus, Forest School is considered to be inclusive, and suitable for all learners. Further, children are encouraged to make decisions about their learning by being allowed freedom to dip in and out of activities, to engage in undirected play and to explore and engage their own curiosity for the natural environment (Ridgers, Knowles & Sayers, 2012).

Research which has explored the impact of Forest School on children's development has noted that children benefit through improved environmental awareness (Nawaz & Blackwell, 2014; Ridgers et al., 2012); increased physical activity, confidence, self-esteem and independence (O'Brien & Murray, 2005, Maynard, 2007); and improved child-adult relationships (Slade, Lowry, & Bland, 2013). Importantly, research also shows that children enjoy the experience, describing it as fun and exciting (Slade et al., 2013).

The remainder of this chapter will consider how Forest School can be used as a tool for facilitating children's physical development, by first considering how different activities offered in a Forest School might promote physical skill development; and then through a close look at how children conceptualise their physical skill development through their experiences of Forest School. This discussion is based around two case studies from a piece of research carried out with my colleague, Helena Pimlott-Wilson (see Coates & Pimlott-Wilson, 2018). First, however, we will consider how Forest School might map onto physical development and PE curricula.

How does Forest School map onto physical education and physical development?

First thing to say is, it doesn't – or at least, it doesn't purposefully map onto PE or the physical development guidelines in the early years. The teachers and Forest School practitioners that we've spoken to are quite clear that Forest School is not PE and I am yet to come across a school who uses Forest School specifically as a substitute for, or supplement to, PE. Indeed, in most cases, when asked "Why Forest School?" the majority of teachers and practitioners we have spoken to say that Forest School offers something more holistic in relation to child development, which goes beyond the teaching of academic or practical skills. Rather, Forest School is an inclusive framework which helps children to develop confidence, problem-solving and collaborative learning abilities in ways which are appropriate and meaningful to them, and which can be transferred into multiple spheres of learning (McCree & Cree, 2017). Being physically active and enhancing understanding about movement and physicality are part of the process of developing these abilities. This is underpinned by the central facet of Forest

School – play, which is naturally physical. Indeed, this is something practitioners are acutely aware of. While Forest School is not designed specifically to target children's physical development, the activities which children engage in provide ample opportunity for children to be physically active and, in turn, opportunities to develop physically. That being said, if we look closely at the objectives for physical development in the Early Years Foundation Stage (EYFS) and the Key Stage 1 curricula, we can begin to understand how activities which children engage in at Forest School might help to achieve those objectives.

Forest School and the EYFS work well together. Both are underpinned by a play-pedagogy where there is a balance between adult- and child-initiated play activity through which children learn (Wood, 2014). In relation to physical development, the EYFS states that a key aim is that children are able to "show good control and co-ordination in large and small movements. They move confidently in a range of ways, safely negotiating space. They handle equipment and tools effectively" (DfE, 2017, p. 11). Forest School provides children in the early years with plenty of opportunities to achieve these goals, through presenting children with a new and often challenging environment to negotiate; offering the opportunity to use tools effectively and safely; and to develop both fine and gross motor skills through the variety of activities presented. These include crafting to develop fine motor abilities, and games to develop gross motor skills, like balance and co-ordination. Further, the EYFS states that children should be given the opportunity to explore a range of environments, as well as opportunity to learn outside of the classroom, which again, Forest School provides opportunity for. Through these opportunities, children not only develop physical competencies which allow them to be active, but that also allow for the development of core skills which act as a foundation for future learning (e.g. hanging from tree branches strengthens the grip needed to write). This is explored in more detail in Case Study 1.

Case study 1: The suburban Primary School

Esthwaite Primary School[1] is a larger than average Primary School in the suburbs of a small market town. The head of the Foundation Year, a Foundation Year 2 (F2) class teacher, had recently completed her Forest School Level 3 training and had secured access to a small area of woodland in a larger wood, a short drive from the school. Our research was carried out with the first group of children to attend Forest School – the F2 class consisted of 28 children (aged 4 and 5). Due to the size of the group, they were split into two Forest School groups, where the first attended Forest School in the autumn term, and the second group attended in the 2017 autumn term (October–November). The Forest School was supported by a lunchtime supervisor from the school, and occurred over a 6-week period, where children attended the Forest School for a half day each week, where they would ordinarily be engaged in classroom activity.

Opportunities offered during this Forest School included:

- Den (re)building (see Figure 13.1);
- Using tools to make art from natural materials;
- Nature exploration/habitat exploration (minibeast and fungi hunting);
- Story-based woodland walks;
- Constructing "furniture" from natural materials;
- Free-play activity;
- Blindfold/eyes-closed trust games;
- Hide and Seek.

During this Forest School, children engaged in a number of activities, which indirectly targeted the development of a range of physical skills through play. When talking to the children about Forest School, many of the children talked about the extra opportunity they had during Forest School to be physically active when compared to being in a school environment, specifically the opportunity to run in a non-restrictive environment. What is interesting is that the children we spoke to were overtly

FIGURE 13.1   Den building during a Forest School session.

(*Continued*)

aware that running in a new and challenging environment came with additional risks they would need to be mindful of in order to navigate the environment successfully. This awareness was facilitated through the games initiated by the Forest School practitioner who encouraged children to engage all of their senses in order to negotiate the spaces. For example, children described a game of hide and seek, where the seeker would shout, "1, 2, 3 where are you?" and the hiding peers would call out to guide the seeker. This encouraged children to listen carefully for the calls of their peers, to translate those calls into directional information and to use this to successfully seek them out. Skills, such as acute listening skills, are useful for children and assist with the development of co-ordination abilities, through the integration of auditory perception and motor output. Engaging with multiple senses is particularly useful in physical development because many of the foundation skills needed for physical development rely on input from the sensory systems (Cheatum & Hammond, 2000).

Another game made use of sensory deprivation to facilitate the use of a range of senses to navigate the environment was an "eyes closed" game, similar to "blind man's bluff" – a game played whilst blindfolded, where the participants seek out their competitors using hearing and touch. One of the children, Lewis, describes this game:

> We done quite a lot of walking bumping into trees. Because we done this game and it was an eyes closed game and you had to not bump into a tree! It was really, really good.

Here, you can see that the objective of this game was to move through the environment using senses other than sight without falling or bumping into trees or other participants. Through the use of sight deprivation, children are encouraged to make use of other senses to understand the features of the environment and their movement through that environment, skills which are fundamental for the development of physical literacy, as described in Chapter 2. Further, these types of games not only assist with the development of co-ordination abilities but also help children develop proprioception, sensory processing and balance, among other skills, necessary for the development of gross motor skills.

While games such as these assist with gross motor skill development, the Forest School also included a range of activities attuned to the development of fine motor skills. If we look at craft activities, for example, children were given the opportunity to use various tools to create artwork. This included the use of saws to cut wood. Using a sharp tool requires precision in order to minimise risk of injury, and so, with the assistance of the Forest School practitioner, children were able to refine their accuracy at cutting materials to execute their desired design. The use of activities which help refine fine motor abilities was not limited to the use of tools but to the range of activities children engaged in, such as handling minibeasts, where children needed to be gentle so as not to harm them; in selecting small natural materials to make faces on trees; and through free-play activities where children used sticks to "draw" pictures on the forest floor.

The activities offered during this Forest School included multiple opportunities for children to refine their physical skills; however, this was achieved in a non-directive manner through the encouragement of children's play in a novel environment. These sorts of play opportunities can be delivered in settings outside of a woodland or Forest School, but for many of the children we spoke to, the natural environment itself, and the risk and challenge that unpredictable surfaces in the environment offered, provided them with a meaningful context to engage with the activities and games. Offering children opportunity to explore new and challenging environments is fundamental for developing their physical awareness and starting this early on in a child's life helps these skills to be refined and to develop over time.

If we turn our attention to the PE curricula for Key Stages 1 and beyond, we see similar, yet more specific aims (see Chapter 9). Whilst, within PE, there is more focus on competitive sporting activity, there are several broader aims that relate more generally to physical activity and physical competencies: First, that children develop competence to excel in a broad range of physical activities; that they are physically active for sustained periods of time; and finally, that they are able to lead healthy, active lives (DfE, 2013). Further, the curriculum suggests that children should engage in activities which build character and help to embed values such as fairness and respect.

Typically, as children move beyond the early years, the kinds of activities offered in Forest School will also change, often becoming more advanced. So, for example, where a four-year-old at Forest School might develop their balance through a sensory deprivation game using blindfolds, an eight-year-old might be given the opportunity to refine their balance skills on a slackline or tightrope. Moreover, where a younger child might do more independent or practitioner-supported activity, an older child will be encouraged to work more with their peers on collaborative activities. Therefore, whilst Forest School does not aim to be or replace traditional PE classes, it provides children with additional opportunity to develop, refine and confidently execute their skills in a novel and demanding environment. Moreover, evidence suggests that engagement with outdoor, natural spaces is a good predictor of later physical activity (Burdette et al., 2004). Case Study 2 explores this in more detail. It is worth noting that the children involved in Case Study 2 were 8–9 years old, but they demonstrated how Forest School can cater to the physical development of older young children. It also shows how the opportunities offered at Forest School can be adapted to suit the physical development needs of children as they grow.

Case study 2: The rural Village School

Rydal Primary School is a smaller than average Primary School in a rural commuter village. This school outsourced the Forest School provision to an independent Forest School practitioner who operated from a woodland area a short walk from the school. In this school, Forest School was an established part of the Year 4 curriculum (eight- and nine-year-old children), having been introduced a decade prior. This Forest School involved six weekly full day excursions during the autumn term and was supported by several Forest School practitioners, parent helpers and the Year 4 class teacher. This Forest School was more structured than the Forest School in Case Study 1. This was to accommodate the number of children in attendance (n = 30) and so involved six "stations" which children rotated around in groups. After the second week, activities become more child-led as children became familiar with the activities and environment. Ordinarily, the number of children at a Forest School would be much smaller, and activities more child-directed, but this is a good example of how it might work where large numbers of children are unavoidable.

Opportunities offered at this Forest School included:

- Fire lighting and cooking over an open fire;
- Rope course/tree-climbing;
- Shelter design and building;
- Scavenger hunt;
- Using tools to create crafts and objects (e.g. whittling using a knife to make a bow and arrow);
- Creating art from the natural environment (e.g. clay tree faces, leaf garlands);
- Habitat exploration;
- Woodland storytelling;
- Free-play.

In this Forest School, the activities involved the use of more advanced physical skills, typical of Forest Schools, which cater to young children beyond the Early Years (Key Stages 1 and 2). For example, children were presented with the opportunity to traverse a slackline (see Figure 13.2), using a long stick or peers to assist with balance; and there was a spiders' web rope course for them to negotiate. In addition to this, where the younger children in the first case study could rebuild an existing den using tree branches and sticks, these slightly older children were tasked with designing and building their own den using tarpaulin, ropes and branches from trees. The opportunities at this Forest School required children to

FIGURE 13.2 Child traversing a slackline.

work closely with their peers to succeed, and this instilled in them a sense of personal and social responsibility, which was mediated through the successful execution of these physical tasks. The development of social awareness through physical activity in a co-operative learning setting prepares children for successful teamworking in other school activities, and this was something discussed by the children at this school. In particular, they discussed how engaging in these activities allowed them to work with peers to develop negotiation and diplomacy skills underpinned by fairness, which they were then able to transfer into other settings, such as at home or school.

Children were aware of the increased opportunity to be active for a prolonged period, and for most of the children we spoke to, the only time they felt inactive was when they sat down to eat lunch. Apart from this, they described Forest School as moving from one physically active task to the next. Further, like the younger children, being in a woodland setting allowed these children to explore their physical awareness through navigating the new environment in which they were exploring.

(*Continued*)

Mai and Beau provide good examples of what this negotiation of the physical dimensions of learning meant to them:

> I knew as I was walking through the woods that I have to be more careful, that I don't want to get stung by nettles or trip over a twig. And I want to be more active and move my body parts but I don't want to go too active and be really silly.
>
> *(Mai)*

> You don't want to get hurt when you're doing something with knives and saws, and you also don't want to be like tripping over twigs and hurting yourself. But you're basically am going to, am going to have fun and all but you want to be safer because like you don't want to trip over something that's not yours and you don't want to hurt anything that's not yours.
>
> *(Beau)*

What was evident from our discussions with these children was that, beyond the development of practical physical skills, Forest School, and the challenging physical environment that Forest School presents to children, provides them with the opportunity to better understand how they use their body appropriately and effectively to minimise risk to themselves, their peers and the environment, thus facilitating the development of personal, social and environmental responsibility through increased physical awareness. Engaging in activities which carried some risk of injury to the self or others, if carried out carelessly, helped children to carefully consider how they used their body. By creating opportunities to both understand and experience the self in an unpredictable and challenging environment presents the opportunity to enhance physical development.

Conclusion

From these two case studies, we can see how Forest School provides children with opportunities to enhance their physical development through the range of play-based activities made available. While Forest School does not attempt to be PE, the ways in which it is delivered through very physical and often challenging tasks allow children to engage with new ways of being active and, through this, develop the skills associated with a physical development or PE curriculum.

This chapter has provided an overview of what Forest Schools are, ways in which they may contribute to a child's physical development and how they might map onto the PE of children. The key message from this is that physical development does not need to be directed or "taught." Rather, through providing children with a range of play opportunities in spaces which challenge them, physical competencies are vicariously and often unintendedly learned by children. Indeed, as stated by Clements (2004), outdoor play not only increases children's liking of physical activity but also improves children's overall physical development as well as stimulating cognitive, emotional and social development.

Summary of key points

- Outdoor play is a necessary tool for children's development.
- Forest School is an initiative which provides children with increased opportunity to play outdoors in a safe environment.
- Forest School presents opportunities for children to develop their physical literacy as well as gross and fine motor skills.
- Activities can be tailored to the age group in attendance with options for more advanced physical skills to be targeted.
- The outcomes of Forest School can help meet the objectives of physical development and PE curricula.

Suggested further readings

Knight, S. (2016). *Forest School in practice for all ages*. London: Sage.
O'Brien, L. (2009). Learning outdoors: The Forest School approach. *Education 3–13, 37*(1), 45–60.

Note

1 Note pseudonyms for both the schools and children have been used to protect the identity of the children involved in this research.

References

Brussoni, M., Gibbons, R., Gray, C., Ishikawa, T., Sandseter, E. B. H., Bienenstock, A., & Pickett, W. (2015). What is the relationship between risky outdoor play and health in children? A systematic review. *International Journal of Environmental Research and Public Health, 12*(6), 6423–6454.

Burdette, H. L., Whitaker, R. C., & Daniels, S. R. (2004). Parental report of outdoor playtime as a measure of physical activity in preschool-aged children. *Archives of Pediatrics & Adolescent Medicine, 158*(4), 353–357.

Cheatum, B. A., & Hammond, A. A. (2000). *Physical activities for improving children's learning and behaviour: A guide to sensory motor development*. Champaign, IL: Human Kinetics.

Clements, R. (2004). An investigation of the status of outdoor play. *Contemporary Issues in Early Childhood, 5*(1), 68–80.

Coates, J., & Pimlott-Wilson, H. (2018). Learning while playing: Children's Forest School experiences in the United Kingdom. *British Educational Research Journal*. doi:10.1002/berj.3491

DfE (2013). National Curriculum in England: Physical education programmes of study: key stages 1 and 2. London: DfE.

Department for Education (DfE), (2017). Statutory framework for the early years foundation stage Setting the standards for learning, development and care for children from birth to five. London: DfE.

Faber Taylor, A., & Kuo, F. E. (2011). Could exposure to everyday green spaces help treat ADHD? Evidence from children's play settings. *Applied Psychology: Health and Well-Being, 3*(3), 281–303.

Gray, P. (2011). The decline of play and the rise of psychopathology in children and adolescents. *American Journal of Play, 3*(4), 443–463.

Hughes, F. P. (2009). *Children, play, and development.* London: Sage.

Knight, S. (2009). *Forest schools and outdoor learning in the early years.* London: Sage.

Maynard, T. (2007). Forest Schools in Great Britain: An initial exploration. *Contemporary Issues in Early Childhood, 8*(4), 320–331.

McCree, M., & Cree, J. (2017). Forest School: Core principles in changing times. In S. Waite (Ed.), *Children learning outside the classroom.* London: Sage.

Moore, R. C. & Wong, H. H. (1997). *Natural learning: The life history of an environmental schoolyard.* Berkeley, CA: MIG.

Nawaz, H., & Blackwell, S. (2014). Perceptions about forest schools: Encouraging and promoting Archimedes Forest Schools. *Educational Research and Reviews, 9*(15), 498.

O'Brien, L. (2009). Learning outdoors: The Forest School approach. *Education 3–13, 37*(1), 45–60.

O'Brien, L., & Murray, R. (2007). Forest School and its impacts on young children: Case studies in Britain. *Urban Forestry & Urban Greening, 6*(4), 249–265.

Powell, S. (2009). The value of play: constructions of play in government policy in England. *Children & Society, 23*(1), 29–42.

Ridgers, N. D., Knowles, Z. R., & Sayers, J. (2012). Encouraging play in the natural environment: A child-focused case study of Forest School. *Children's Geographies, 10*(1), 49–65.

Sallis, J. F., Prochaska, J. J., & Taylor, W. C. (2000). A review of correlates of physical activity of children and adolescents. *Medicine & Science in Sports & Exercise, 32*(5), 963–975.

Slade, M., Lowery, C., & Bland, K. (2013). Evaluating the impact of Forest Schools: A collaboration between a university and a primary school. *Support for Learning, 28*(2), 66–72.

Stone, M. R., & Faulkner, G. E. (2014). Outdoor play in children: Associations with objectively-measured physical activity, sedentary behaviour and weight status. *Preventive Medicine, 65,* 122–127.

Taylor, A. F., Wiley, A., Kuo, F. E., & Sullivan, W. C. (1998). Growing up in the inner city: Green spaces as places to grow. *Environment and Behaviour, 30*(1), 3–27.

Valentine, G., & McKendrick, J. (1997). Children's outdoor play: Exploring parental concerns about children's safety and the changing nature of childhood. *Geoforum, 28*(2), 219–235.

Veitch, J., Bagley, S., Ball, K., & Salmon, J. (2006). Where do children usually play? A qualitative study of parents' perceptions of influences on children's active free-play. *Health & Place, 12*(4), 383–393.

Veitch, J., Salmon, J., & Ball, K. (2007). Children's active free play in local neighborhoods: A behavioral mapping study. *Health Education Research, 23*(5), 870–879.

Wells, N. M., & Evans, G. W. (2003). Nearby nature: A buffer of life stress among rural children. *Environment and Behaviour, 35*(3), 311–330.

Whitebread, D. (2017). Free play and children's mental health. *The Lancet Child & Adolescent Health, 1*(3), 167–169.

Wood, E. (2014). The play-pedagogy interface in contemporary debates. In L. Brooker, M. Blaise, & S. Edwards (Eds.), *The Sage handbook of play and learning in early childhood* (145–156). London: Sage Publications.

14

ENHANCING PHYSICAL DEVELOPMENT THROUGH PLAY

Pat Preedy

Personal reflection

I have worked in education for over 40 years as a teacher, head teacher, inspector and researcher. As head of one of the first Beacon schools in the United Kingdom, I became interested in finding out what the research evidence suggests makes a difference to children's learning. I was delighted when Professor Peter Tymms from the Centre for Evaluation and Monitoring (University of Durham) invited me to be part of the team that developed PIPS (Performance Indicators in Primary Schools). Having completed my PhD in twin studies, I got to know Dr Rebecca Duncombe, who was a mother of twins and a PE specialist working at Loughborough University. We discussed my concerns about gaps in the Early Years Foundation Stage and weaknesses in the Early Years Foundation Stage Profile assessments. This led us to develop the "Movement for Learning" Project, which highlighted how children's physical development has declined, particularly during the past ten years, and how a specific intervention programme can enable children to develop the balance, gross and fine motor skills that they need for effective learning. At the same time, I was also working with Dr Kay Sanderson on the "Parents and Carers as Play Partners" Project through Middlesex University (Dubai) and have continued to focus on meeting the needs of young children.

The world has changed and is rapidly changing. Children are moving less, eating more and experiencing the impact of a digital revolution. This chapter draws together my work as an early childhood specialist and researcher into physical development and play – key elements required for children's development and learning.

Introduction

Children around the world play, even in circumstances that are extremely challenging, such as war or deprivation. Play is essential for the healthy physical, social, emotional and cognitive development of children and is considered to be so important for children that it is included in the United Nations Convention on the Rights of the Child (1990). For example, Article 31, part 1, p. 10 states that "parties recognise the right of the child to rest and leisure, to engage in play and recreational activities appropriate to the age of the child and to participate freely in cultural life and the arts." Although Article 31 highlights the rights of the child to play and engage in recreational activities, the right of the child to move and develop physically is implicit. Knowing how important movement is to cognitive and all-round development, perhaps it is time to re-word the Article to include: *enabling the child to engage in play, physical and recreational activities appropriate to the age of the child.*

On the surface, children's play may seem to be simple. However, Hughes (2012), a leading play theorist and practitioner in the United Kingdom, suggests that there are at least 16 different play types, displayed by children including social, socio-dramatic, rough-and-tumble, exploratory, object, creative, communication, deep, recapitulative, symbolic, fantasy, dramatic, imaginative, locomotor, mastery and role play. Erikson (1963) highlighted the "make-believe" element of play which enables children to learn about their social world and their cultural role within it. He gave great emphasis to play based on the recognition that young children have limited ability to communicate their problems in the way adults may.

There has been much written about how play situations provide opportunities for children to develop socially and emotionally but there is much less information about how play supports children's physical development and enables them to develop balance, gross and fine motor skills and the mature postural reflexes needed to automatically maintain the body's position relative to gravity. The focus of this chapter is to consider the importance of play to children's physical development with particular reference to "The Parents and Carers as Play Partners Project" developed by Dr Kay Sanderson and myself through Middlesex University (Dubai).

How is play linked to physical development?

When babies are born, they spend a great deal of time sleeping and feeding. Through play and movement, the baby's brain makes synaptic connections using information provided through the sensory systems. It takes 9–12 months to develop the mobility skills needed for independent living and life. Early exploratory movements and interactions with people are the beginnings of play enabling the baby to learn and make sense of the world (see Figure 14.1). This very informal and primitive form of play is, nonetheless, essential for a baby's overall development. The following sections detail the contribution that play could have to physical development as babies and young children pass through different ages and stages.

FIGURE 14.1 Early exploratory movements and interactions with people are the beginnings of play.

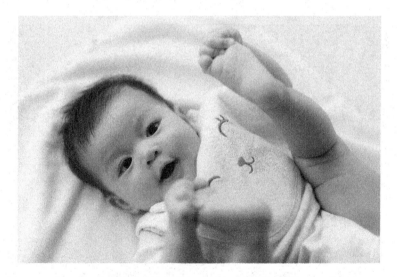

FIGURE 14.2 Playing with your hands and feet helps to develop body awareness (proprioception) as well as gross and fine motor control.

By about two months, the baby can smile and will react to noises and faces made by adults. At about this time, the baby also discovers her hands and will spend time watching them move and sticking them into her mouth (Figure 14.2). From about three months of age, the baby becomes much more aware of the world around her and begins to recognise and react to people when they enter the room. At this stage, it is important to turn down background noise, so the baby can "tune in" to the language being used by the adult. Using small toys to play with the baby encourages him/her to develop his/her body awareness and hand-eye co-ordination, which will later become important components of overall physical development. Whilst play at this age is still somewhat removed from a more conventional view of play, it marks the start of both early interactions with other people and a developing enjoyment of "toys," both of which will be important as the baby passes through each developmental stage, and opportunities to interact with others and objects become more frequent and often sought after.

Although it is important to put babies on their backs to sleep, early play experiences also need to provide opportunities for children to be on their fronts (tummy time) and to play on the floor (see Figure 14.3). This enables the baby to move all of his or her limbs including naturally rolling over on to the tummy. The following picture helps to illustrate how floor time is also play time and may enable all-round physical development. Playing with the baby on the floor encourages him or her to naturally practise the movements needed in the right sequence for cognitive development. Spending long periods of time restricted in chairs, walkers and buggies prevents opportunities for babies to progress through the developmental stages they need to.

FIGURE 14.3   Tummy time play enables babies to move all of their limbs and enables them to roll over.

By about five months, the baby should be able to sit up on his or her own. She will bang toys that make a noise and should know how to use a rattle. As the baby interacts with toys (stretching out to reach for things or moving toys about, for example), she or he is building core strength, postural control, balance, and gross and fine motor skills (see Figure 14.4).

FIGURE 14.4 Playing on the floor enables the baby to develop postural control and core body strength.

   From 6 to 12 months, the baby uses a pincer grip (thumb and first finger) to pick things up (see Figure 14.5). This movement is essential for inhibiting the palmar grip that a baby is born with but that restricts the thumb by enclosing it inside the fingers when a fist is made. Children encouraged to play on the floor will spend long periods of time picking up the tiniest items and examining them. Playing with small toys and "posting" objects through holes enable the child to drop and pick up toys and to turn the pages of a book.

FIGURE 14.5 A mature pincer grip enables the young child to pick up and manipulate objects.

At this stage, floor time is particularly important as it enables rolling, commando crawling and creeping on all fours (see Figure 14.6). Play that encourages these movements enables the baby to control and integrate movements from left to right and top to bottom.

FIGURE 14.6   Floor time enables a baby to find the position required to crawl.

From one to two years, play involves further development and refinement of fine motor skills and hand-eye co-ordination. The child should be able to build a tower with small blocks (see Figure 14.7), put pegs into a pegboard, scribble, paint with strokes, manipulate play dough, turn knobs, drink from a cup and eat a variety of textured food (see Figure 14.8).

FIGURE 14.7   Building a small tower with blocks.

If the child has had sufficient opportunities to play and move, by three he or she will be able to hold a crayon with the thumb and forefinger (not fist), copy a circle, cross and square and may even be able to write his or her first name. Walking becomes a smooth movement with the ability to turn corners and to stop without sitting down. Climbing without assistance, running and propelling a tricycle enable the child to further refine and develop gross and fine motor movements.

FIGURE 14.8   Good hand-eye coordination and proprioception are needed to feed oneself.

During the Reception Year of school (four to five years), many children can copy letters and write their family name. They can dress and undress independently, use scissors and bring their thumbs into opposition with each finger in turn. Running around obstacles, balancing on tip-toes, hopping, jumping, skipping forward and catching a ball extend both the play and opportunities for physical development.

It is important to know the stages of child development in order to provide the child with the play opportunities needed for physical, social, emotional and intellectual development. As has been outlined in this section, play is important for all aspects of a child's development, not least his or her physical development. Despite this, providing sufficient opportunities for play can be challenging for practitioners and parents.

Barriers to play

The play opportunities that parents and carers provide for their children are influenced by cultural and societal norms, values and beliefs. There can be significant barriers preventing children from developing physically and cognitively through play. Barriers to physical development are listed and explained in a number of the chapters within this book, and two barriers that have particular significance to play are added: the increased use of technology and the use of nannies in the home (this is particularly relevant to the play study we conducted in Dubai and outlined later in this chapter).

Technology – barrier or learning tool?

Common Sense Media (2011) reported that approximately 72% of iPad applications in the Educational Category are marketed for pre-schoolers and these applications frequently claim an educational value for young children. This may be so but the impact on movement and active play opportunities should not be overlooked (especially in an age group who, arguably, do not need to be starting formal education). The following statistics provide much food for thought:

- 60% of parents do not supervise their child's technology use;
- In a typical day, children consume just over three hours of media. This includes computer use, cell phone use, tablet use, music and reading. Two thirds of this time is spent with *screen media* (TV, computers, the Internet, etc.) while reading is less than 20 minutes per day;
- 75% of children are allowed technology in their bedrooms (www.common sensemedia.org).

A range of research (Sigman, 2017) is now indicating that excessive screen time is linked to obesity, poor sleep, language delays and inattention. Recommendations vary regarding the amount of screen time that should be allowed for children, and there is a growing consensus that children under two years of age should not be allowed screen time at all and that children aged between two and five should be limited to no more than an hour a day in total. This information highlights the importance of managing and monitoring technology use by our young children. We need to ask ourselves:

- What learning opportunities are being provided?
- Is time spent on devices at the expense of active and creative play that enables children to develop physically, socially, emotionally and intellectually as nature intended?

There are some positive studies published citing the benefits of hand-held devices in developing literacy skills for children experiencing disability (Flewitt, Kucirkova, & Messer, 2014). However, where technology use is found to be beneficial, this is frequently linked to adult support and interactions with the child, rather than the child engaging with technology in isolation.

Childcare – support or barrier?

In the Gulf Region (the location of the Parents and Carers as Play Partners study reported later in this chapter), many local and expatriate families employ housemaids and nannies to help with childcare and life in the family home. Many parents do not have extended families to call upon for help and are left with no alternative but to employ housemaids/nannies.

Most of the female workers employed as housemaids and nannies originate from Sri Lanka, Philippines, India and African sub-continent. They usually live in the family home or in an adjacent maid's room, and many work long hours for little money. The majority are untrained and unqualified, lacking the experience, skills and knowledge to meet the physical and emotional needs of babies and young children. All too often electronic hand-held devices and the television are used to keep children occupied. Research is limited in this area, but a study published in the *Journal of Childhood Research* conducted in 2005 on housemaids and nannies indicated that 58% of children under the age of 3 in the region spend on average between 30 and 70 hours a week with housemaids and nannies. The report stated that, although not always a positive or enriching experience, there was an economic benefit to parents using their domestic help as childcare.

Although the study was located in the UAE, it prompts the question, *can childminding and day care settings negatively impact the physical and cognitive development of children?* For example, in the United Kingdom parents of two-year-olds can now claim 30 free hours per week of early education and childcare. Steve Biddulph, an Australian psychologist (Biddulph, 2015), refers to a range of studies including those in the United Kingdom and United States indicating that children younger than three in nurseries are at risk of damaging their mental health. Levels of cortisol reach double the level of when the child is at home and are an indicator of stress (which may lead to aggression, antisocial behaviour and the inability to develop close relationships later in life). He particularly considers inexperienced staff with minimal qualifications as a strong contributory factor to children's emotional deprivation and stress.

The Parents as Play Partners project

When Dr Rebecca Duncombe and I conducted the *Movement for Learning* project (Duncombe & Preedy, 2018), we found that most children in our sample started school with limited gross and fine motor skills and a high level of retained primitive/baby reflexes. The children simply did not have the skills necessary for effective learning particularly for reading and writing. Understanding how play incorporates movements necessary for the development of balance and gross and fine motor movements is important for parents, practitioners and teachers. It is essential that all those caring for young children enable them to have strong and secure attachments with play opportunities enabling them to develop physically, socially, emotionally and intellectually.

The Parents as Play Partners research, conducted by Kay Sanderson and me, was based in the UAE and attempted to address the concerns outlined earlier. As many children were spending large amounts of time with housemaids/nannies, we wanted to provide parents with an easy method of engaging with their children rather than leaving childcare almost entirely to the maid or nanny. We introduced parents to the "ten-minute rule," limiting the time expected for each Play Partners session to ten minutes – providing a little of the right input every day (see Figure 14.9). In reality,

FIGURE 14.9 Providing a little of the right input every day can have a huge impact.

once parents experienced the benefits of playing with their children as Play Partners they extended the time allocation, encouraging their nannies and housemaids to also adopt the method. Although the focus of this research project is on supporting parents in using the Play Partners method, it is intended to expand the project as part of training for nannies and housemaids in the region. Likewise, it has applicability and relevance to parents and carers across the world.

The project focussed on four families who had all been residents within the UAE for many years. All of the children in the study attended nursery school. Two of the sample group had an older sibling. All parents involved in the study worked and had assistance with childcare within the home. Each of the families involved had volunteered independently of each other. Taking this into account, families from different nationalities and socio-economic groups were selected to provide a balanced representation, as detailed in the following:

Participants

Table 14.1 details the participants in the study:

TABLE 14.1 Participants in the Parents as Play Partners project

Nationality of family	Child's age	Parental involvement	Siblings	Environment	Location
Greek	2 years, 1 month	Both	No	Apartment	Dubai
Egyptian	2 years, 6 months	Both	Yes (older brother)	Villa	Dubai
British	2 years	Both	Yes (older brother)	Villa	Dubai
Nigerian	2 years, 4 months	Both	No	Bedsit	Dubai

The families who volunteered to take part in the study did so for various reasons including:

- To improve the communication of their child;
- To change some unruly behaviours and attitudes of their child;
- To strengthen the attachment between themselves and their child;
- To develop engagement and play skills between themselves and their child.

The resource

A booklet was designed for parents in electronic form and hard copy detailing the importance of play as well as the "Play Partners" method. This included the importance of movement and how to use everyday activities and natural resources to engage with their child through play. A number of sections were covered in the booklet including: the importance of play; Parents as Play Partners; using everyday activities as play opportunities; providing play opportunities at home; and being active together.

Research methods

The research included the following:

- Pre-questionnaires administered to families to obtain general information about the family unit and determine the interpretation of play by parents;
- Pre-intervention filming (15 minutes) to capture the ways in which parents played with their children prior to seeing the "Parents as Play Partners" booklet. No guidance was given to the child or the parents in terms of what to play and how to play, so communication, engagement and attachment were all under the control of the child and the parents;
- Post-intervention filming. Following the first session of filming, one parent was taken aside and the *Parents as Play Partners* booklet was explained to them (20–30 minutes) and the activities that would form the intervention. Whilst this was taking place, the other parent was asked to distract the child, so that all plastic and technological items could be removed from the play area being filmed. These toys and games were replaced with a selection of household objects and items and materials found naturally in the home, for example; pans, spoons, socks, baskets, cushions, throws and dried food items such as pasta and beans. In addition, all technology was removed from the play area - all mobile devices had to be turned off and hidden and televisions switched off. A second session of play was then filmed. The play on this occasion was to be led by the child, with the parent communicating, joining in the play and offering encouragement – at no time were they to take the lead. Types of play activity included dinners

being made, dens being built, food being created, washing being emptied, hide and seek within boxes and reading in tents made from throws over table and chairs;

- Diaries or blogs;
- Interviews;
- Post-questionnaire.

Findings

The findings from this research were, on the whole, positive and indicated that the "Parents as Play Partners" resource was effective in increasing both the quality of play and time parents spent actively playing with their child. Figure 14.10, for example, shows a child taking the lead in a play session.

FIGURE 14.10 The child takes the lead, and the parent joins in the play as a partner.

Findings from the pre-questionnaire

The questionnaire administered at the start of the research (i.e. before the play intervention) potentially reflects the understandings and views of wider society in the UAE and internationally, and is summarised in Table 14.2.

TABLE 14.2 Parents' responses to the pre-questionnaire

1	What do you understand by play?	All answers referred to children using play as part of their development and learning – particularly language development. Physical development was not mentioned.
2	How important do you think it is for children to play?	All agreed it was very important.
3	What sort of play does your child engage in?	All responses involved toys, balls, cars and anything available.
4	Who is involved in your child's play?	This had a mixed response: nursery staff, nanny, friends, teachers, mother and father.
5	What does your child enjoy playing with?	Commercial toys/media.

Interestingly none of the respondents mentioned home-made learning materials or activities and materials centred around what is available at home or in the garden. This was reflected in the analysis of the pre-intervention videos.

Findings from the pre-intervention videos

During the home visit, parents were asked to play with their child as they would normally do. The play areas were crowded with plastic toys both big and small, TV, musical instruments, books and a variety of toys and games. The footage was analysed by Dr Jaqueline Harding from Middlesex University using an observation schedule that she had developed in 2015 as part of her PhD. The following were observed:

- The children's body language revealed high levels of frustration and anxiety;
- Play was individual although parents were present;
- Concentration was limited – children drifted from toy to game to book to toy and no sustained play took place;
- Anxiety showed on parents' and children's faces, tantrums started and aggressive behaviour was sometimes displayed – hitting with cars and throwing toys;
- Parents tried to control situations and offer another toy to replace the one thrown, and the same action occurred again and again;
- All four children were in tears, showing aggression by the end of the 10 minutes with parents looking exhausted and frustrated.

Findings from the post-intervention videos

When the parents began to use the play partners method the following changes were highlighted:

- The children's body language revealed high levels of engagement, activity and involvement in the play with their parents;
- Children turned their trunk towards parents and a close triangle was formed between parents, object (of play) and child;
- Body movements by parents and children became more purposeful suggesting a greater depth of interest and involvement in the activity;
- In terms of "flow and immersion in the moment" (Harding, 2014) all children exhibited signs of deep play or "wallowing in play" (Bruce, 1996) in close proximity to their parents;
- Frequently, footage clearly revealed the compelling nature of conceptual development through play involving trajectory; enveloping; transforming; transporting;
- Increased frequency of moments of spontaneous laughter from parents and children.

The change in the quality of engagement and the relationship between parents and children were striking after the intervention. Through play, parents and children could engage for sustained periods of time in a relaxed and meaningful way (see Figure 14.11). Although filming was stopped after the allocated time, the children and parents were so engaged in a state of play that they continued oblivious that filming had ceased.

FIGURE 14.11 Through play, parents and children could engage for sustained periods of time in a relaxed and meaningful way. Developing posture and fine motor control is a natural part of play.

Findings from the post-intervention questionnaires and interviews

The post-questionnaire focussed predominantly on the *Parents as Play Partners* module and the project itself. The first four questions related to the ease of use of the module and if it was understandable. All agreed that the module had been easy to use and understand. A key question, which the researchers were interested to review, concerned the impact of the module and the answers are outlined in Table 14.3:

TABLE 14.3 Impact of the Parents as Play Partners project on families

	Family 1	Family 2	Family 3	Family 4
Yourself	It has helped me to consciously create more time for play with my son and help him learn every day.	Very positively, new ideas, approaches. Happy to make something more creative, happy to see our son being more creatively and constructively entertained.	I want to change a bit of my day to be more involved in playing.	I feel less tired and stressed. I make time to play and read and life is better, I have my maid read also, things are better. I can now spend time with my younger son.
Your child	It has helped our son to play more and be confident to try new things and to play with other kids nicely and share.	Very positively. He can now engage with us more effectively and us with him. There is a better sense of continuity between home and pre-school.	He is so happy, he loves his new den and his sock puppets and bath times are so much fun with the kitchen utensils.	He is talking so much more and is not aggressive any more. The school is happy with him.
Your spouse	It has helped him learn how to play more and create time for our son.	Very positive, quality time spent as a family instead of one on one.	Very happy, he has made dens in the bedroom and now they read every night together, it is wonderful!	He now plays with our children as he has ideas. They make paper aeroplanes and models together.

(Continued)

	Family 1	Family 2	Family 3	Family 4
Your family	We all had fun playing together and it helped us to come up with new ideas and things to do every day.	Very positively, quality time is spent together, more creativity, more enjoyable, more productive, created some time for togetherness.	We are happy and thank God that we found you. Our home is full of paintings and we have less and less tantrums.	It was an amazing experience for our little family. Thank you for enlightening us through it. We definitely have a different perspective to playing now!

Findings from the diary entries

The diary entries were equally positive about the resource, and a few illustrative entries have been listed in the following:

> He loves reading the book with the penguin travelling in an umbrella, so we thought it would be a great idea to make an umbrella today. We started off for an umbrella, but, along the way he decided to create a hat instead. We then played the game to keep the hat on our heads for as long as possible, this was really good fun!!!

> Today daddy and me played let's cook dinner together. I learnt how to use the knife and I chopped up the vegetables. Our little chef in the making, amazing!

> We made a den from an old curtain. My son didn't want me to go out of it! He loved spending time with me in there even if we are just sitting doing nothing! But as a change it is the only place he lets me hold a book to read it for him for more than two minutes!!

> Dressing up, both my boys (6 and 2.6) wore my high heel shoes and baby blankets as capes to pretend to be Elsa with ice paws from Frozen! Yes, boys like Frozen movie too. My little one came to say a lot of new words as he played pretending, examples; ice, here I am, anyway, let it go, was so much fun, we laughed lots.

> We had a beautiful day today. The weather was perfect and we spent the whole day outdoors strolling around the city. The beautiful day was complete with my son and his dad playing puppet socks in the bath, he loves them and talks so much when using them!

What next for the project?

Following on from the success of the pilot study, the *Parents as Play Partners* findings were shared at the BSME (British Schools of the Middle East) conference in Qatar 2016. The project has been extended through workshops organised by schools within the UAE and is now available free to schools who register at www.playpartnersproject.co.uk.

Conclusion

Despite all of the research into the benefits of play, both broadly and in relation to physical development, we are still having to justify the role of play in early childhood provision. This book highlights the physical development needs of young children and this chapter has illustrated the contribution of play to helping children reach their physical development potential.

In addition, the research presented earlier illustrates the simplicity and importance of engaging in effective play opportunities. Being a "play partner" enables children to engage in sustained activity that is led by their needs. The floor, natural everyday materials and a little time (as little as 10 minutes a day) are all that are needed (see Figure 14.12).

FIGURE 14.12 Play does not need expensive equipment.

The challenge for parents is how to remove barriers to enable them to engage with their children within what is often a busy and challenging life. *The Parents as Play Partners* project gives parents an easy-to-use tool that is inexpensive and not time-consuming. Becoming play partners enables them to engage with their children rather than being a supervisor or instructor. They are able to tune in to their children's interests and extend them, deepening the relationship as well as enhancing the child's physical and cognitive development.

Summary of key points

- Play is essential for the healthy physical, social, emotional and cognitive development of children and is considered to be so important for children that it is included in the United Nations Convention on the Rights of the Child (1990).
- It is important to provide opportunities for play and movement in order that a baby/child can complete the necessary stages of physical development that are directly linked to later cognitive development.
- Early exploratory movements and interactions with people are the beginnings of play, enabling the baby to learn and make sense of the world. This very informal and primitive form of play is essential for a baby's overall development.
- The Parents and Carers as Play Partners Project highlighted that there can be barriers to play including the lack of time and the impact of technology and childcare.
- Parents under pressure to work long hours were pleased to find that just 10 minutes a day being a play partner with their children could have an enormous impact on the relationship they had with their children. The focus on natural materials and opportunities for child-led play indoors and outdoors enabled children to be physically active and to lay the foundations for successful learning.
- The challenge is to ensure that parents, carers and all those responsible for young children know the importance of play and movement to children's all-round development and learning.

Suggested further reading

Brown, S. (2010). *Play: How it shapes the brain, opens the imagination and invigorates the soul*. London: Penguin.
Duncombe, R., & Preedy, P. (2018). Movement for learning. In P. Preedy, K. Sanderson, & C. Ball (Eds.), *Early childhood redefined: Reflections and recommendations on the impact of start right*. Oxford: Routledge.
Moyles, J. (2013). *Play and early years: Birth-to-seven-years*. Cardiff: Play Wales.

References

Athey, C. (2007). *Extending thought in young children: A parent teacher partnership*. New York, NY: Sage.
Biddulph, S. (2015). *The Complete Secrets of Happy Children*. Berwick-upon-Tweed: Martins the Printers Ltd.
Bruce. T. (1996). *Helping Young Children to Play*. London: Hodder and Stoughton.

Duncombe, R., & Preedy, P. (2018). Movement for learning. In P. Preedy, K. Sanderson, & C. Ball (Eds.), *Early childhood redefined: Reflections and recommendations on the impact of start right.* Oxford: Routledge.

Erikson, E. (1963). *Childhood and Society.* New York: W.W. Norton and Company.

Common Sense Media (2011). www.commonsensemedia.org

Harding, J. (2014). *The Institute of Maternal and Child Health (and wellbeing).* Retrieved from https://prezi.com/-nv99m11kqca/the-institute-of-maternal-and-child-health-and-wellbeing/

Flewitt, R., Kucirkova, N. & Messer, D. (2014). Touching the virtual; touching the real: iPads and enabling literacy for students experiencing disability. *Autism Journal of Language and Literacy,* 37 (2), 107–116.

Hughes, B. (2012). *Evolutionary playwork.* London: Routledge.

Moyles, J. (2013). *Play and early years: Birth-to-seven-years.* Cardiff: Play Wales.

Sigman, A. (2017). *Screen dependency disorders: A new challenge for child neurology.* JICNA. Retrieved from http://jicna.org/index.php/journal/article/view/67. ISSN 2410-6410

15

PHYSICAL DEVELOPMENT PROGRAMMES AND APPROACHES

Content and impact

Rebecca Duncombe, Pat Preedy, Cathy Parvin,
Kim Pott and Ruth Smith

Personal reflection (Rebecca Duncombe)

I was asked to present some of the "Movement for Learning" data (a research project I conducted in collaboration with Dr Pat Preedy) at a conference on Early Years Physical Development in 2017. I outlined the key features of the programme and presented some of our preliminary impact data. In doing so, I highlighted that Movement for Learning was not Physical Education (PE) and therefore did not share many of the features that people working in this area might expect to see. This was the whole point. Movement for Learning was never designed to replace PE; rather, it was meant to enable children to develop the physical skills that they needed to do well in the classroom and later in PE.

An additional presentation and a number of workshops followed my own. As I listened and participated in these later sessions, two things struck me: first, there are many different ways in which to provide effective physical development opportunities for young children and, second, it must be hard for practitioners and parents to choose the "best" or most appropriate approach for the child or children in their care or setting. I later approached two of these speakers (Ruth Smith and Kim Pott) to ask them to contribute to this chapter. The purpose of this chapter is, therefore, to outline four different approaches (two movement interventions, one music and movement class and one school's relatively novel approach to physical development in the Early Years). Additionally (and where possible) impact data or illustrative quotes are provided to help practitioners and parents establish which approach or programme may be most relevant to them. Whilst Movement for Learning has taken over my life in recent years and I have seen the positive impact that it has had on young children, I have always been careful never to portray it as the best or only approach available. Indeed, on a number of occasions, I have (sometimes controversially) argued that this and similar programmes would not be needed if physical development was "done" properly before children got to school! The four approaches are now detailed in the following.

Movement for Learning (Dr Rebecca Duncombe and Dr Pat Preedy)

Movement for Learning is a daily movement programme for reception children and is delivered by class teachers in school time. The programme is expected to take approximately one school year to complete with six progressive units lasting four weeks each. Due to the time taken to settle into a new school as well as disruptions at Christmas and towards the end of the summer term, it was felt that 24 weeks of activities would enable schools to implement the programme more easily. Each unit consists a warm up, main activities and a cool down and, apart from the main activities, which are rotated, the children do the same activities each day for the four weeks (see Figure 15.1). As was mentioned in the personal reflection, Movement for Learning was never designed to be PE or to replace PE and we stressed this to the teachers

FIGURE 15.1 Movement for Learning "in action".

involved right from the start. The children do not change for the sessions but are expected to take off their shoes and socks (an enormous challenge for many children and their teachers, certainly in the early weeks of term) but necessary to allow sensory feedback and improve balance. Further details can be found on the Movement for Learning website: www.movementforlearning project.co.uk

The programme was piloted for a year in two schools (one state and one independent school). The programme was revised slightly based on feedback from the teachers from these two schools and then rolled out to approximately 30 schools across the United Kingdom (there are now over 100 schools delivering the programme). The two schools from the pilot year and a further two schools selected in the second year were involved in the Movement for Learning Research project and data were collected on approximately 120 children from the four schools (data solely from the pilot year, 46 children, are presented in the following). The data collection included baseline and end of project physical development scores using the Movement Assessment Battery for Children (Movement ABC-2; Barnett, Henderson, & Sugden, 2007) and a selection of primitive reflex tests (further information about primitive reflexes can be found in Chapter 10). Comparison data were available in three of the schools (these children participated in normal school life and followed the EYFS as delivered in their schools). The baseline data have already been presented in Chapter 8, so the impact data will be presented here.

The Movement ABC-2 is a standardised test pack that assesses balance, throwing/catching and manual dexterity as well as allowing an overall physical development score to be calculated. Raw scores are converted into percentile scores and those scoring below the 16th percentile are seen to have or be at risk of developing a movement difficulty. Clearly, we would want as many children as possible to be scoring towards the 100th percentile as this would indicate a very good level of physical development (we would certainly want to see our own children at or above the 50th percentile). The data presented in Chapter 8 show that many children are starting school with low levels of Physical Development but, more worryingly, those children who solely followed the Early Years Foundation Stage (EYFS) finished with worse physical development scores than when they started (as a mean for the cohort). Yet, those who participated in Movement for Learning showed an improvement. Interestingly, 12.2 per cent improved enough to no longer have or be at risk of a movement difficulty (compared to an increase of 4.5 per cent from the comparison group). Primitive reflex scores also improved slightly for the intervention group whilst getting slightly worse for the comparison group. These data are presented in more detail in Duncombe and Preedy (2018).

At the end of the academic year, the teachers involved participated in a focus group and the following comments help further illustrate the impact of the programme:

We've got three out of twenty-seven this year who are finding letter formation tricky, whereas normally, at this point, there are still ten who are spider-writing and you can't read what they have written. So I think it has made an impact on their writing, particularly their letter formation.

I have seen a great difference in some children's balance and coordination from taking part in daily MfL. It amazes me how quickly you can fit it into your daily routine.

The potential that Movement for Learning (and other similar programmes) has to improve physical development in young children as well as helping to reduce the incidence of retained primitive reflexes is outlined earlier. However, it should be noted that a number of teachers who were initially interested in the programme were unable to deliver it due to contextual constraints (time, space, support and other priorities linked to inspection), and those who were able to deliver it, found it hard to squeeze into the school day (often not managing all of the five sessions each week). For some schools, the approach outlined later in the section titled "Prioritising Physical Development in the preschool setting" may be more suited to their own individual context.

Jimbo Fun: a handwriting intervention (Cathy Parvin)

During my work for the Dyspraxia Foundation and subsequently running Dyspraxia Education, I have visited hundreds of schools. One common thread consistently emerges: teachers raising concerns about handwriting. Similarly, it is the most frequent request for help on our helpline at Dyspraxia Education by both teachers and parents. On a personal level, I have witnessed the long-lasting impact of handwriting difficulties, on my own daughter's painful educational experience. As my involvement in schools increased, viewing the children as a trained general and orthopaedic nurse, I noticed that most of the children who struggled with handwriting appeared to have underdeveloped pre-writing motor skills. On closer observation, I noted that these children displayed certain compensatory behaviours for the lack of these basic skills. The children were having to stabilise themselves prior to handwriting by wrapping their legs around the leg of the chair, flopping their head onto the table, or leaning heavily on their non-writing hand. They were clearly experiencing pain from the physical exertion of writing and it seemed to take immense effort for them. Despite this immense effort, the writing produced was poorer in both quality and quantity, compared to many of their peers.

On further investigation, I identified that, out of a class of 30 children, approximately five would struggle to master handwriting. Of these five, on average, three of them would show signs of having an underlying motor difficulty such as dyspraxia (DCD developmental co-ordination difficulties) or would have a diagnosis of other co-occurring neuro diverse conditions such as ADD (attention deficit disorder), dyslexia and/or ASD (autistic spectrum disorders). These conditions frequently have associated motor difficulties which accounted for their handwriting challenges. This raised the question as to why the remaining two children would be struggling with handwriting, with no apparent underlying SPLD (specific learning difficulty) or motor condition.

A number of further reflections and observations led me to realise that a number of foundational skills were required before handwriting could be successful. In particular, I had observed that many children who struggled with handwriting had low muscle tone and weak core stability, yet these children were expected to do more advanced skills (writing), despite not yet having mastered the basics. Thus, interventions from class teachers (or others) that solely targeted the more advanced skill of handwriting were failing to address the actual cause of the problem and there was little recognition that children need to go through developmental stages to be ready for handwriting. Attempting to correct fine motor skills, whilst overlooking the child's poor gross motor skill and core stability, was akin to focussing on a child's football skills when he could barely walk. A further problem appeared to be a lack of understanding relating to "letter movement" (starting the letter in the right place, going in the right direction and most importantly ending it in the right place). In collaboration with a number of professionals and experts who kindly gave their time to this project, Jimbo Fun was developed to address these two concerns. That is, it was designed to help children "catch up" on underdeveloped pre-writing skills and embed correct letter movement (see Figure 15.2). In addition, there was a recognition that it needed to:

- Target children aged seven years and above as an intense "catch up" intervention;
- Be quick and easy to use for schools who struggle with time to deliver these programmes (we decided on just 15 minutes a day);
- Be in a "grab and go" case containing all the equipment needed to deliver the programme, therefore saving teaching staff time in rounding up equipment;
- Be affordable for schools;
- Be engaging for children who were totally disengaged with handwriting;
- Be safe for most children to use;
- Be comprehensive and easy to use for untrained professionals. A training video to ensure accuracy and negate the need for staff to complete expensive pre-programme training was included;
- Offer an after-sale helpline;
- Be adaptable to meet the huge range of children who struggle with handwriting;
- Be easy for schools to evidence their intervention for OFSTED;

FIGURE 15.2 A child working through the activities in Jimbo Fun.

Profit is used to support children with dyspraxia through Dyspraxia Education. For more details, see: www.jimbofun.co.uk

The programme was piloted and then a larger trial conducted and early feedback was encouraging. The children completely engaged with it and showed positive benefits, not only in handwriting but also in the children's focus, self-esteem and many other areas. On average, it took between 8 and 12 weeks before benefits were effective. Due to the positive impact of Jimbo Fun, I was contacted and asked to produce a version of Jimbo Fun that was more suited to younger children; thus, "Junior Jimbo Fun" was developed for children in reception and Year 1.

Potential impact of Jimbo Fun: quantitative data

As part of the intervention, children were assessed on their pre-writing skills using an observational checklist designed for the project. The average pre-writing motor skill improvement score of those who completed Jimbo Fun was 11 points. Individual data from children aged between 6 and 10 (17 boys and 1 girl) are provided in Table 15.1. As a score of around 60 would be about average for children of this age, you can see from the table that all but one of these children was below average at the start of the programme. Experience has shown that children with a starting score of between 40 and 60 should engage with Jimbo Fun for six weeks and that children who start with a score of less than 40 should do the programme for 12 weeks.

TABLE 15.1 Pre- and post-"Jimbo Fun" pre-writing motor skills scores

Child	Pre score	Post score	Progress score	Evaluation
A	33	55	22	Positive
B	21	31	10	Positive
C	32	48	16	Very positive
D	30	57	27	Very positive
E	23	35	12	Positive
F	43	53	10	Mainly positive – found challenging in places
G	28	37	9	Positive
H	32	41	9	Mainly positive
I	24	33	9	Positive
J	25	26	1	Found it difficult, but Mum felt he'd made more progress than shown due to the furniture he was using when post assessed.
K	36	55	19	Very positive
L	38	53	15	Positive
M	63	64	1	Unsure
N	38		Child ill	Only half completed but TA said it was beneficial and was disappointed not to be able to complete
O	34	36	2	Only done a few times a week
P	26			Not completed lack of TA
Q	21	38	17	Very positive
R	21	32	11	Very positive

Potential impact of Jimbo Fun: qualitative data

Tom was seven years old when his mother first contacted our helpline. She described him as an exceptionally bright and articulate little boy but who was very frustrated that he could not write down what was in his head. He had frequent outbursts when asked to do homework or write anything. On assessment, he showed signs of low muscle tone, poor core stability and motor skills. His letter formation was difficult, many letters being formed using incorrect letter movement. He admitted his hand hurt when he wrote and that it tired him. He used many avoidance tactics and got upset when asked to write.

We started the Jimbo Fun programme. His mum did the exercises and letter formation every day before school and I visited once a fortnight to see how he was doing. He willingly did the exercises and really engaged with it. As his muscle tone increased, he stopped complaining of pain and gradually both the quality and quantity of his writing increased. On one of my visits, his mum became quite emotional when she showed me a letter he had written to her all of his own volition. Once he had improved his motor skills, he was able to easily form the letters and, as the programme progressed, he naturally took pride in forming his letters well. His teacher noticed an improvement not only in his handwriting but his attention, self-confidence and behaviour. He had even observed Tom helping other children with handwriting. Tom was rewarded in assembly for much improved handwriting. After completing Jimbo Fun, Tom's mum said his overall behaviour had improved and he was far less frustrated because he could write his thoughts down. I continued to monitor him for six months and his mum reported he had continued to make progress and was finding schoolwork considerably easier. He was a much happier child than he had been when she had first contacted me.

Jimbo Fun and Junior Jimbo Fun are interventions aimed at many children who struggle with handwriting and motor skills but who are waiting for Occupational Therapy or who would not necessarily meet the criteria for Occupational Therapy referral. It is ideal for children whose teachers and parents feel need some help but are unsure of how to provide this. Similarly, if a school has completed the programme and the child has not made progress, this would be a strong indication they need a higher level of assessment and intervention. However, the vast majority do make good progress.

Kimble's music and movement classes (Kim Pott)

I started a local music group with my three young children 14 years ago and was overwhelmed by the demand for the classes. As the numbers increased, it didn't take me long to realise that incorporating movement was an essential ingredient to the mix of what we offered. Central to the classes is the development of skills that will later help with reading and writing in the classroom. For example, in order to be good at reading and writing, children first need to be able to:

- Listen and follow instructions;
- Control large and small muscles (gross and fine motor skills);
- Have good core strength, postural control and neck strength to sit comfortably in a chair;
- Have good eye strength (to focus close up on the paper and then far away when copying from the board);
- Have the confidence to use their imagination to write an interesting story;
- Remember and be able to sequence in order to put their ideas into a logical order.

Numerous activities were devised to develop these skills and also to provide parents with "take home" ideas to use between sessions. The reasoning behind the inclusion of some of these is included in Table 15.2.

TABLE 15.2 Example activities used in Kimble's session and reasons for their inclusion

Activity	Reason for doing
Bouncing 3D objects in a parachute, popping bubbles and batting balloons	Encourages vertical and horizontal eye movements. Both of which are required when reading, writing and in maths. Building eye strength in order to support tracking words across a page
Role play songs (e.g. pretending to be a pirate: scrub the deck, climb the rigging, make pirate noises)	Expands vocabulary and starts to enable the child to use their creativity and imagination as well as improving their ability to imagine what it would be like to be someone else
Singing Using songs with short, simple repeated phrases is much easier for a child to learn, remember and repeat	Develops language skills: • Children learn to sing at the same time as they learn to speak • Vocal exploration can help to tune our ears to important sounds
Music and movement activities that require actions and/ or remembering sequences. For example, Marching on Mondays, Tip-toe on Tuesdays	Supports the development of memory: • Learning the days of the week, months of the year or the ABC (despite being made up of 26 abstract sounds, most four-year-olds can recite this through song)
Activities performed in a group environment and/or with a partner	Promotes personal, social and emotional development: • Working together towards a common goal can promote a sense of belonging and inclusion • Build social confidence • Helps develop more positive relationships
Weight bearing activities (e.g. jumping, hopping, crawling) Jumping like a kangaroo or crawling on all fours like a tiger	Develops gross motor skills: • Develops muscle strength • Weight bearing activities increase bone density • Fitness and agility may be improved The big muscles exercised during gross motor activities need to be well developed before those used in fine motor control. Thus, lots of big movements will ultimately help smaller movements to become more controlled and automated
Travelling in different ways (forwards, backwards, changing direction, different heights, different speeds, etc.)	Develops gross motor skills, movement vocabulary and proprioceptive awareness
Using the claves (tapping sticks). Dough dancing (squeezing, pinching or splatting play dough to the music)	Develops fine motor skills

Activity	Reason for doing
Songs that encourage the children to pat their opposite knee with their hand or tap their opposite shoulder	Encourages children to cross the "midline": • When reading, our eyes must track from left to right and cross over an imaginary midline. Many children find this hard and repeating this can help to build the necessary neural connections in the brain to make the movement more "fluid"
Songs with rhythms	Develops Literacy Skills: • Rhythms based on syllables of the lyrics help children to break down words; developing skills to aid in reading and spelling
Songs about location (e.g. a teddy who is placed in, above, below and to the side of a cardboard box)	Develops vocabulary, understanding, communication and proprioceptive awareness: • Doing the actions to the song helps develop meaning • Positional and directional language is essential for a child to understand in order to form letters and numbers

Thus, Kimble's Music and Movement classes evolved to incorporate activities that would develop these skills and our core moto became "Movement through play the musical way." I have also developed and published songs and music based on my knowledge and experience under the brand of "Funky Feet Music." The following photos illustrate some of the ways in which children can enjoy and develop in a range of areas during a Kimble's session (Figures 15.3–15.7):

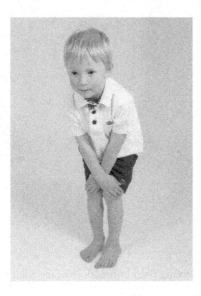

FIGURE 15.3 A child learning the names of his body parts and successfully crossing the midline.

FIGURE 15.4 Children enjoying a role play activity.

FIGURE 15.5 Children driving their bodies developing their spatial awareness.

FIGURE 15.6   A child immersed in following his creative interests.

FIGURE 15.7   Children jumping using big motor muscles and building bone density.

A typical Kimble's session lasts 45 minutes and consists of pre-session free-play, where parents can come together to get to know each other before the session starts and to familiarise themselves with equipment; a welcome song that is familiar to the children and signals the start of the session; introduction of the theme for the day; the main session itself; a calm down song and a drink; and finally a familiar goodbye song, which would signal the end of the session. Each activity is referenced to the EYFS framework and Table 15.3 outlines an example of a theme as well as identifying the links to the EYFS. The theme in this example is the zoo/jungle:

TABLE 15.3 Example of a Kimble's theme and accompanying activities

Song and activity	Observation opportunities	Instructions
Song: "A Day at the Zoo" – an action song that builds memory and sequencing skills	Perform actions to the song	Clap along and sway to the chorus
Jumping on the spot or whilst travelling (Physical Development)	Come up with their own ideas for movement	Point to yourself and the children when you sing "me" and "you"
Singing (Expressive Arts and Design)	Negotiate space	Perform actions by moving like the animals
Linking animals to country of origin (Understanding of the World)	Ability to move, stop and keep still and balance	Have the children echo each phase whilst performing the actions
Echo singing (Communication and Language)	Get into character, role play	
Picking out rhyming words (Literacy)	Echo singing	
Working with others (Personal, Social and Emotional Development)	Contrasting movement	
Counting number of animals in the song and memory and sequencing (Maths)	Recognising different animals and their characteristics	
	Remember the order as the sequence builds up	

Extensions		
Add tuned percussion to parts of the song, for example, the chime bars when you sing the animal part, e.g. a jumping wallaby	Split the children into groups and take turns to be the animals. Get them to act out their own character when it is their turn	Find different ways to move for different animals
At Setting or at home activity. Make tickets for the zoo. Try different shaped tickets, for example, map shaped tickets and group animals that come from that part of the world		

The following quotes taken from Facebook reviews illustrate some of the ways in which both parents and teachers have experienced the sessions as well as hinting at the impact they have had on children:

> My 2 sons both attended Kimbles when they were younger and loved it – the songs are original and fun allowing the children to enjoy themselves while learning and developing in so many ways.
>
> *(Teacher)*

> I absolutely love Kimbles. Every child and parent should experience this very special journey, great themes, music and movement with fundamental movement skills whilst developing literacy/numeracy in a FUN ENJOY-ABLE way. Keep up the great work Kim and team.
>
> *(Sports teacher)*

> We have been taking part in Kimbles sessions for many years and I cannot recommend it enough. Really high quality activities that are fantastic fun as well as being really good for supporting so many areas of child development. Staff are so enthusiastic too and really love what they do!
>
> *(PE teacher)*

> My three kids all love Kimbles and really get a lot out of it. They are having so much fun they don't even realise how much they are learning and what a good workout they are getting – highly recommend!
>
> *(Parent)*

> My son really enjoyed this morning's bug session. He is sometimes a bit unsure going to new places but was happy to join in straight away! Kim is so enthusiastic and had loads of fantastic ideas. Lots of different songs and props used too. Will definitely go again.
>
> *(Parent)*

Chapter 4 identifies a number of "enrichment" activities that parents may choose to take their young children to. Kimbles is an example of such an activity, and it is hoped that the information provided previously will help practitioners and parents to realise and understand the benefits of a music and movement programme that places child development through play, and specifically the joy of movement, at the heart of its rationale.

Prioritising physical development in the pre-school setting (Ruth Smith)

The final "programme" under the spotlight is more of an approach or "philosophy" than an intervention but has been included in this chapter as it represents what is possible in Early Years settings as well as providing an example of how academic outcomes can be improved by increasing opportunities for young children to engage in physical development opportunities. In 2008, Ruth Smith from Woodland Grange Primary School in Leicestershire was delivering the EYFS to her pupils in much the same way as many practitioners across the United Kingdom, but, following a meeting where the focus was on "barriers to learning," this all changed. Within the meeting, the conclusion was that the biggest barrier to learning was the children's physical development (or lack of it) and, from this meeting, Ruth has played a very active part in changing this by enabling appropriate and adequate opportunities for children to move. In 2009, the school was involved in piloting "Meaningful Movement," a floor-based programme for young children that aims to improve physical development and reduce the incidence of retained reflexes. Ruth eventually integrated these movements into games and music to make the movements more "child-friendly" and more in line with her EYFS ethos. The "light bulb moment" came when Ruth realised that physical development should not be an intervention or a tag-on activity but it should be part of everything. This realisation led to a number of dramatic changes in the setting, but, despite academic activities suddenly becoming less of a focus, the children were progressing and being "ready to learn" much quicker than in previous years. The biggest development was the opening of Woodland Grange Pre-School in September 2015 which meant that Ruth was able to start targeting physical development even earlier. This resulted in children being "ready to learn" even sooner and the physically strong children that were developing within the preschool environment were proving academically ready at an earlier age.

It has been highlighted throughout the book that children's play has become less "risky": they are less active than in previous years; they have less access to unsupervised, outdoor play; and they engage more with electronic "screens." Ruth's approach set to counteract many of these issues and she recalled the following as examples of activities they had introduced:

- Play dough – using dough as big as a child's head to really work gross motor movements and targeting specific "pivots" and muscles for handwriting;
- Getting parents on board:
  - Explanations at first visit to school;
  - Letters home – article of the month (e.g. OT guidelines for PD and self-help skills);
  - Explaining that children will get dirty plus strategies to enable this (i.e. clothing, wellies, etc.);
  - Making children carry own book bags and take responsibility for their belongings;
  - Electronic Learning Journeys used to explain the direct links between physical and academic ability.
  - Videos and photos of physical activities that parents could do at home, to improve their child's arm strength, visual tracking, body awareness.
- Making everything physical – removing chairs, using furniture as a physical resource, for example, a tunnel, a boat, a train, a den;

- Pre-mark making activities – a focus on Gross Motor activities before writing is even introduced: stick fighting, tyre rolling, shed painting, tug of war, monkey bars, wringing out sheets and cloths;
- Muddy activities – encouraging children to explore mud and engage in sensory play;
- Forest school – initially teaching children how to walk on uneven terrain, step over logs and under branches. Taking the ethos back into the school setting so that, like physical development, Forest School is also an integral part of our practise;
- Muddy clothes hung on the fence for parents to see, including those of the adults;
- Teachers model behaviours:
  - Get dirty themselves;
  - Always trying to make play more physically challenging.
- Introduction of open-ended resources, e.g. "junk" (tyres, guttering, pipes, cable reels), sand, water, sticks, woodwork tables and tools (including saws!);
- Very few rules:
  - Can't climb higher than 1.3 m;
  - Long sticks must be dragged along the floor;
  - Children must walk indoors, and save "big voices" for outdoors.
- Designing things like water walls and mud kitchens so that children have to travel, stretch and lug resources around a wide area (Figures 15.8–15.11).

FIGURE 15.8 Children using real hammers and developing their fine motor skills.

FIGURE 15.9 A child adding his contributions to the graffiti wall and developing the shoulder and arm strength to support future writing activities.

FIGURE 15.10 Pumpkin painting – using heavy objects to develop strength.

FIGURE 15.11 Water walls to encourage investigative skills, sensory play and gross motor movements.

The approach is arguably simple but is it effective? Likewise, is there a cost to children's learning by adopting an approach so heavily weighted towards just one core area of the EYFS? In Ruth's experience, focussing more on the "physical" has not been detrimental to the children's learning. In fact, she feels that the children who have experienced this approach are often more ready to learn than the children who experienced the previous (less physical) approach. Indeed, the school data is supportive of this belief and can be seen in Tables 15.4 and 15.5 (where "pre-changes" refer to the situation prior to the opening of the pre-school attached to the main school, and post changes refer to the time after the pre-school opened when the emphasis on the physical starts at age 3 rather than age 4, as it had been prior to the changes):

TABLE 15.4 Children obtaining a good level of development at the end of the reception year

	Pre-changes: mean of children starting school in 2012–2015 (per cent)	Post-changes: children starting school in 2016 (per cent)
All children	61.0	82
Boys	56.3	73
Girls	69.5	93

TABLE 15.5 EYFS end of year profile data – children at age related expectations or above

	Pre-changes: mean of children starting school in 2012–2015	Post-changes: children starting school in 2016	Increase since changes were made
Number	75.5%	97%	21.5%
Shape space and measures	82.5%	100%	17.5%
Writing	65.5%	82%	16.5%
Being imaginative	84.3%	100%	15.7%
People and communities	84.5%	100%	15.5%
The world	84.5%	100%	15.5%
Speaking	85.8%	100%	14.2%
Understanding	86%	100%	14.0%
Exploring media and materials	85.6%	98%	12.4%
Technology	89%	100%	11.0%
Listening and attention	88%	98%	10.0%
Managing feelings and behaviour	88.8%	98%	9.2%
Moving and handling	89%	98%	9.0%
Self-confidence and self-awareness	91.3%	100%	8.7%
Health and self-care	91.5%	100%	8.5%
Making relationships	91%	98%	7.0%

These data, whilst only representing a small number of children from just one school, illustrate that gains do seem to have been made in a wide range of areas since the changes were implemented and physical development was made more prominent in the curriculum at this setting.

Concluding comments

The two interventions, the music and movement classes and the approach to physical development in the pre-school setting outlined earlier, illustrate a number of different ways in which physical development opportunities could be improved and increased for young children. It was never the aim of this chapter to highlight any one as better or more effective than another. Rather, the aim was to outline what might be possible in different contexts and enable practitioners and parents to select the approach that may work for them. Of course, numerous other similar programmes and approaches are in existence and their exclusion here has not been because they are not worthwhile or worthy of further attention. The four previous sections were "opportune" inclusions (in that the editor was already in touch with the individuals involved). That said, the thinking behind each one does fit well with the overall messages of this book and the evidence provided (albeit sometimes limited) does suggest that, with a bit of effort, improvements can be made in physical development and that these can translate into academic success in the classroom and improvements in physical skills.

Summary of key points

- There are a number of different ways that physical development opportunities could be increased and improved for young children:
  - Two of the approaches outlined here involve an intervention to put right what has already gone wrong and two try to prevent problems from occurring in the first place.
- Context is important. What works in one setting may not be possible in another. It is doing "something" that is important.
- Opportunities for movement and for appropriate movement at the right time in a child's development may improve their academic success.
- Example activities provided in this chapter could be used by parents and practitioners in their own homes and settings.

Suggested further readings

Duncombe, R., & Preedy, P. (2018). Movement for learning. In P. Preedy, K. Sanderson, & C. Ball (eds), *Early childhood redefined: Reflections and recommendations on the impact of start right*. Oxford: Routledge.

Smith, R. (2012). *The little book of gross motor skills: Little books with big ideas*. London: Featherstone Education.

Reference

Barnett, A., Henderson, S. E., & Sugden, D. A. (2007). *Movement assessment battery for children* (2nd ed.) (Movement ABC-2). London: Pearson.

CONCLUSION

Rebecca Duncombe

Meeting the physical development needs of young children is clearly a complex task and one that requires careful planning, supported by appropriate policy documentation and adequate knowledge and understanding of the area. Chapters 1, 8 and 9 outline key policy and provision in relation to early years physical development and Physical Education in Key Stage 1 of primary school in England, and the shortcomings of these are identified. Chapters 2, 3 and 4 define and discuss key terms and concepts in relation to meeting the physical development needs of young children: physical literacy, fundamental movement skills and physical activity. It is argued that fundamental movement skill development relies on a strong foundation of physical development and that physical activity, whilst important for its health benefits and contribution to lifelong physical activity, may not always, in itself, provide appropriate and adequate opportunities for physical development.

Young children span the age range from 0 to 8 years and the needs of a very young baby differ from those of an eight-year-old engaging successfully in a PE lesson at school. Indeed, their needs differ quite dramatically from those of children much closer in age to them. This is partly why providing appropriate physical development opportunities for young children is so complex. From a very early age, babies develop at different rates and some are even born with different levels of physical development (compare a premature baby with a full-term baby, for example). Despite this, all children need to pass through each stage of development (as detailed by Dorothy Marlen in Chapter 6). The key point that Dorothy makes is important – babies should be left to pass through each stage unassisted and in their own time. That is not to say that babies should be left entirely on their own to complete their physical development journey but that they should not be assisted by being propped up, supported by, strapped into or entertained by various energy-saving and supposedly baby-friendly devices, or given physical help to reach the next developmental milestone. Picture, for example, the four-month-old who is not yet capable of sitting without support and who, despite this, is put into a high chair to be weaned, or the ten-month-old who is being held up by his or her arms by proud parents as he or she demonstrates his or her new-found "walking skills" to family and friends. In Dorothy's experience, children left to develop at their own pace and without unnecessary assistance will meet all physical development milestones in their own time and without retaining their baby or primitive reflexes beyond a time when they are no longer helpful.

The information from Dorothy's chapter helps us to meet the physical development needs of babies right from the start. Other chapters in the book have outlined what we can do when a child's physical development journey has been interrupted or remains incomplete. For example, Chapter 10 discusses the role of retained primitive reflexes in preventing some children from reaching their physical development potential and outlines an approach that can help these children to re-visit missed stages or spend more time practising a certain developmental movement. For some children, such a drastic intervention may not be needed and, when this is the case, plenty of advice is offered in Chapters 7, 11, 12, 13 and 14. These chapters identify ways in which resources and environments might be structured to better suit the physical development needs of young children. For example, in Chapter 7, Sue Gascoyne offers us a delightful insight into the ways in which messy play and collections of objects can both engage young children, whilst also offering opportunities for them to practise their gross and fine motor skills. Using play to facilitate physical development is then further explored in Chapter 14 by Pat Preedy who describes the ways in which seemingly simple play opportunities are essential for overall development. In Chapter 13, Janine Coates explores the potential of outdoor play and the Forest School approach and identifies the benefits of this as an approach in the early years as well as in primary schools. Carol Archer, in Chapter 12, provides a framework for practitioners to assess their physical development provision in terms of the layout of the physical environment and the resources provided within it, and identifies how simple changes to these can facilitate physical development opportunities. Whilst Carol outlines ways in which the environment might be adapted to suit the physical development needs of young children, Carolynne Mason, in Chapter 11, explores whether and how more traditional forms of sport may be adapted to be relevant to younger children.

Further advice and practical examples are offered in Chapter 15, which outlines and evaluates four different approaches – all designed to meet the physical development needs of young children. The first – "Movement for Learning" is a daily movement programme delivered to children in reception; the second – "Jimbo Fun" is a handwriting intervention that offers opportunities to practise gross and fine motor skills; the third – "Kimbles" is a music and movement programme; and the fourth was an approach taken by one school to better suit the physical development needs of their children. This final example shares many effective features with the examples given in Chapter 5, which overviews the Finnish approach to physical development in young children. The examples from Chapter 15 were all developed following recognition that young children's physical development was lower than desirable and that something needed to be done. Data from each of these interventions/approaches reveal improvements following participation and provide further support for the argument that levels of physical development can be improved.

There does seem to be a lack of guidance in policy documents in the UK (the EYFS and Development Matters) around why physical development is important and how appropriate and adequate opportunities can be provided for young children to develop their gross and fine motor skills. Likewise, the national curriculum for PE at Key Stage 1 largely ignores the relevance of a strong physical foundation and focusses more on developing the fundamental movement skills of running, throwing, catching, striking and jumping. All of these skills rely on balance, proprioception, good visual tracking, an ability to cross the midline, coordination and spatial awareness and all of these, in turn, require a child to have had good physical development experiences earlier in childhood. As a former PE teacher and with many years of experience researching in PE, I am all too aware of the pressure to produce children who are good at sport but, by focussing on the skills required for sports, we are at risk of forgetting the physical foundations that these are built upon. My argument would be that we need to take some children back a few stages to complete their physical development journey before we expect them to be able to move forward and succeed in PE and in the classroom. I remind the reader here of my earlier analogy about allowing children to walk before they can run (or to crawl before they can walk or to roll before they can crawl). Thus, if opportunities are not provided when children are babies or toddlers, they need to be provided at a later date. In order for this to happen, there needs to be recognition of this fact within official policy and accompanying training provided for early years practitioners and primary school teachers. Likewise, parents, health visitors and those involved more widely in the education and health of young children need to be reminded of the importance of providing appropriate and adequate physical development opportunities as well as being provided with information to explain how these opportunities might be offered. In this way, my hope is that we will get closer to fully providing for the physical development needs of young children.

INDEX

Note: **Bold** page numbers refer to tables; *italic* page numbers refer to figures and page numbers followed by "n" denote endnotes.